The
LEGENDS

The LEGENDS

BUCKEYES

THE MEN, THE DEEDS,
THE CONSEQUENCES

MARK REA

ORANGE *frazer* PRESS
Wilmington, Ohio

ISBN 978-1939710-109
Copyright©2014 Orange Frazer Press

Orange Frazer Press
P.O. Box 214
Wilmington, OH 45177
Telephone: 800.852.9332 for price and shipping information.
Website: www.orangefrazer.com
www.orangefrazercustombooks.com

Book and cover design: Brittany Lament, Orange Frazer Press

Library of Congress Cataloging-in-Publication Data

Rea, Mark, 1958-
  The legends : Ohio State Buckeyes : the men, the deeds, the consequences / Mark Rea.
    pages cm
  ISBN 978-1-939710-10-9 (alk. paper)
  1. Ohio State Buckeyes (Football team)--Biography. 2. Football players--United States--Biography. 3. Ohio State University--Football--History. I. Title.
  GV958.O35R42 2014
  796.332'630977157--dc23
                          2014021130

First Printing

DEDICATION

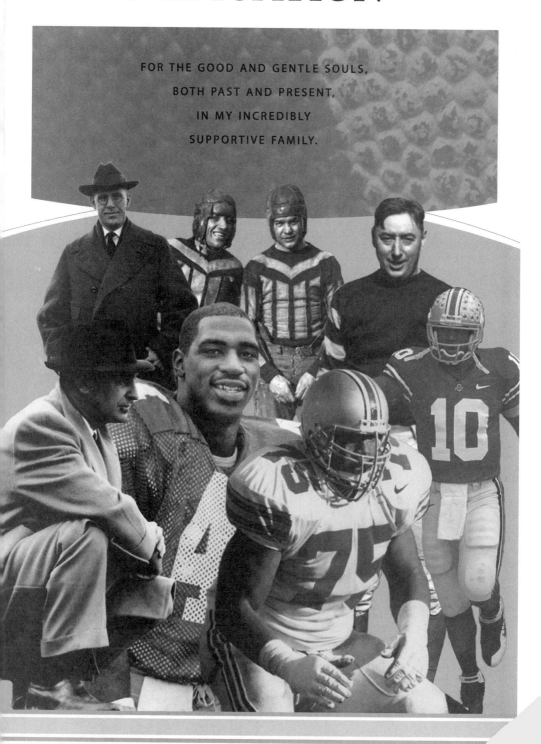

FOR THE GOOD AND GENTLE SOULS,
BOTH PAST AND PRESENT,
IN MY INCREDIBLY
SUPPORTIVE FAMILY.

ACKNOWLEDGEMENTS

Several years ago, while I was trying to explain a typical day at the office, I told my wife Lisa that one of my duties was to talk to fans. "Fans?" she said rather excitedly. "You have fans?" I chuckled at the thought and told her they were not fans of me personally, but of Ohio State football.

That story provides a little insight into my wife's personality. Because she was such a fan of mine, it never occurred to her there wouldn't be others. In addition to being my rock, my foundation, my confidant and the best friend I'll ever have, Lisa has always been my biggest fan. For those reasons and countless others, I am eternally grateful and infinitely blessed.

James Thurber once wrote, "Editing should be, especially in the case of old writers, a counseling rather than a collaborating task." With that in mind, I would like to thank John Baskin at Orange Frazer Press for the tone he set during our first meeting together. John challenged me to explore new depths with my writing, a challenge I accepted—albeit somewhat reluctantly at first. When one has been doing anything as long as I have been writing and editing, it is often difficult to think outside the box. Yet, thanks to John, I learned to embrace a more literary style and with his help was able to paint a much more vivid portrait of the subjects contained in this book.

Thanks also to the other talented professionals at Orange Frazer, including Marcy and Sarah Hawley, who helped shepherd me through the process, and Brittany Lament, whose design talents help set the book apart.

The photos which appear within these pages are due to the many outstanding photographers who have used their expertise over the years to leave a visual history of Ohio State football. Many thanks to those talented artists as well as Michelle Drobik at OSU Photo Archives and Matthew Hager at *Buckeye Sports Bulletin* for being extremely helpful with this project.

I have had the good fortune to spend a great deal of my professional life doing what I love, and for that I owe gratitude to *Buckeye Sports Bulletin* publisher Frank Moskowitz. In the summer of 1988, Frank decided to take a chance on someone he didn't know to help his company take the next step in its evolution. More than twenty-five years later, thanks to Frank's drive, determination and vision, *BSB* remains one of the most popular publications of its kind in the country. I am proud to have played a small role in the company's success, and have always been honored to consider Frank as my good friend.

Jack Park is the consummate gentlemen, always willing to give of his time and vast knowledge of Ohio State football history. His encyclopedic memory, easygoing charm and one-of-a-kind voice make Jack one of my favorite people, and I am honored that he considers me a friend and colleague.

A huge thank you to everyone at the Ohio State Sports Information Department, past and present, most especially Jerry Emig and his staff. Also special thanks to the late D.C. Koehl for his invaluable help over the years whenever I sought historical information. From his eclectic hobbies to his passion for Ohio State athletics, D.C. was truly a unique presence that is sorely missed.

Thanks to the countless Ohio State football players and coaches with whom I have interacted over the years. They provided not only insight and colorful background information for these pages, but hours upon hours of entertainment on cool and crisp autumn afternoons. Without their contributions, this book would never have been possible.

To my daughter Jessica, who emanates life and love through her flashing green eyes and radiant smile. I am so very proud of you, Jess, and despite your already impressive list of achievements, I know you have barely scratched the surface in what you will accomplish in your life.

Finally, I would like to pay tribute to my late parents. My father was stoic and very carefully weighed each word while my mother was a gregarious woman who could talk the ears off a statue. In other words, you couldn't find two more divergent personalities.

Yet, they walked hand in hand through more than fifty years of marriage, and along the way provided my brothers and me with a nurturing environment in which to grow as well as a lifetime of warm memories.

They are only two of the good and gentle souls to whom I referred on the dedication page of this book, but they have been and always will be the two most important influences in my life.

CONTENTS

FOREWORD

The Ohio State football program is steeped deeply in tradition. For 125 years, it has provided incredible enjoyment and memorable experiences for fans of all ages—lifelong friendships, national championships, thrilling victories, agonizing setbacks, abundant individual awards, and that noteworthy encounter each season with "That Team Up North."

Mark Rea has done a remarkable job of "personally introducing" you to some of the prominent players and coaches that helped develop this great tradition. You'll learn about their childhood backgrounds and environment, their mentors and who influenced them, and why they chose to play football for the Ohio State Buckeyes.

This is one of the most thoroughly researched Ohio State football publications ever produced. Mark's long hours of delving deep into this rich history brings to light an abundance of fascinating information never before revealed. It is a notable compliment to Coach Woody Hayes' famed quotation, "You win with people."

I've known Mark for nearly twenty years, and have always admired his insightful stories and thorough attention to detail. He is a dedicated professional, and this book is one of his finest efforts.

Enjoy *The Legends; The Ohio State Buckeyes.* You will be uplifted and feel a personal connection with many of the players and coaches who helped create the great tradition of Ohio Sate football.

—*Jack Park*
Ohio State Football Analyst and Author
Commentator, The Ohio State Football Radio Network

The LEGENDS

JOHN W. WILCE

OSU COACH 1913–1928

NICKNAME: Jack

HOMETOWN: Rochester, New York

RECORD: 78-33-9

BIG TEN CHAMPIONSHIPS:

1916, 1917, 1920

John Wilce is credited
with coining the phrase
"intestinal fortitude."

Most fans credit Woody Hayes with shining the national spotlight on Ohio State football as it is known today. In reality, the foundation for the program as a perennial powerhouse began to be put in place in 1913, the year Hayes was born in tiny Clifton, Ohio, and its architect was Jack Wilce, a bespectacled bookworm of a man who looked more at home in a library than on the gridiron.

Jack's parents, John Watkins Wilce and Rosetta Maria Woodworth, had met and fallen in love in Mequon, Wisconsin, a tiny town near Lake Michigan about thirty miles north of Milwaukee. But shortly after the couple was married, John was lured to Rochester, New York, in the late 1880s as the city was experiencing an industrial boom. German immigrants John Jacob Bausch and Henry Lomb had begun manufacturing medical instruments in Rochester in 1861, and entrepreneur George Eastman was launching his newest venture, a photography business that would eventually become known as Eastman Kodak.

With each new industry came a sharp increase in construction, perfect for a skilled stonemason such as John Wilce, and unable to resist the attraction of what seemed like easy money, he eagerly moved his wife and baby daughters Anna and Mary to western New York to seek his fortune. Soon the family had a new addition, a son born May 12, 1888, and christened John Woodworth, although everyone knew him as "Jack."

Life was good in Rochester as Jack's mother, a lighthearted woman known as Marcy to her friends, filled the house with the sounds of laughter and classical music, as well as the aroma of home-cooked meals. There was one thing missing, however. It wasn't home, and after only a year in Rochester, the family packed its belongings and moved back to Wisconsin. There, Jack was exposed along with his older sisters to an old-fashioned Midwestern American upbringing, a nurturing, morality-based environment that molded the stern-principled character and personal conviction he would exhibit the remainder of his life.

Jack was an avid reader from an early age, devouring page after page of everything from dime-store novels to the works of Shakespeare and Thoreau. "I read anything I could get my hands on," he said years later. "If I didn't have anything new, I would go over what I'd already read." Reading his precious texts by the dim light of a candle put such a strain on his eyesight that he was fitted for large, round glasses at an early age. But any boy who dared make fun of Jack's horn-rimmed appearance did so at his own peril. In addition to his studies, he was quite an athlete and more than able to take care of himself.

A strapping young man just over six feet tall and weighing a rock-solid 180 pounds, Wilce seemed born to excel at every athletic endeavor he tried. He was equally adept at baseball, football, basketball, and track, quickly becoming a high school star of renown in and around the Milwaukee area. He decided to attend the University of Wisconsin to pursue a degree in teaching, and as a freshman in the fall of 1906 anchored the school's crew team to a victory in the prestigious Poughkeepsie Regatta.

While at Wisconsin, Wilce became a three-sport letterman, although his true calling seemed to be football. He earned All-Conference honors as a fullback with the Badgers in 1909, and then was fully prepared to leave his athletic career behind after graduation. He had landed a job teaching history at a high school in La Crosse, Wisconsin, a city of about fifty thousand in the western part of the state. Just before the fall semester began, however, school officials approached him to ask if he would be interested in coaching. As a young man of meager means fresh out of college, Wilce eagerly accepted the extra few dollars that came with the additional duties. He wound up spending only one year in La Crosse as his school's football coach and athletic director, but a fire had been ignited.

Wilce returned to his college alma mater after being offered positions as assistant professor of physical education and assistant coach on John R. Richards's football staff. That triggered an unlikely chain of events that began with Richards leaving Wisconsin after only one season to take over the program at Ohio State where he would assume additional duties as the school's first director of athletes. But "Big John" quickly decided Columbus was not to his liking, and he resigned immediately following the final game of the 1912 season. That left the university without a football coach or athletic director as the Buckeyes prepared to compete the following season as full-fledged members of the Western Conference.

Ohio State acted quickly, promoting Lynn St. John from business manager to director of athletics and opening a nationwide search for a new football coach. The school quickly narrowed its focus to Carl Rothgeb of Colorado College and the University of Chicago's John Schommer, but both men eventu-

young Jack Wilce, who at twenty-five had never been a head coach on any level. He more than seemed equal to the challenge, however.

During the new coach's initial season in 1913, the Buckeyes turned in a 4-2-1 overall record including a 58–0 win over Northwestern in the season finale. That represented the team's first Western Conference victory, and it wound up its first season of league membership with a 1-2 conference mark and sixth-place finish.

Wilce saw incremental improvement the next two years as Ohio State finished in a fourth-place tie in 1914 and a third-place tie in 1915 before the program's breakout season. The coach had signed

"When Wilce finally resigned, he was quoted as saying that if he ever coached again, it would only be the team at the Ohio Penitentiary, because that was the one place where the alumni never wanted to go back."
—*Chester Smith*, Citizen Journal

ally turned down the job. That left the university in the position of being forced to offer the position to

one of the country's top prospects from East High School in Columbus, and Charles "Chic" Harley led the Buckeyes to the 1916 Western Conference championship as a sophomore. OSU set a host of school records that season, including a 128–0 win over Ohio Wesleyan—the most points ever scored by the Buckeyes in a single game.

Wilce would guide Ohio State to two more conference titles in 1917 and 1920 as well as runner-up finishes in 1919, 1921, and 1926, all the while transforming the Buckeyes into a national power. However, while coaches such as Knute Rockne, Glenn "Pop" Warner, and Amos Alonzo Stagg are more renowned today for the impact they had on football's early days, Wilce doesn't receive nearly enough credit for being one of the game's top tacticians of his time. For example, he was one of the first coaches ever to adopt the strategy of rushing the passer, and he is believed to be the first ever to utilize a five-man defensive line, unveiling it during a game at Princeton in 1927.

In addition to his innovative pass defense, Wilce also specialized in a wide-open passing attack. While most teams of the era played ball-control with their triple-option formations, Wilce allowed his players to throw extensively throughout the game. During the 1920 season, the Buckeyes defeated Illinois when quarterback Harry "Hoge" Workman passed to Cyril "Truck" Myers for the winning touchdown on the final play of the game. The play not only gave the Buckeyes a 7–0 win, it also won them the conference championship.

Wilce also tried to marry the physical and mental aspects of the sport. He was constantly trying to reform the way his players talked on and off the field, and he is credited with coining the phrase "intestinal fortitude," first using the term in 1916 while lecturing to his team on anatomy and physiology.

Wilce coached at Ohio State for sixteen seasons, a record that wouldn't be surpassed until Hayes surpassed his achievement. Wilce might have coached longer, but he abruptly resigned following the 1928 season, citing a personal struggle of trying to balance the ideals of athletics with the increasing financial requirements needed to field a team that could compete annually for national honors.

"I figured football was becoming more and more of a business proposition than I wanted to go into," Wilce said years later. "I saw the game being taken away from the boys. I was a faculty-type coach. I had always stressed educational aspects of the sport. This, to me, was far more important than winning the game. I don't want to give the impression that I'm critical of football the way it is played today. It came about through no one's fault in particular. It followed the normal trend of things and was brought about by the public's demand. I just didn't want to become an active part of that type of football, so I quit."

Wilce could have ridden off into the sunset with his legacy intact. He was inducted into the College Football Hall of Fame in 1954 and wrote several books on football, many of which became primers for coaches who followed him into the profession. He was an honorary life member of the American Football Coaches Association, served as the group's first secretary, and received the Stagg Award in 1959, the association's highest honor for "perpet-

uating the example and influence of the great coach in football."

But Wilce went on to another career and had as much success—if not more—than he enjoyed on the gridiron. He had continued his study of medicine at Ohio State while serving as head coach and received his medical degree in 1919. After his resignation as coach, Wilce took postgraduate classes at Columbia and Harvard as well as the National Hospital for Diseases of the Heart in London, then returned to Ohio State in the 1930s to become a professor of preventive medicine at the university's College of Medicine.

Regarded as one of the country's leading heart specialists, he served as director of Student Health Services at OSU from 1934 until his retirement in 1958. Eleven years later—six years after he died at the age of seventy-five—the John W. Wilce Student Health Center was completed on the Ohio State campus and named in his memory.

CHARLES (CHIC) HARLEY

OSU HALFBACK, SAFETY, PUNTER, KICKER 1916–1917, 1919

NICKNAME: Chic

HOMETOWN: Chicago, Illinois

HEIGHT: 5 ft 8 in WEIGHT: 150 lb

ALL-AMERICAN: 1916, 1917, 1919

47

Chic Harley (right) was the reason the Horseshoe Stadium was built.

*O*ctober 21, 1916.

With just a few seconds left, a 5-foot-8, 150-pound sophomore named Chic Harley carried his upstart Ohio State football team to victory by kicking the extra point after scoring the game-tying touchdown against Illinois, the heavily favored defending champions of the Western Conference. It was by far the biggest victory in program history, and unknown to anyone then, an outcome that sparked the drive to build one of the grandest sports arenas of all time, transforming a sleepy little town into one of the college football capitals of America.

Although Harley played his final game for the Buckeyes in 1919 and died forty years ago, his exploits on the football field have far outlived him—one of the definitions of a true legend. For those who are unaware of the long shadow cast by that legend or how important his legacy was—and still is—to the university, understand that Ohio Stadium itself would likely never have been built had Harley not wound up in a Buckeye uniform.

It took just three seasons— only twenty-three games—during the early part of the twentieth century for Harley to singlehandedly transform Ohio State football from little more than a club sport to a major player on the national stage. When he arrived on the scene, Ohio State had only recently joined the Western Conference (the predecessor of today's Big Ten) and was searching for its identity in intercollegiate athletics. It was also searching for a player that would justify its membership in that conference.

Enter Charles William Harley, a slightly-built, often clumsy young man who always seemed to wear a wry smile—as if he knew something you didn't. Born September 15, 1895, in Chicago, he moved with his family—parents Charles Sr. and Mattie, three brothers and three sisters—to Columbus when he was twelve and quickly earned fame as a football star at East High School, leading the Tigers to several City League championships. Harley had two distinct personalities. Off the field he was reserved, almost painfully shy in the company of strangers. On the field, surrounded by his teammates, he came alive as he exhibited the heart of a lion, the graceful moves of a gazelle, and the guts of a cat burglar.

Nicknamed "Chic" by his teammates because of his Chicago roots, Harley never missed a beat as he made the transition from high school to college. Despite his slight build, Harley spent his freshman season at Ohio State often practicing with the varsity players. When he joined the varsity as a sophomore the following season, it was the final piece of the championship caliber program head coach John W. Wilce

had been trying to establish. From the moment he first set foot on Ohio Field, Harley was the featured star for the Buckeyes from his halfback position, running and throwing the ball with equal success.

His first game as a collegiate player came in 1916 and was a 12–0 win over old Ohio Conference foe Ohio Wesleyan. The contest drew only 4,889 fans to Ohio Field, which was located near the intersection of 18th and High Streets. Ohio State rolled to victory the following week with a 128–0 pounding of Oberlin that still ranks as the highest point total ever in school history. But the third game of the season was when Harley's legend began to grow.

In their first Western Conference game of the season, the Buckeyes traveled to Illinois to take on legendary coach Bob Zuppke and the powerful Fighting Illini. "This was one of the biggest games up to that time in Ohio State football history," OSU football his-

Not a lot of people knew that Ohio State had a football team until Chic started to play.

torian Jack Park said. "The Buckeyes had played Illinois four previous times and never beaten them. In fact, Illinois had shut out Ohio State in three of those games, and Ohio State had only scored three points in the other."

The 1916 game was drenched in rain as well as déjà vu with the Buckeyes once again struggling to put points on the scoreboard. But with Illinois desperately clinging to a 6–0 lead in the fourth quarter, Harley broke off a twenty-yard touchdown run on a sloppy field and tied the score. Under the rules of the era, the scoring team punted the ball from the end zone to a teammate and the extra point was attempted from the spot on the field where the punt was caught. Harley punted to teammate Fred Norton on the 22-yard line. Then after calling timeout and changing his muddy shoes to clean ones, Harley calmly drop-kicked the extra point to give the Buckeyes a 7–6 victory. It was the Illini's first loss at home in four years, Ohio State's first win against Illinois after four previous losses, and a legend was born.

Years later, team manager Bill Dougherty, who ran out onto the field to hand the clean kicking shoe to Harley, put the enormity of the win into perspective when he said, "I would like my part in it remembered on my tombstone." Daugherty ranked that in importance over his other contribution to Ohio State, that of composing the team fight song *(Fight the Team) Across the Field.*

By the time, he was a senior, Harley had become a larger-than-life figure. He had helped Ohio State win its first Western Conference baseball championship, hitting better than .400 as a switch hitter. He held several school track records and also lettered in basketball. He played soccer during the offseason and even had offers to become a professional boxer. But it was on the gridiron where Harley enjoyed his greatest fame. Known by such glowing nicknames as "The One and Only" and "The All-American of All-Americans," he had led the Buckeyes to their first Western Conference championship in 1916, then repeated the feat the following year as the team outscored nine opponents by a combined margin of 292–6 to easily win a second consecutive league title. Following a year in military service with the U.S. Army Air Corps, Harley returned to Columbus for his senior season in 1919 and the atmosphere surrounding Ohio State football was at an unprecedented fever pitch.

During the years before Harley arrived on the scene, residents of Ohio's capital city barely knew the game of football itself existed, much less that the little college just

The 1919 season finale at Ohio Field against Illinois was to be Harley's final game as a Buckeye, and ticket demand reached an all-time high. The game was a sellout five days before kickoff—OSU athletic director Lynn St. John estimated sixty thousand could have been sold—and nearly twenty thousand people tried to jam into Ohio State's home stadium, a facility that had been built to hold only about one-fourth of that crowd. Fans filled the wooden bleachers long before game time and stood

> "He was an ordinary boy in an ordinary town. There was nothing all that unusual about him, at least in appearance, and there was nothing all that special about the town. Young Chic Harley and middle-aged Columbus seemed made for each other."
> —*Bob Hunter,* Chic

north of downtown had a football team. Now, as the victories stacked one on top of another—including the first-ever win against archrival Michigan—Ohio State football was the hottest ticket in town, and it was only getting hotter.

fifteen to twenty deep in both end zones. Others stood in windows of buildings across the street while several more climbed trees to catch a glimpse of the game. When the Buckeyes took the field, the *Ohio State Monthly* reported that resi-

Chic was so athletic, he even had offers to become a professional boxer.

dents as far as a mile away could hear the roar.

Illinois kicked a field goal with just eight seconds remaining for a come-from-behind 9–7 victory, but the outcome of the game mattered little in an evolution that had already taken place. The day of Harley's final game, university officials met to vote for construction of a new football stadium, an ambitious project to be built on the banks of the Olentangy River for the then-unheard-of sum of $1.3 million. Ohio Stadium, completed in 1922, became one of college football's earliest Meccas and was referred to for many years as "The House That Harley Built."

Following his final game as a Buckeye, Harley found nothing in his life to replace the game he loved so much, and the transformation from mythical football hero to tragic figure didn't seem to take very long. He tried his hand at several endeavors, including playing one season for the Chicago Staleys in the American Professional Football Association, the forbearer of the National Football League. Harley also returned to Ohio State for a charity football game in 1923 and was talked into serving as a volunteer assistant coach under Wilce. Later, he took a job piloting a plane that carried the U.S. Mail and dabbled in several other business ventures. But he simply could not shake the demons that accompanied a life that he evidently considered a failure. In 1938, after what was termed in those days a "nervous breakdown," Harley entered the Veterans Administration Hospital in Danville, Illinois, and with very few exceptions, it was his home for the next thirty-six years.

Chic's mental collapse put him in an asylum for the rest of his life.

Harley visited the stadium for the first time in more than a decade a year later and was mobbed by friends and well-wishers. Because of health problems, he didn't return until 1948 when he was coaxed into attending the annual Captains Breakfast. When his train arrived from Chicago at Union Station in

Columbus, more than a thousand people stood in the rain just to catch a glimpse of the man who had put Ohio State on the college football map. By the time the procession made it to the State Capitol building, it had turned into a full-fledged ticker tape parade with a crowd estimated at seventy-five thousand—one-fifth the total population of Columbus at the time.

Harley returned to Ohio Stadium only a handful of times after that. He was honored in 1951 for his induction into the College Football Hall of Fame and continued to follow the Buckeyes into the middle 1960s until declining health and his chronic depression kept him hospitalized during most of his final years. Chic died due to complications from bronchial pneumonia on April 24, 1974, in Danville, Illinois, at the age of 78, and in accordance with his final wishes, the body of the man once known as "The Immortal" was returned to Columbus for memorial services and driven past Ohio Stadium on its way to burial at Union Cemetery on Olentangy River Road. Two-time Heisman Trophy winner Archie Griffin served as one of Harley's pallbearers.

In the years since his passing, Chic Harley and his legacy have largely receded into the shadows. There are times, however, when the memories of his exploits are dusted off for new generations. As new books are written and faded newsreel footage is uncovered, football scholars are once again tasked with describing just how much Harley meant to the inexorable force that Ohio State football has become.

Perhaps James Thurber, the acclaimed American humorist who was Chic's classmate at both East High School and Ohio State, put it best when he wrote in 1940, "If you never saw Chic Harley run with a football, we can't describe it to you. It wasn't like Grange or Harmon or anybody else. It was kind of a cross between music and cannon fire—and it brought your heart up under your ears."

GAYLORD (PETE) STINCHCOMB

19

NICKNAME: Pete

HOMETOWN: Sycamore, Ohio

HEIGHT: 5 ft 10 in WEIGHT: 165 lb

Pete was not built for football as he was small. But he had huge hands.

*H*ad Chic Harley not been the most radiant star in the Ohio State football firmament during the early part of the twentieth century, Ohio Stadium might have been referred to as "The House That Stinchcomb Built." Pete Stinchcomb was a diminutive do-everything quarterback and defensive back alongside Harley on the successful Scarlet and Gray teams of 1917 and 1919, and then became the focal point of a Western Conference championship team in 1920, the first in school history to go to the Rose Bowl. But while Harley's life spiraled out of control following his illustrious football career, the extremely popular Stinchcomb seemingly had the Midas touch.

No player from the first half-century of Ohio State football had as much impact on the program as Harley, whose exploits first at East High School in Columbus and then at tiny Ohio Field for the Buckeyes led to the construction of mammoth Ohio Stadium, still one of the largest on-campus stadiums in America. Yet a case could be made that Harley's immeasurable popularity was due at least in part to the fact he was a local boy playing for his hometown team. Had Stinchcomb been from Columbus rather than a tiny village in northwestern Ohio no one had ever heard of, could the history of Ohio State football been written differently?

"That's impossible to say," said Ohio State Athletics Hall of Fame member Marv Homan, who spent forty years in the university's sports information department, including the last fifteen as director. "There isn't much question in anyone's mind the impact Harley had on Ohio State football. He has always been credited with putting the program on the map, and rightfully so. Pretty much anyone who played with him would have played in his considerable shadow at that time. But I can remember some people who saw both of them play who claimed that Stinchcomb might have been every bit as good as Harley. If that were true, or even close to being true, Stinchcomb must have been some kind of player."

That assertion was shared by more than a few fans of the era. "A ninety-something fan once told me he thought Stinchcomb was better than Harley," longtime *Columbus Dispatch* sportswriter and columnist Bob Hunter wrote in his 2012 book *Saint Woody: The History and Fanaticism of Ohio State Football*. "I listened, nodded, and respectfully declined the temptation to question the old gent's sanity. But for anyone to even consider the possibility of that says a lot about Stinchcomb's ability."

Gaylord Roscoe Stinchcomb was born June 24, 1895, the middle child to James Grant Stinchcomb and Emma J. Milligan, a couple of English and Irish descent who lived in Sycamore, Ohio, a tiny dot on the northern Ohio map covering less than a square mile of mostly rural Wyandot County. Gaylord's father was a teamster, an occupation much in demand around the steel mills of nearby Tiffin and Upper Sandusky. Anyone who owned a team of horses and a wagon could earn a good wage by hiring himself to any of the dozens of mills needing materials transported to and from the mills. It was a job that often took the elder Stinchcomb away from his family for long periods of time, however, and James soon followed a new opportunity about thirty miles northwest to Fostoria where he became a contractor for a relatively new industry in the early 1900s—road construction.

Moving from the rural tranquility of Sycamore to Fostoria with its railroads, flour mills, and glass factories was a culture shock for young Gaylord. Known as Pete, a nickname given to him by little sister Isabelle who could pronounce neither Gaylord nor Roscoe properly, Stinchcomb kept mostly to himself until entering Fostoria High School. Once there, he quickly came out of his shell and became one of the most popular students in the hallways and classrooms. His popularity soared through the community as well when he became an All-State halfback while playing for the undefeated Redmen.

Pete was an unlikely football star at just 5-foot-8 and 157 pounds, but he was extremely fast and quick-thinking, and he possessed huge hands with spider-like fingers, perfect for gripping the bigger and slipperier football of the era. After another thrilling touchdown run, one local account reported, "What a sight to behold was Stinchcomb. The whirling dervish must have seemed a blur to the big-city boys as he danced his way around them and over the goal, pigskin securely tucked away."

gridiron pedigree to speak of and certainly not one worthy of comparison to the mighty Maize and Blue. OSU had become a Western Conference member only in 1913 and had never finished higher than fourth in the final standings. But

"Of course, he was fast. His name was 'Gaylord,' for gosh sakes. What kind of name was that for a jock?"
—*Buckeye Notes*

After graduating from high school in the spring of 1916, Pete was all set to join his father's road crew, but he had been such an outstanding athlete in so many sports at Fostoria High that he had drawn the attention of several college recruiters. The University of Michigan, with its campus less than a hundred miles from Fostoria, seemed a logical choice. Fielding Yost had been head football coach since 1901 and built a Midwestern powerhouse, winning four national championships and churning out a steady stream of All-America players.

About one hundred miles to the south of Fostoria was Ohio State, although the Buckeyes had no

head coach John W. Wilce, a professorial figure who enjoyed dabbling in psychology, offered a unique opportunity for Stinchcomb.

Years later, Pete recounted how Wilce appealed to his sense of pride. "He told me I would become just another number in Yost's football factory, but at Ohio State, I would be one of the final pieces of a championship puzzle he was trying to put together. He said he had this boy Harley already in school, and together he thought we would make a pretty good combination."

It might only have been a routine sales pitch to prevent one of Ohio's best high school players from escaping north to Michigan, but Wilce proved uncannily prophetic. Harley led the Buckeyes to their first conference championship in 1916, and the team repeated the feat the following year when Stinchcomb joined the varsity squad. In the words of a local sportswriter, "Harley and his team- 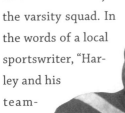 mate Stinchcomb outstepped their rivals and made the greatest pair of backs ever seen in the Western Conference."

Military service in World War I interrupted both young men's college careers, but when they returned to the Buckeyes in 1919, the Ohio State football program returned to prominence, even knocking off Yost's powerful Michigan squad for the first time in sixteen tries. Harley made his third All-America team that year while Stinchcomb was named to the All-Western Conference first team, the first OSU quarterback in history so honored.

Harley's college eligibility had been exhausted following the 1919 season, but Stinchcomb had one more year and Pete made the most of it. He was named to the All-Conference first team again, was a consensus first team All-America, and led the Buckeyes to their third league championships in five years. The 1920 team was

The ever literary Pete helped found the student bookstore on OSU's campus.

also the first Ohio State squad invited to the Rose Bowl, although it took some begging on the part of the university before Western Conference officials agreed to allow the Buckeyes to accept the invitation.

Waiting in Pasadena for the Midwestern powerhouse was the University of California, a team that had won each of its eight games and outscored its competition by a lopsided 482–14 margin. Ohio State entered the game as favorites, mainly because of what was considered stronger competition in the Western Conference, but the Buckeyes proved no match for the Golden Bears. In front of a Tournament Park crowd of nearly 42,000, California rolled to a 28–0 victory. Ticket demand for the game was so high that Tournament of Roses officials decided their annual event needed a larger venue, leading to construction of the current 100,000-seat Rose Bowl stadium nestled at the foot of the majestic San Gabriel Mountains.

The 1920 game also featured one of the most talked-about plays in the early history of the Rose Bowl, a second-quarter touchdown pass that caught Ohio State flat-footed.

After a first down run, Cal's Archie Nisbet feigned an injury, writhing on the ground for a few moments while his teammates appeared to be milling around. In fact, they were lining up for the next play. Center George "Fat" Latham took Harold "Brick" Muller's position at right end, right halfback Albert "Pesky" Sprott moved six yards behind the line and then Muller stood a few yards behind and slightly to the right of Sprott. Nisbet quickly rose from the ground, moved to the center spot and snapped the ball to Sprott, who turned and lateralled to Muller. At the same time, left end Brodie Stephens ran full speed down the field while Ohio State stood stationary with their hands on their hips.

As Stephens streaked by, a quizzical Stinchcomb yelled, "Where do you think you're going?" The words were no sooner out of his mouth when the OSU defender watched Stephens gather in a 53-yard touchdown pass from Muller. After the game, when asked why he hadn't covered Stephens, Pete laughed and replied, "Frankly, I didn't think anybody could throw the ball that far."

Once he returned to Columbus, Stinchcomb remained one of the most influential undergraduates on the Ohio State campus. Despite the fact his football career was over, he played baseball and ran track for the Buckeyes, winning the NCAA championship in the broad jump as a senior. And his accomplishments weren't limited to athletics. In addition to winning the presidency of his senior class as well as the Ohio State Student Council, Pete helped found the Student Book Store on campus. When he wed his fiancé, Anne Jane Summers, in the fall of 1921, university president Dr. William Oxley Thompson officiated at the marriage ceremony.

Following his college years, Stinchcomb rejoined former OSU teammates Harley and John "Tarzan" Taylor on the Chicago Staleys of the American Professional Football League and helped the team win the 1921 championship in only its second year of existence. Pete played a total of four professional seasons and then returned to Columbus where he went into private business as the owner of a lumber company in Upper Arlington.

He also became involved in an ongoing campaign to help his old teammate Harley, whose health had begun deteriorating rapidly. Stinchcomb helped organize fundraisers and chaired steering committees to make sure the Harley name was never forgotten. When Chic became a charter member of the College Football Hall of Fame in 1951, one of the first congratulatory telegrams he received was from his old pal Pete.

Stinchcomb got his own rightful place in the college hall in 1973 although he wasn't able to enjoy the accolade to the fullest. A few months before induction ceremonies, he passed away at the age of seventy-eight. Later that year, as Pete's widow Anne accepted his official hall of fame plaque during halftime of an Ohio State football game, she watched as the marching band's famous Script Ohio morphed into the word "Pete."

It was a fitting tribute to the lightweight football player who was a heavyweight of a man.

WESLEY
FESLER

OSU END 1928–1930 **OSU COACH** 1947–1950

NICKNAME: Wes

HOMETOWN: Youngstown, Ohio

HEIGHT: 6 ft 0 in **WEIGHT:** 160 lb

ALL–AMERICAN: 1928, 1929, 1930

RECORD: 21-13-3

BIG TEN CHAMPIONSHIPS: 1949

30

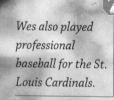

Wes also played professional baseball for the St. Louis Cardinals.

Wes Fesler could have easily related to the protagonist in Thomas Wolfe's best-selling novel *You Can't Go Home Again*. After a tremendously successful collegiate career at Ohio State that garnered nine varsity letters in three sports, as well as three consecutive All-America honors in football, Fesler returned to Columbus as head coach of the Buckeyes only to be driven out just four short years later by a rabid fan base much more interested in victories than celebrating bygone heroes.

Fesler had for almost two decades looked forward to returning to the site of his greatest accomplishments, and for a man who had never been associated with anything but winning, tendering his resignation was tantamount to admitting defeat. He later remarked it was like choking on the bitterest of pills.

Wesley Eugene Fesler was born June 29, 1908, the third son of a welder who worked amid the blast furnaces of the steel mills in Youngstown, Ohio. Young Wes was protected by his older siblings Raymond and Donald, who were nine and six years older than their baby brother, but Wes quickly made friends of his own due of a friendly, easygoing nature and a bright smile that served as a sharp contrast to the soot-filled skies of his hometown.

Like most of the youngsters growing up in the Roaring Twenties, Wes sampled just about everything Youngstown had to offer. His tastes ran the gamut from classical music and literature—major influences from his English-born mother Sarah—to bowling and shooting an occasional game of pool.

But organized sports was where Wes flourished, and his achievements in football, basketball, baseball, and track at South High School quickly earned him renown throughout the Midwest. As good as Fesler was at every sport, he was especially accomplished as an All-Ohio receiver for the Warriors, and that led several of the best-known coaches in college football to make a pilgrimage to the coal and limestone-filled shores of the Mahoning River. Fesler was polite and accommodating to the various coaches who made pitches for their individual schools, but he was interested only in following the footsteps of older brother Ray, who had been a starting center fielder for the Ohio State baseball team from 1921 to '23.

As he did in high school, Wes played three sports for the Buckeyes. He was an All-Big Ten selection as well as a Helms Athletic Association All-American in basketball and outdid his three-year letterman brother in baseball by earning four varsity sweaters. He also excelled in the classroom, was a Phi Beta Kappa, and would likely have been an Academic All-American had the honor been around in those days.

Above all other endeavors, football seemed tailor-made for Wes, and he became one of Ohio State's most decorated players. His career began with a flourish when he caught a 16-yard touchdown pass during a 19–7 victory against Michigan in 1928, a game that broke OSU's six-game losing streak against the Wolverines. The following season, Fesler played every minute of every game, appearing at offensive and defensive end, fullback, and punter. He also caught a 22-yard pass to account for the only touchdown in a 7–0 win over Michigan.

During his senior year, Fesler once again served as the backbone of the Ohio State team. He scored the season's first touchdown during a 59–0 win over Mount Union, and threw eight yards for a touchdown in his final college contest, a 12–9 victory at Illinois. At the end of the season, he was voted the Big Ten's Most Valuable Player and earned his third consecutive All-America honor, becoming the first OSU player to accomplish that feat since Chic Harley in 1916–1917 and 1919.

Following graduation, Fesler spent the summer of 1931 playing professional baseball in the St. Louis Cardinals organization, then returned to Ohio State in the fall to become an assistant football coach. What followed were stints at several schools as a head basketball coach, football assistant, or both, a résumé-building period interrupted only by two years of service in the Office of Strategic Services in Washington, D.C., at the end of World War II.

Fesler returned to college coaching as head of the football program at Pittsburgh in 1946, but his career took a turn following that season when Ohio State head coach Paul Bixler resigned. The university went through the motions of forming a search committee and leaking the names of several potential candidates to the press, but committee chairman Richard Larkins had only one name on his list. The assistant athletic director, who was soon to succeed longtime director of athletics Lynn St. John, had been a close friend of Fesler since the two were teammates on the OSU football team. But Larkins had to play things close to the vest in fear of showing favoritism.

"I never saw Dick so serious for so long a time in my life," Fesler said of the meeting when he was formally offered the job. "He did almost all the talking after he arrived. Saint just sat and smiled. Lending moral support, he called it."

The hiring of Fesler appeared a masterful move by the university, and the handsome, dark-haired 38-year-old enjoyed an enthusiastic homecoming response. "Needless to say, I am happy to be home again," he said. "When I left Columbus back in 1933, I left with the hope that someday I would return. The time has arrived and I'm plenty thrilled. I know that I have a tremendous job confronting me,

but I am confident there are a lot of people in Columbus, and all of Ohio, willing and anxious to help me along the way. Without a united front, it will be impossible for me, or any other coach, to be a success. I promise all of you that I am going to work extremely hard to get the backing of the entire state."

It was a short-lived honeymoon.

Newly installed offensive and defensive schemes as well as a wartime-depleted roster conspired for a last-place finish in the Big Ten standings in Fesler's first year. His second team improved to 6–3 overall and 3–3 in the conference, but a preseason interview Fesler had granted to an Ohio newspaper threatened to destroy whatever emotional capital he had banked over the years with many Ohio State fans. "To me," he said, "it isn't important how many games we win. To the best of my ability, I intend to fight for and help bring about a leveling-off of this great program until football becomes strictly an extracurricular activity. Maybe I'm cutting my own throat, but as head football coach, I want to say to the boys of Ohio that you can't eat footballs. What counts after your football playing days are over is what kind of education you have, and whether you can hold your own in the tougher competition of business life that follows. I say it now, and I'll say it as long as I have a voice, that no boy will come to Ohio State with the primary thought of playing football."

To say the townsfolk were ready to storm the castle was an understatement. Any initial grumbling grew into full-throated criticism when Fesler's 1949 team stumbled from the starting gate with a 2-1-1 record that included an embarrassing 27–0 loss to Minnesota. But the coach frustrated his detractors when the Buckeyes won their next four games and then forged a 7–7 tie with Michigan to win a share of the Big Ten championship and a trip to the Rose Bowl that resulted in a 17–14 victory against the University of California.

Though the 1949 season had ended successfully, rumors of player dissatisfaction with Fesler began to circulate, and stung by the criticism both inside and outside his program, the coach began to entertain thoughts of stepping away. A few weeks later, however, university officials offered a raise, as well as a lifetime position in the physical education department should he elect to retire from coaching, and Fesler decided to return for the 1950 season.

It was a decision he would come to regret. Junior halfback Vic Janowicz won the Heisman Trophy that year, but the Buckeyes didn't have a particularly good season as a team. The year began when the team squandered a late 27–13 lead and wound up losing a 32–27 decision against Southern Methodist University, and the campaign ended with a 9–3 loss to Michigan in what has become known as "The Snow Bowl." Played in blizzard-like conditions at Ohio Stadium, the game's outcome hinged on Fesler's decision to punt during the final seconds of the first half. Janowicz's kick was blocked and recovered in the end zone by the Wolverines for the game's only touchdown, a play that sealed Fesler's fate.

His critics second-guessing him mercilessly, Fesler decided he'd had enough. Unable to sleep and nearly incapacitated by blinding headaches, the haggard and red-eyed coach crafted a four hundred-word letter of resignation in which he explained two reasons for his action. One was a purported business opportunity, but the second was "the tension brought about by the tremendous desire to win football games for Ohio State which has reached the point where definite consideration for my health has become involved."

He couldn't resist taking a swipe at his critics for what they had done to him and to the game that he loved. "Somewhere along the line," Fesler wrote, "the responsibility of a coach as a father and teacher combined have been forgotten. The fans have forgotten that college football is a game for kids, played by kids against kids. Successful seasons seem to be the only thought in mind now."

Six days later, the Athletic Board accepted the resignation, paving the way for the hiring of Woody Hayes and the beginning of a new era of Ohio State football. Meanwhile, Fesler quickly realized he was going to miss football too much, and in late January accepted the head coaching job at the University of Minnesota. Three years with the Golden Gophers produced only a 10-13-4

record, and Fesler began facing the same criticism that had driven him from Columbus. Following the 1953 season, the man who would be inducted into the College Football Hall of Fame the next summer wanted nothing more to do with the sport that had shaped his life.

Fesler moved to California and became a successful real estate broker for more than three decades. He occasionally watched professional football games on television, but rarely attended games in person.

Before his death in 1989 from complications due to Parkinson's disease, Fesler confessed he was a football dinosaur whose time had come and gone, run out of the city that made him famous, and forced from the game he loved so much. Football had made Wes Fesler, but it had also broken a part of him—the part that couldn't go home again.

WILLIAM BELL

OSU LINEMAN 1929–1931

NICKNAME: Big Bill

HOMETOWN: Akron, Ohio

HEIGHT: 6 ft 0 in WEIGHT: 192 lb

42

William Bell was the first black football player for Ohio State University, where he played from 1929 to 1931. He earned All Big Ten and Honorable Mention All-American honors his final season.

Ohio State football began its evolution from small-town curiosity to collegiate powerhouse during the early part of the twentieth century, riding the exploits of such luminaries as Chic Harley, Pete Stinchcomb, and Wes Fesler to nationwide fame. Harley, Stinchcomb, Fesler, and countless other star players during the program's fledgling years had one thing in common besides being athletically gifted. They were all white.

During the first forty years of their existence, the Buckeyes had welcomed only a handful of African-American players to wear the Scarlet and Gray. Frederick Douglas Patterson, the light-skinned son of a Greenfield, Ohio, carriage manufacturer became the first black football player at Ohio State when he joined the Buckeyes for the 1891 season. Five years later, Julius B. Tyler, the son of a prominent Columbus businessman, became the first black player to score a touchdown as a Buckeye. But while the achievements of Patterson and Tyler were significant, they were quickly relegated to little more than footnotes in Ohio State football history. It was certainly nothing out of the ordinary for the era, but after Tyler left the team in 1896 after only one season, it wasn't until 1929 when the Buckeyes would have another black player on its roster.

He couldn't have known it at the time, but William Bell became the man who squeezed through the crack in the racial door left ajar by Patterson and Tyler, eventually swinging it open for the glorious modern-day history of Ohio State football that features the exploits of Heisman Trophy winners Archie Griffin, Eddie George, and Troy Smith not to mention multi-decorated All-America performers Bill Willis, Jim Parker, Bob Ferguson, Jack Tatum, John Hicks, Korey Stringer, Orlando Pace, and Mike Doss.

"In my opinion, I don't believe William Bell gets the recognition he deserves in terms of what he meant to Ohio State football," long-time OSU football historian Jack Park said. "At that time, there were very few black players in college football, and there hadn't been any black players at Ohio State in more than thirty years. His background, where he came from, what he was and what he became and all he accomplished after he left Ohio State, it's a truly remarkable story about a remarkable man."

William McNeil Bell—future educator, administrator, and coach—was born in the Deep South during the early part of the twentieth century, the great-grandson of a former slave. He was named for William Christopher, an unorthodox Georgia slave owner unbound by the prevailing philosophy among slave owners of the time. William Christopher not only defied the laws prohibiting the education of slaves, he taught them how to read and write as well as the skills of masonry and blacksmithing. Before the enactment of the Emancipation Proclamation in 1863, he had already freed dozens of slaves, including a thirty-year-old man and his family, providing them with money, a sliver of land, and, most important, identification papers attesting to their free status.

That young man, John Nathan Christopher—William Bell's great-grandfather—adopted his former owner's surname and began making an earnest new life for his family as the self-taught craftsman of fine furniture. At first, he made furniture exclusively for the Christopher family, but his workmanship attracted such demand that he soon opened his own shop. He was so successful that when the Christophers' main house was burned during the Civil War, John Nathan loaned the family $2,000 to refurnish the home when it was rebuilt.

John Nathan later dabbled in gold mining, served two post-Civil War terms as justice of the peace in Blairsville, Georgia, and his descendants eventually settled in Polk County near Cedartown, where Bill was born in 1912, the fifth of nine children to Thomas Henry Bell and Maggie B. Adrine.

"I owe a great debt to William Christopher," Bill said. "He taught John Nathan to read and write, as well as so many other things. And he gave him his freedom. My great-grandfather in turn taught *my* father all his skills, and my father taught me. William Christopher had a direct influence on my life and everything I accomplished."

As a toddler, Bill spent his days running barefoot over the orange

Georgia clay as a sharecropper's son. But his carefree life as a farm boy quickly changed when the family uprooted and moved to Akron, Ohio, shortly before the outbreak of World War I. By the time he reached high school age, the war was over and Bill was looking to further his education by attending college. In the late 1920s, most of the opportunities for higher learning available to African-American youngsters were at historically black colleges throughout the South. There were, however, certain allowances made if the youngster was athletically as well as academically gifted. Bill was both.

There was no official policy at Ohio State in 1928 prohibiting black players from participating in football, but an unwritten rule had kept the program all-white during much of the preceding three decades. John W. Wilce was embarking upon the final season of a sixteen-year tenure as head coach of the Buckeyes, and while Wilce was tired of the increasingly commercial nature of college football, he continued to view the sport as vital to the development of young men. Although his superiors in the OSU athletic department expressed their misgivings, warning Wilce of the possible ramifications of putting an African-American player in uniform, the longtime coach agreed to allow Bell to try out for the freshman team.

Blessed with the strength of an ox and the gracefulness of a gazelle, Bill made a quick ascension up the freshman depth chart at tackle. He impressed his coaches with his ability to bulldoze his way through defenders while earning new friends among his teammates with an infectious laugh and grim determination. "He was definitely a people person," said his only son, William M. Bell Jr. "That was always his emphasis—on people."

Bill was ready to take his place on the varsity team during his sophomore season of 1929 but was forced to prove himself again that fall for a new coaching staff. Sam Willaman, a star halfback, fullback, and end for the Buckeyes from 1911 to '13, had taken over as head coach for the retired Wilce but had received the same warning about what might happen if the Buckeyes fielded a black player.

Willaman understood perhaps more than any other college coach at the time what was at stake. He had been hired following a successful four-year stint as head coach at Iowa State where one of his star players was lineman Jack Trice, the proud son of a former slave and Buffalo Soldier. Trice, who had played football under Willaman at East Technical High School in Cleveland and was the first black player in Iowa State history, died of complications from injuries he had sustained during a game against the University of Minnesota in 1923. Trice, who had continued to play after suffering a broken collarbone early in that contest, died from internal bleeding that likely occurred in the third quarter when he was knocked to the ground and intentionally trampled by three Minnesota players.

Mindful of the risks of putting a black player on the field during that era, Willaman met with Bill before the 1929 season to express his reservations. "But it never occurred to me that I wouldn't play," Bell said years later. As a result, the player who become known simply as "Big Bill" became the anchor of the offensive line for the Buckeyes in each of the next three seasons, opening holes for the likes of quarterback Carl Cramer, as well as Fesler and fellow three-time All-American Lew Hinchman. During his senior season in 1931, Bill was named to the All-Big Ten second team and earned honorable mention All-America honors as well, a first for a black player at Ohio State.

Football was far from Bill's only campus activity. He was a member of the African-American fraternity, Alpha Phi Alpha, served as its sergeant at arms, and was a member of the Varsity "O" as well as the Collegiate Council and the Interracial Council. During his senior year, the Upper Class Cabinet of the OSU chapter of the YMCA selected him to lead a new committee on interracial relations.

Bell graduated from Ohio State in 1932, and embarked upon a rich and successful career in education and coaching that crisscrossed the country. Beginning in 1936, he began an eight-year stay at Florida A&M where he was athletic director and head football coach, leading the Rattlers to three black college national championships, a tenure interrupted by military service with the U.S. Air Force in World War II during which he served as football coach at Tuskegee Army Air Field and its famed Black Fliers Warhawks team. He returned to civilian life in 1946, and won another national title at North Carolina A&T, a school at which he also served as athletic director for twenty-three years. Bell retired from athletics in 1968, but he continued his career in education as associate dean of students and professor of physical education at Iowa State before taking over as chair of the physical education and recreation department at Fayetteville State University in North Carolina.

"That physical education department was his baby," said Ike Walker, a former high school basketball coach who studied under Bell at North Carolina A&T in the 1950s. "He never said phys ed. He always said health and physical education. He wanted it to be a profession."

So much so that Bell organized physical education departments at several universities and later assisted in the development of Fayetteville's National Youth Sports Program, a summer organization for disadvantaged youths. Bell also continued his own education, earning his doctorate in health and physical education from Ohio State in 1960, and serving on numerous local and national health and physical education committees.

"Dr. Bell was part of a vanishing breed," Walker said. "In all my years with him, I never read or heard of anything shady. That's why I remember him as such a gentleman. The man was affable. He was courteous. He was kind. He didn't separate himself from students. I remember him fondly."

As should every Ohio State football player of African-American descent whose path toward stardom with the Buckeyes was paved by the great-grandson of a former slave.

SIDNEY GILLMAN

OSU END 1931–1933

27

NICKNAME: Sid

HOMETOWN: Minneapolis, Minnesota

HEIGHT: 5 ft 11 in **WEIGHT:** 188 lb

Sid formed a jazz band when he was a teenager. He played piano.

Supremely confident, overtly ambitious, and blessed with more than just a dash of chutzpah, Sid Gillman had the kind of personality that made him a success in nearly any endeavor he tried. Accomplished musician, aspiring lawyer, football star, innovator, hall of fame coach—Gillman was all of those and more.

Born October 26, 1911, in Minneapolis, Gillman was the fourth child of David and Sarah Gillman, a Jewish couple who bestowed the Hebrew name of Yisra'el on their newborn son. It was the same name given to Jacob after he had wrestled God's angel, and seemed appropriate for a headstrong child eager to make his own way in the world.

Sid's father was an Austrian immigrant who had once worked in New York City as a police detective, but he quickly soured on the tedium of police work and living in the cultural melting pot of America's largest city. He decided that a move to the northern part of Minneapolis with its Midwestern small-town way of life was perfect for his young family.

A friendly man with a firm handshake and an easy laugh, David ran a neighborhood grocery, then a pair of movie theaters. He was an extremely popular figure, a fair man who instinctively knew how to make people happy. Those were personality traits he apparently did not pass on to his son.

Young Sid was more interested in making himself happy. He neglected his studies, including studying the Torah, wiling away hours on the sandlots of Minneapolis while dreaming of becoming a major league baseball player. By the time he had graduated from North High School, however, football had surpassed everything as the teenager's passion—well, almost everything.

When Sid was seven, he began piano lessons and every spare minute he didn't have a ball in his hands was spent practicing at the family spinet. Eventually, he became so proficient with the instrument that he formed a small combo of jazz players, and they played at nearly every wedding and bar mitzvah in the Twin Cities area. During a Sweet Sixteen party at which the band was playing, Sid met Esther Berg, a petite brunette who shared Sid's interest in music as well as sports. They quickly became inseparable, and Esther became as much a passion for Sid as football.

Gillman, an all-city selection each of the three seasons he played varsity football at North, seemed bred to play the game. He wasn't tall, but his broad shoulders and big, meaty hands made him perfect for line play, and he also had enough speed and leaping ability to become a pass-catching threat at offensive end.

It seemed a foregone conclusion Gillman would play his college football at the University of Minnesota, but he was eager to escape Minneapolis and its culture of anti-Semitism. In those days, Jews were forbidden from holding memberships in such civic groups as the Kiwanis or Rotary clubs, and they were prevented from owning houses and being hired for certain kinds of jobs. So, Sid made the most difficult decision of his young life, leaving his hometown as well as Esther to move 750 miles and attend Ohio State.

"I felt that she and I had to separate for a while," Sid said years later. "I would have said, 'Let's get married,' and she would have said, 'No, we're not getting married until you get your degree and make some-thing of yourself.' I knew that if I went to Minnesota, I wouldn't have lasted long. (Going to Ohio State) was the smartest thing I ever did."

Gillman went to Ohio State to major in political science with the ambition of becoming a lawyer. Practicing law, playing a little piano on the weekends and raising a family with Esther would be a pretty good life, he reasoned, so he concentrated on studies and found himself a band called the Miserable Five that needed a piano player.

By the time he began his sophomore year, music was going much better than football. After participating on the freshman team in 1930, then undergoing surgery to correct a painful thumb injury, he was nowhere to be found on the preseason depth chart the following year. Somehow, though, Gillman found his way into the lineup by week two and never left. The following season was even better when he finished second on the team in tackles and earned first-team All-America honors. He was elected to serve as a senior captain in 1933, and the Buckeyes finished 7–1, good enough for a second-place finish in the conference. But the lone defeat was to Michigan, and the result sealed Sam Willaman's fate as head coach. Two months after the season ended, Willaman gave into pressure and offered his resignation.

Gillman didn't know it at the time, but his life was about to

immediately hit it off. From that day through the next four decades, Gillman would perfect Schmidt's innovative schemes and use them to win championships at the college and professional levels. In addition to copying many of Schmidt's intricate formations, Gillman paid

Gillman: "How can you possibly make a call like that? You stink, you know that? You stink."

Official, walking off a 15-yard penalty: "Hey, Sid, how do I smell from here?"

change. He was about to meet Francis Albert Schmidt. Schmidt was a tall Texan with a penchant for expensive suits and bow ties, and his slow drawl lulled listeners to sleep with its Southern charm before shocking them awake again with the vilest of profanity. Schmidt had been successful as a head coach everywhere he had been, and Ohio State officials eagerly lured him from Texas Christian University to become Willaman's successor.

Schmidt and Gillman first met at a luncheon shortly after the new coach had been hired, and the two

further homage to his mentor by beginning the practice of wearing a bow tie while coaching on the sideline. He also adopted Schmidt's often prickly attitude toward players, administrators, and rival coaches.

After serving as a student assistant under Schmidt in the spring of 1934, Gillman landed a full-time assistant's job at Denison University in the fall. He spent four seasons there, continuing to work part-time for Schmidt at Ohio State. They spent hours together strategizing and drawing up outlandish alignments, trying to figure out how to best utilize Schmidt's eclectic penchant for razzle-dazzle.

Gillman left Denison in 1938 to become a full-time assistant at Ohio State and was instantly Schmidt's favorite. In fact, he was the only staff member the increasingly-paranoid head coach would allow full access to the playbook. Even then, Gillman was forbidden from discussing plays or strategy with his fellow assistants.

After Schmidt was fired following the 1940 season, Gillman returned to Denison before landing his first head coaching job at Miami University in 1944. He led the Redskins to a 31–6–1 record over four seasons, then produced three Mid-American Conference championships at the University of Cincinnati from 1949–1952.

In the midst of that run, Gillman felt the tug from his alma mater. Ohio State head coach Wes Fesler had resigned and university officials focused their attention on Gillman. They eventually offered him the job and he accepted. Shortly thereafter, however, Gillman received a phone call from the university, rescinding the offer. Nothing was ever said on the record, but the inference seemed clear.

"I just had a sneaking suspicion that religion might have entered into it," Gillman said later. "Every time a job would open up in the Big Ten, I would (make a) play for it. But as soon as they found out I was a Jew, that was the end of it."

There was another possibility. Gillman had gained the reputation of being difficult to deal with, and he had a long line of administrators, former players, and fellow coaches whose dislike for him was deep-seated. Despite his string of championships, Sid left in his wake a string of tactless statements to boosters or administrators, extravagant demands on athletic department budgets, and denials that he was leaving for another job just before he left for another job.

When he left Oxford following the 1947 season, Gillman burned several bridges by resurfacing at Cincinnati in the spring of 1949 with several former Miami assistants on his staff. He had also coaxed several of Miami's most promising prospects to join him in the Queen City.

"I remember there was a lot of animosity," said College Football Hall of Fame coach Ara Parseghian. "Leaving the way he did...there was some anger that developed for Sid trying to recruit kids to go to Cincinnati. That's a no-no in coaching. That was a huge situation. A lot of words were spilled over that."

After Gillman left Cincinnati, the school was hit with NCAA sanctions stemming from allegations the football program gave more than the allowable amount of financial aid to its players and paid the expenses of potential recruits during campus visits between 1951 and 1953. Gillman denied any wrongdoing, but the Bearcats were hit with a one-year probationary period during which the team was barred from competing in a bowl game.

If any animus on the part of Miami or Cincinnati officials bothered him, Gillman never let it show. He left the college ranks in 1955 and became head coach of the National Football League's Los Angeles Rams, guiding the team to the league championship game that first season. After five years with the Rams, Gillman jumped to the

Los Angeles (later San Diego) Chargers of the upstart American Football League and produced five division championships and one league title in ten seasons.

Along the way, Gillman tutored and influenced several assistants who would go on to enjoy hall of fame coaching careers themselves, including Chuck Noll, Bill Walsh, and Dick Vermeil, who between them captured a combined eight Super Bowl titles.

Gillman was inducted into the Pro Football Hall of Fame as a coach in 1983.

"Sid Gillman is the father of the modern-day passing game at all levels of football—the National Football League, collegiate football, high school football, and even down to Pop Warner," said longtime NFL quarterback and ESPN analyst Ron Jaworski, whom Gillman tutored for three seasons. "The concepts that he developed are still being used at every level of football."

Not bad for a Jewish kid who just wanted to practice a little law and play the piano on weekends.

FRANCIS A. SCHMIDT

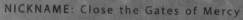

OSU COACH 1934–1940

NICKNAME: Close the Gates of Mercy

HOMETOWN: Downs, Kansas

RECORD: 39-16-1

BIG TEN CHAMPIONSHIPS:

1935, 1939

Francis was obsessed with writing plays. He wrote them everywhere—on cocktail napkins and even envelopes.

*E*qual parts innovator, absent-minded professor, and paranoid monomaniac, Francis A. Schmidt was one of the most unusual personalities in the history of the Ohio State football program.

He earned a law degree but never practiced law. He dressed like a captain of industry, yet peppered his speech with enough profanity to make a longshoreman blush. He laughed and partied with his players, apt to be seen strumming his banjo in a fraternity house late on a Saturday night. Still, the man who coached the Buckeyes for seven seasons from 1934 through 1940 was so paranoid he refused to share his vast playbook with those same players. Success so consumed Schmidt that the relentless pursuit of it often hamstrung his ability to attain it, something that very likely led to the coach's premature death.

Francis Albert Schmidt was born December 3, 1885, in Downs, Kansas, a tiny dot of a town that rose out of the northern Kansas prairie only because locomotives for the Central Branch of the Union Pacific Railroad had to have somewhere to turn around.

Schmidt's father, Francis Walter, was a studio photographer during a time when not many Kansas farmers had the means or wherewithal to sit for portraits. Therefore, he uprooted his family every few years in search of a new customer base. That kind of restlessness seemed to have an impact on young Francis Albert, who never remained very long in one place his entire life. He did stay long enough in Fairbury, Nebraska, to graduate from high school there and earn his first measure of success. He was elected senior class president, captained the football team, and helped his two-man track team finish second at the state meet, a single point behind a much larger team from Lincoln.

Second place wasn't good enough for Schmidt, though, saying that he "cleared those hurdles with too much room to spare." It was the beginning of a chase for perfection that would ultimately destroy him.

Following his high school graduation, Schmidt continued the life of a vagabond, but he seemed successful nearly everywhere he went. He won a varsity letter at Nebraska during the only season he played college football, and he completed his academic work toward undergraduate and law degrees simultaneously in just three years.

He fully intended to pursue a career as an attorney, but his mother, Emma, had fallen ill in the summer of 1907 and young Francis chose to help care for her. By then, the Schmidt family was in Arkansas City, Kansas, and he took turns caring for his mother and running his father's business, making himself into an excellent photographer.

Emma Schmidt died later that year, and Francis stayed in Arkansas City to help at the family photo studio. Still, he knew his hyperactive mind wouldn't allow him to settle for such a mundane existence. He began taking long walks around town during the early evening as he tried to clear his head and ease his restlessness. During one of those walks, he stumbled upon the city high school football team as it began fall practice. Not long after, Arkansas City High School had itself a new football coach.

It was the beginning of a new career for Schmidt, one that evolved rapidly. In the fall of 1915, he spent the first of two seasons as an assistant football coach and head men's basketball coach at Henry Kendall College (now the University of Tulsa). He left Kendall to join the U.S. Army during World War I, quickly rising to the rank of captain. Upon his discharge, he returned to Kendall where he was named head coach of both the football and men's basketball programs.

Schmidt eventually concentrated his career solely on football, but it was at Kendall that the man known for his bombastic personality began to develop the kind of frenetic offensive philosophy that earned him such nicknames as "Frantic Francis" and "Close The Gates Of Mercy." After winning a pair of conference championships in only three seasons at Kendall, Schmidt's coaching career skyrocketed. Seven years at the University of Arkansas was followed by five seasons—and two more titles—at Texas Christian University before Schmidt finally hit the big time.

Ohio State had dismissed head coach Sam Willaman following the 1933 season and settled upon Schmidt as the man to replace him. Still, many in the Columbus community were skeptical about the tall, angular man who came north armed with little more than a bow tie and a distinctive Southern drawl.

The day the coach was formally hired by the university, he sat through a battery of questions from Columbus newspapermen until the inevitable was asked. "Michigan is pretty tough," a reporter offered. "How concerned are you about them?"

"How concerned should I be?" Schmidt replied slowly, flashing a wry smile. "Don't forget they put their trousers on one leg at a time just the same as anyone else."

No one knew it at the time, especially since the coach was simply repeating an old Texas aphorism. But somewhere along the line "trousers" were substituted for "pants," and the genesis of one of Ohio State's oldest and most cherished traditions—the Gold Pants Club—was born.

Not only did the new coach lead his team to victory over archrival Michigan later that fall, Ohio State defeated its hated archrivals in each of Schmidt's first four seasons in Columbus—a feat still unmatched by any other head coach in program history.

While victories against the Wolverines seemed to come easily, each of Schmidt's first two seasons with the Buckeyes was marred by a single defeat, costing the team a chance to win its first national championship. An 18–13 loss at Notre Dame in 1935 was particularly disheartening after Ohio State held a seemingly safe 13–0 lead heading into the fourth quarter.

Schmidt was roundly criticized following the game because he had taken out several of his best defensive players at the beginning of the final period, and substitution rules in those days prevented those players from re-entering the game in the same quarter. As a result, Notre Dame scored three touchdowns, including the eventual game-winner with only fifty seconds remaining.

"Smitty felt he was completely responsible," Ohio State backfield coach Floyd Stahl said later. "I've never seen a man so disconsolate."

Determined to make up for his blunder, Schmidt redoubled his efforts to shape Ohio State into the most potent offensive team in college football. Unfortunately, that effort became a 24/7 obsession and he began to blur the line between colorful eccentric and compulsive neurotic.

There was the time Schmidt took his car to a garage for repairs. Because he was in a hurry, the coach said he would wait in the car while the mechanic put the vehicle on a hoist to determine the problem. Several minutes later, after becoming engrossed in diagramming new plays, Schmidt opened the driver's side door and tumbled six feet to the concrete floor below, spraining his ankle.

"At practice, he would have plays sticking out of his belt and pockets and everywhere," halfback Tom Kinkade said. "At a banquet, he'd be writing plays, or I'd see him on campus walking through a flowerbed looking at his plays. He was a little crazy."

Some estimated the coach had devised more than five hundred plays, some of which he had scribbled on cocktail napkins or the backs of envelopes—any slip of paper available at the time.

"There were so many plays. We had cards with the plays written on them that we stuck underneath our helmets," three-year starting quarterback Tippy Dye said. "During timeouts, we took them out and looked at them. During a punt return against Michigan one year, I got cocked pretty good. It knocked me out a little, my helmet flew off and the plays scattered all over the field. I was still a little out of it, but I made sure and picked 'em up."

"He was kind of neurotic, strange and private. He didn't have close friends or curry favor. He was just a bizarre guy—he probably could have used medication. Everything with him was just overboard."
—*Brett Perkins,* Frantic Francis

Whereas most college offenses of the era ran about eight basic plays, Schmidt devised more than fifty, each of which had several variations. Sometimes, the variations even had variations, making it difficult for the players to keep track of every nuance of so many

the Faculty Club, they'd sneak in and look because they didn't always know what was coming. He was very secretive. He thought everyone was cheating him, afraid someone was going to steal his offense."

Finally, Schmidt's fanaticism about offense caught up with him.

His concentration on offense made it difficult for him to relate to personnel during a game. There was the tale of two Ohio State tackles, who shall be known here as Nitro and Oxman.

"Nitro," said Schmidt, "go in for Oxman."

"Nitro's already in there, Coach," said Oxman. "I'm Oxman."

After a brief pause, Schmidt said, "Okay, whoever you are. Go in for whoever he is."

—*Tim Cohane*, Great Football Coaches of the Twenties and Thirties

formations. Neither did it help when Schmidt often refused to share his playbook long enough for everyone to get on the same page.

"The assistants didn't even have all the plays," fullback Jack Graf said. "He had them on big pads of paper, and at lunch when he went over to

The Buckeyes compiled only a 4-3-1 record in 1938 and suffered their first defeat against Michigan after four straight victories. Losses to the Wolverines would follow during the next two seasons, including a 40–0 loss to Michigan that completed a four-loss campaign in

1940. The Buckeyes had fallen victim to a rebuilding season, a number of injuries to crucial players, and a brutal schedule that included three of the top eight ranked teams in the nation.

But a lot of influential boosters had grown increasingly tired of Schmidt's antics. Following the 1940 season, *Ohio State Journal* editor Robert E. Hooey quoted an "unimpeachable source" as saying the coach's contract would not be renewed because "on frequent occasions and especially during the last three seasons, Schmidt has been the storm center of numerous arguments throughout the coaching and player ranks."

The university immediately debunked the report, and Schmidt continued to enjoy the support of key allies within Ohio State's athletic department, most notably director of athletics Lynn St. John. Nevertheless, Schmidt's nature wouldn't allow him to wait until things blew over. He offered a hastily written letter of resignation to the university Athletic Board, and then hoped the board would reject it.

On December 16, however, the board unanimously voted to accept Schmidt's resignation despite an overall seven-year record of 39-16-1. Five weeks later, the Buckeyes announced Schmidt's successor—thirty-three-year-old Massillon (Ohio) High School coach Paul Brown.

For all intents and purposes, Schmidt's demise in Columbus signified the beginning of the end of what had been a superlative career. He resurfaced at the University of Idaho during the spring of 1941 but posted two losing seasons before the Vandals suspended their football program for the duration of World War II.

Years of neglecting his health in favor of his coaching career finally began to take its toll, and Schmidt was hospitalized in Spokane, Washington, in early September 1944. Without football, it seemed he had nothing left to live for, and less than three weeks later, he was gone at the age of fifty-eight.

The cause of his death was a brain tumor—as well as a broken heart.

WILLIAM H.H. DYE

OSU QUARTERBACK 1934–1936

NICKNAME: Tippy

HOMETOWN: Harrisonville, Ohio

HEIGHT: 5 ft 7½ in **WEIGHT:** 145 lb

NFL DRAFT: 1937, Cincinnati Bengals

50

Tippy played for the very first Cincinnati Bengals team in 1937. The team lasted for only a few years.

Football has always been a rough-and-tumble enterprise populated by gladiators with such ominous nicknames as Dick "Night Train" Lane, Clyde "Bulldog" Turner, and Johnny "Blood" McNally, monikers used to strike terror in opponents before the players bearing those names ever took the field.

It wasn't quite that way at Ohio State in the mid-1930s, especially when the Buckeyes had a quarterback whose name seemed more suited for a character from a Shakespeare comedy. Yet Tippy Dye achieved a feat that remained unparalleled for seventy years before going on to lead one of the most successful careers in college coaching and sports administration.

A charismatic bundle of charm, guile, and natural athletic talent packed into a tiny 5-foot-6, 130-pound package, William Henry Harrison Dye was named after an uncle who was named after the ninth President of the United States. William Henry Harrison served the shortest term of any U.S. President, dying just thirty-two days after delivering his two-hour inaugural address amid a cold drizzle. Although Harrison's presidential term was a short one, he had a long and storied military career, which included leading an 1811 victory against a Native American uprising at the Battle of Tippecanoe. Henceforth, Harrison became known as "Old Tippecanoe," and any youngster named in his honor picked up the same moniker. Since young William's uncle already went by "Tip," the newest addition to the Dye family immediately became known as "Tippy."

Tippy grew up in Pomeroy, Ohio, a small town just across the Ohio River from West Virginia known mostly for its coal and salt mines. His parents had separated, and Tippy and his older brother and sister lived with their mother, Mayme, who operated a tearoom out of a three-story building on Main Street. The tearoom was on the ground floor while the family lived on the third floor, a fortunate thing as the Ohio River flooded Main Street on a regular basis.

There wasn't much glamour attached to a Pomeroy childhood, but Tippy didn't seem to care. He participated in every kind of sandlot game he could find, which invariably led to some unknowing bigger kid picking on him because of his size. "I never started a fight in my life," Tippy once said. "But I finished quite a few."

By the time he reached high school, his status among his peers was much more impressive than his physical stature. Nevertheless, he found success in every sport Pomeroy High offered, winning an astounding fourteen varsity letters by starring in football, basketball, baseball, and track. It was also during high school when the typically reserved Tippy summoned enough courage to ask Mary Kennedy Russell if he could walk her home after school. Mary, the beautiful youngest daughter of a local attorney, giggled and said yes, and it was the beginning of a relationship that would last for the next seventy years.

Like her older sisters and brother, Mary was blessed academically and she planned to follow her siblings to Ohio State after graduation from high school. That presented a dilemma of sorts for Tippy, who had planned to follow his brother and sister to Ohio University and play basketball there. He weighed his decision only long enough to tell his mother he had changed his mind and would attend Ohio State in the fall.

Basketball was the sport Tippy enjoyed most, but he also liked football and decided to try out for the freshman team at OSU. He soon discovered he wasn't the only campus newbie to have that idea as enough freshmen to field twelve full teams showed up for the first day of practice. Because of his size, the coaching staff suggested that Tippy might be more suited for the role as team manager, but he insisted upon playing. The coaches begrudgingly relented, putting him on the seventh-string roster. By the time the season was over, however, he had become the top-ranked quarterback on the freshman team.

Despite the progress he made, Tippy was forced to start over again as he entered his sophomore season. He was small compared to his fellow classmates, but his diminutive frame was even more exaggerated among his older varsity teammates. Additionally, he was being asked to learn an entirely new system. Ohio State had replaced five-year head coach Sam Willaman with the innovative Francis A. Schmidt, who quickly installed a complex offense that placed special emphasis on the quarterback position.

College football rules in 1934 were much different from those of today, most notably regarding the calling of plays. Coaches could not signal from the sideline, nor were they allowed to send in plays with substitute players. That put the onus for calling plays squarely on the shoulders of the quarterback.

Despite the complexity of his overall offensive scheme, Schmidt preferred to keep Dye out of harm's way as much as possible, often instructing his quarterback to run to the opposite side of the field from where the play was being run. There were several advantages to that philosophy. First and foremost, running Dye away from the action was an effective misdirection fake for the Buckeyes while it also protected a diminutive player from the physical pounding a quarterback of that era would normally absorb. Schmidt also liked the idea of his quarterback being able to survey

the field and quickly concentrate on the next play, rather than having his brains repeatedly scrambled by blocking and/or being tackled on every play.

Now, the only problem was learning Schmidt's voluminous playbook. But Tippy was a quick study, thanks in part to Mary, who had become his late-night study partner at the campus library. Impressed by Tippy's quick grasp of his system, as well as his confidence and fearlessness, Schmidt installed the sophomore as a co-starter at quarterback with junior Stan Picura.

Dye thrived for the Buckeyes as a deceptive runner, deft passer, and elusive kick returner, helping the team win nineteen games and two Western Conference championships from 1934 to 1936. Most notably, he helped Ohio State to three consecutive victories over archrival Michigan, becoming the first starting quarterback in program history to beat the Wolverines three years in a row. It was a feat that would not be matched until Troy Smith did it seven decades later from 2004 to 2006.

During his time on campus, Tippy became a sort of surrogate

son for Schmidt and his wife Evelyn. Thanks to Schmidt's vagabond life as a coach, the couple never had children, so they would often form a familial connection to one of Francis's players. "I thought he was a great, great coach and a fine individual," Tippy said. "He treated me like a son—both he and Evelyn did—and I loved both of them. They had me to dinner sometimes, and I don't think they ever had anyone to dinner."

In addition to his football exploits at Ohio State, Dye was a three-time All-Big Ten selection and second-team All-American in basketball as well as a two-year letterman in baseball. As if his sporting life didn't occupy enough of his time, Tippy lived at the Phi Delta Theta house for three years and paid for his meals by washing dishes. He also sold Pontiac automobiles until he had enough money to buy one for himself. Along with teammate Charlie Ream, he worked at the sprawling downtown Lazarus department store, and he also worked for a time at the State House of Representatives, earning three dollars a day as a page and making new friends such as fellow page Jesse Owens. Any spare time

was devoted to Mary, who was president of the Pi Beta Phi sorority on the OSU campus.

After graduation, Tippy played professional football for one year with the first incarnation of the Cincinnati Bengals of the old American Football League before embarking upon a coaching career in college basketball. He was an assistant at Brown University and Ohio State before serving in the U.S. Navy in World War II. While in the service, he found time to coach a little football, teaching the T-formation to future Pro Football Hall of Fame quarterback Otto Graham.

Upon his discharge from the Navy, Dye returned to his alma mater and spent four seasons as head coach of the basketball Buckeyes, leading them to the 1950 Big Ten championship. Fred Taylor, the winningest coach in Ohio State history, was a starting forward on that '50 team, and Taylor often said he benefitted greatly from the way Dye carried himself on the sideline as well as in public.

"There's no question Tip influenced Fred," said Dick Schnittker, an All-America forward who also played for Dye at Ohio State. "You could see that in Fred's players when his ball clubs played. They were very calm, very tough, never got upset, never got mad. That's a direct influence of Tip."

Following the 1950 title season, Dye took over the basketball program at the University of Washington, and in 1953 guided the Huskies to their only NCAA Tournament Final Four appearance. He remained at Washington for nine seasons before beginning his career in sports administration, serving as director of athletics at Wichita State, Nebraska, and Northwestern. While at Nebraska, he laid the foundation for a college football dynasty by hiring Hall of Fame coach Bob Devaney in 1962. Over the next eleven years, Devaney and the Cornhuskers won eight Big Eight Conference championships and two national titles.

Dye spent his later years in California, living with his daughter and son-in-law following Mary's death in 2001. But he was asked to receive one final curtain call in 2006 when he was invited by Ohio State to watch from the Ohio Stadium press box while Smith tried

to equal his feat of three straight victories against Michigan. He was 91 at the time and figured he was simply a long-forgotten name on a yellowed page of history. "He never talked about any of his stuff unless you weaseled it out of him," said his son William III, who is nicknamed Tippy Jr. "He was so modest and humble. He knew how good he was, but it was like he was no better than a guy living in a box under a bridge."

Dye decided only at the last minute to accept the invitation, and was glad he did. During the game, a thrilling 42–39 victory by the top-ranked Buckeyes over number two Michigan, Tippy received a standing ovation from the record crowd of more than 105,000. Then he got a heartwarming bonus on his trip home. "People recognized him at the airport in Chicago," said his niece Lindsey Ein. "He got a big kick out of that."

Dye returned to northern California where he lived until his death in 2012, slipping away at the age of 97. His final request was granted a few days later when he was laid to rest next to his beloved Mary in their hometown of Pomeroy.

ESCO SARKKINEN

OSU END 1937–1939 **OSU ASSISTANT COACH** 1946–1977

HOMETOWN: Rochester, New York

RECORD: 78-33-9

BIG TEN CHAMPIONSHIPS:

1916, 1917, 1920

25

Due to an accident involving Esco, a scooter, and a milk truck while at OSU, Esco never got his driver's license and refused to drive a car.

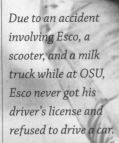

The nickname "Super Sleuth" doesn't seem to fit a man who stood more than six feet tall, weighed in excess of 200 pounds and refused to drive a car. Yet, that was the moniker Woody Hayes hung on longtime assistant coach Esco Sarkkinen for his detailed scouting reports filed during reconnaissance missions from behind enemy lines.

Sarkkinen had been an All-American end at Ohio State in 1939, then returned to his alma mater seven years later to become one of college football's most acclaimed coaches of offensive and defensive ends. But as good as he was at tutoring young linemen, Sarkkinen was even better at scouting. His descriptive accounts of a rival's tendencies, specific to the tiniest detail, were invaluable to Hayes and the rest of his staff as they prepared game plans for upcoming opponents.

"Sark was acknowledged as the best football scout in the Big Ten certainly, and probably in the country," said longtime Michigan head coach Bo Schembechler, who served with Sarkkinen on Hayes's staff at OSU from 1958 to 1962. "I can't emphasize how much a good scout meant to our football program when I was an assistant coach. It was a critical resource."

Gene Fekete, who like Sarkkinen was an All-American performer for the Buckeyes who returned to Columbus as an assistant coach, remembered a scouting report on Michigan one year that was so minute in specificity, Hayes had trouble digesting its intricacies.

"Woody asked if we could beat them," Fekete said. "Well, if you said yes, before you could hardly get it out of your mouth, the old man would ask, 'How?' So, Sark answered, 'Well, Woody, if we do thus and so...' Woody asked again, 'Can we beat 'em?' and again Sark says, "If we do thus and so...' Woody was getting mad by this time and told Sark, 'I want you to go out that door and come back in, and I'm going to ask you once more!' Sark went out the door, came back in and Woody asked, 'Can we beat 'em?' and Sark said, 'If we do thus and so...'

"Well, Sark went out that door and came back in two or three more times that morning, and they kept on yelling at each other. It finally went to a no-decision. Time was being wasted, which Woody didn't like, and the other assistants could no longer hide their amusement, which Woody also didn't like."

Sarkkinen was one of only a handful of assistants who could go toe-to-toe with the legendary Hayes temper and not be swept away in a hot rush of molten lava. But his coaching style was in stark contrast to his famous boss's fire-and-brimstone approach, a trait that earned Sarkkinen the affection and respect of his fellow assistants as well as his players.

"Sark had an effective diplomatic air about him that put him in good stead with Coach Hayes and all of us," said former OSU head coach Earle Bruce. "Sark was the greatest assistant coach ever at Ohio State. Knowledgeable and hard-working, he covered every detail. He was soft-spoken, humorous and fun to be with. Sark was one of the most positive individuals I have ever known."

Two-year starting defensive end Tom Marendt said, "Sark had the one quality that everyone playing under him appreciated. Whenever you goofed up, he never corrected or criticized you in front of the other players. He would take you off to the side for privacy. Coach was not a wimp. He could be very demanding and get in your face—but never within earshot of your fellow team members. That considerate kind of one-on-one coaching was rare and all of us appreciated it."

Sarkkinen also had a wry sense of humor, an encyclopedic knowledge of Ohio State football trivia, and a deathly aversion to driving an automobile. The first two of those personality traits served him well during his thirty-two years as an OSU assistant. The third proved problematic, even though Sark had a pretty good reason for his fear of motor vehicles.

During his days as an Ohio State student, a devil-may-care Sarkkinen could be seen tearing around campus on a motor scooter, his tousled blond hair flowing in the breeze. One day, late for a class, Sark sped around a blind corner toward his usual parking space behind the physical education building, a spot on a loading ramp that served one of the dormitories. At the same time, a fully-loaded milk truck was backing up that same ramp. Sark saw the truck as he rounded the corner, but it was too late. He lost control of the scooter, smashed through one of the truck's glass doors, and wound up sprawled among a mixture of broken glass and spilled milk.

and Central Ohio where he could get around much easier. His wife, Freda, took turns with other assistant coaches performing chauffeur duties, and whenever they were not available, Sark improvised.

"Sark had his own polite way of dealing with potentially explosive situations, through cigarette smoking. Whenever Woody asked him a question, Sark would slowly keep on puffing, pensively, as if conjuring up an answer. After a while, Hayes would become impatient and move on."
—*Earle Bruce*

"It was pure luck he wasn't killed or seriously injured," Fekete said. Sarkkinen never again drove any vehicle, including a car, later boasting that he was the answer to a trivia question of which modern-day OSU football coach never had an Ohio driver's license.

Having an assistant coach that refused to get behind the wheel proved challenging at times, especially when Sark was assigned to the fertile Cleveland recruiting area. When Hayes hired Lou McCullough in 1963, however, McCullough reassigned Sarkkinen to Columbus

"We used to say if you see an empty taxicab standing in front of a high school building in Columbus, Sark is inside recruiting," said Bill Mallory, who served with Sarkkinen at Ohio State from 1966 to '68.

Before he was reassigned, Sarkkinen did extremely well recruiting in and around Cleveland, perhaps because he knew the lakefront area so well. He was born April 9, 1918, in Conneaut, Ohio, a small Lake Erie town located in the northeastern tip of the state about seventy miles from Cleveland. Esco attended Harding High School in nearby Fairport Harbor and became a star in basketball, track, and football for the Skippers. He later found the same kind of success at Ohio State, despite the fact he had not been actively recruited by the Buckeyes. Sark became one of the rare sophomores under head coach Francis A. Schmidt to earn a starting berth, playing end positions on both offense and defense, and by the time he was a senior, he had been honored with first team All-American recognition.

Sid Gillman, who would go on to a Pro Football Hall of Fame career as a head coach, was Sarkkinen's position coach for the Buckeyes in 1938 and '39, and said the All-American award was well-deserved.

"He was a great blocker, hitting hard and clean," Gillman said. "He was a near perfect pass catcher and could make yards after a reception. He was always in position to help the runner downfield. On defense, Sark piled up the interference if he didn't make the tackle himself... He was just the kind of player who sensed where trouble might be and made sure to be there."

Sarkkinen was selected by the Green Bay Packers in the third round of the 1940 National Football League draft, but by that time he had no desire to continue playing the game. The coaching bug had bitten and bitten hard, and Esco found himself in Lancaster, Ohio, in the fall of 1940, serving as a high school assistant under E.J. Wilson. When Wilson retired the following summer, Sarkkinen was promoted to head coach and led the Golden Gales to their first conference title since 1933. For meritorious service to youngsters, a citizen committee in town named the 23-year-old their "Man of the Year."

Despite his initial success as a head coach, Sarkkinen could not escape the harsh realities of the time. After only two seasons at Lancaster High School, he enlisted in the Coast Guard and attended its Officer Candidate School. He graduated in ninety days with the rank of lieutenant junior grade and was assigned to the Coast Guard station in New London, Connecticut. There, he played end on the Coast Guard football team and later became its line coach.

Years later, Sarkkinen's daughter Sandy said she believed enlisting in the Coast Guard provided insightful commentary regarding her father's character. "He was always a cautious person and not a big risk-taker," Sandy said. "This caution, I believe, was reflected in his choice of military service. Curious as it may seem for the coach of a contact sport, my father was a gentle person and somewhat of a pacifist. Even so, as the son of immigrant parents (from Finland), he deeply appreciated living in America. His decision to serve in the Coast Guard was, I believe, a way of being true to his character while providing honorable service to his country."

That caution might also have led to Sarkkinen's reluctance to move around during his coaching career. "Esco's coaching potential was exceptional," Gillman said. "He had everything needed to become a top head coach. For a coach like myself, who had a driving need to keep moving up in the coaching ranks, it is extremely difficult for me to understand how Esco—or any other coach—could be satisfied with assistant coaching as a career.

"But Esco was very satisfied to be an assistant coach at Ohio State. He loved the university and its football program and was content to con-tribute his coaching talent to them."

Following his discharge from the Coast Guard, Sarkkinen was back on the OSU campus in 1946 as an assistant coach under Paul Bixler. It was the beginning of a thirty-two-year run as an assistant under Bixler, Wes Fesler, and Hayes.

"It's true that I had a lot of offers to move on," Sarkkinen said, "but once I got the Ohio State job, with all the great tradition and great players and great coaches and great fans, nothing else appealed to me."

When Fesler was forced out following the 1950 season, Sarkkinen never made it any secret that he preferred several other potential candidates over Hayes. He immediately made peace with his new boss following their initial staff meeting, however. Sarkkinen expected a dissertation on football and coaching philosophy, and instead received a half-hour discourse on loyalty.

That was all Sark needed to hear and it began a twenty-seven-year partnership with Hayes that produced thirteen Big Ten championships, five national titles, and countless All-American players.

DONALD
SCOTT

OSU HALFBACK AND QUARTERBACK 1938–1940

NICKNAME: Don

HOMETOWN: Canton, Ohio

HEIGHT: 6 ft 1 in **WEIGHT:** 208 lb

ALL-AMERICAN: 1939, 1940

NFL DRAFT: 1941, Chicago Bears

Ohio State University's airport was named Don Scott Airport in Don's honor.

*T*he date was October 4, 1943, and no one at Ohio State felt much like celebrating.

Two days after Ernie Parks and Dean Sensenbaugher had combined to rush for 338 yards and four touchdowns during a 27–6 victory over Missouri in a half-empty Ohio Stadium, the university got word that former quarterback Don Scott's bomber aircraft had crashed during a routine training flight near a U.S. Marauder Base in Great Britain. Scott was killed instantly along with his co-pilot and a flight engineer.

Scott's death was front-page news in Columbus as well as his Canton, Ohio, hometown during an era when hundreds of thousands of American families were mourning loved ones killed in action in World War II. Scott's death seemed more meaningful, though. If he could be taken, no mother's son seemed immune to the horror of war.

Born May 4, 1919, Scott lived a storybook life and had the boyish charm and good looks to match. As a youngster, he attended Worley School where he was regarded as the best at any game he chose—

football, basketball, golf, bowling. He was even considered the best marbles player. Later, he would spend his ninth and tenth-grade years at Lehman High School, playing defensive tackle on the football team and center on the basketball team, before transferring to Canton McKinley in 1935 and leading the McKinley basketball team to the state semifinals twice. He was a two-way tackle for the Bulldogs his junior year of football before switching to quarterback as a senior, and that year he completed forty-eight of ninety-three passes for 991 yards and eleven touchdowns. He also rushed for 657 yards and kicked thirty-four extra points.

When Scott decided to attend college at Ohio State, success followed him from Canton to Columbus. He lettered in basketball in 1939, the year the Buckeyes lost a 46–33 decision to Oregon in the first NCAA Tournament championship game, and he earned three varsity letters on the football team from 1938 to 1940. He led the Buckeyes to the Big Ten championship in 1939 and earned All-America honors in both '39 and '40, but his football career at Ohio State was a rocky one.

Head coach Francis A. Schmidt was an ahead-of-his-time offensive tactician who was constantly tinkering with his already-voluminous playbook. Unfortunately, the fidgety Schmidt also liked to tinker with his players and Scott had become one of his pet projects. Intrigued by Scott's size—thick shoulders, muscular thighs and quick feet packed onto a 6-foot-2, 210-pound frame—Schmidt tried to place his prodigy at the all-important left halfback position. The experiment progressed throughout Scott's freshman season, but Schmidt's penchant for restlessness caused him to lose interest, and after playing nearly the entire season opener in 1938, Scott saw his playing time increasingly diminish until he appeared in only nine minutes of action against Michigan in the season's final contest.

The following spring, Schmidt had changed his mind about Scott, this time switching him to the quarterback spot in the middle of the Ohio State offense. The transformation was amazing as Scott took on the responsibility of operating Schmidt's intricate philosophy, and he led the Buckeyes to the conference title. He was among the nation's leaders in passing and punting and remained a lethal threat to opposing defenses while running with the ball. He also continued to possess exceptional blocking skills—honed during his years as a lineman—and following a 61–0 rout of the University of Chicago in early November, Schmidt remarked, "I can't remember a back so dangerous in so many departments of play."

The era of good feeling between coach and quarterback would be short-lived, however.

Two weeks later, the Buckeyes were seeking to put the finishing touches on an undefeated conference campaign with their traditional season finale against Michigan. Unfortunately, the outcome seemed predetermined. The arrival of Ohio State's train into Ann Arbor was delayed, sending the already high-strung Schmidt into a lathered frenzy. When the Buckeyes finally made it to the stadium just minutes before kickoff, their coach blew another fuse when his plea to push back the starting time of the game was rebuffed. The players ran onto the field, many of them improperly taped and none of them in their usual game-time mindset, but they had adrenaline and anger working for them, which paid off early.

Ohio State raced out to a 14–0 lead on the strength of two touchdown passes from Scott, one to end Frank Clair and the other to Vic Marino, a guard who had lined up at an end position before drifting to the back of the end zone to snare an easy pass thrown against misdirection. But the Buckeyes couldn't sustain their initial emotion, and Michigan came back to tie the game midway through the third quarter.

The teams remained deadlocked until the final minute of the game when Michigan scored a 24-yard touchdown off a fake field goal. Scott did his best to rally the Buckeyes in the final fifty seconds of the pitched battle, picking up 38 yards on back-to-back scrambles to move the ball to the Wolverines' 23-yard line. But with time left for only one more play, Scott's desperation throw toward the end zone was intercepted and Michigan was able to secure a 17–14 victory.

Despite the loss, the Buckeyes were still Big Ten champions and Scott and his teammates tried their best to celebrate their triumph. But the idiosyncratic Schmidt wouldn't allow it. His solution to the loss at Michigan was to make marathon practice sessions even longer, riding and deriding players so mercilessly that many began plotting against him.

Scott was never in that camp, but with so much dissension on the team his production began to suffer. What no one knew was that Schmidt had entrusted his quarterback to call his own plays in 1940, but while Scott was attempting to direct his team's attack, the normally quiet huddle had become a place for teammates to air personal grievances against their coach. Scott didn't enjoy the role of dictator or arbiter, and Schmidt felt Scott didn't have the work ethic or commitment to gain a strong enough grip on the coach's complex system.

By the time the season finale against Michigan was played, the Ohio State team was a fractured mess and the Wolverines took full advantage. Halfback Tom Harmon solidified his frontrunner status in the Heisman Trophy race by accounting for five touchdowns during a 40–0 victory that marked the final game of the Schmidt era. Several weeks later, growing increasingly tired of Schmidt and his antics, the university voted not to renew the coach's contract, replacing him with Paul Brown, the vibrant young high school coach from Massillon, Ohio.

Despite his challenging senior season, Scott earned his second All-America honor and was selected by the Chicago Bears with the ninth overall pick of the first round of the 1941 NFL draft. Entering his sophomore season at Ohio State, Scott had joked, "Upon graduating, I would like to enter into an engineering practice, but would consider a 'palm-greasing' pro football offer." That tongue-in-cheek comment never came to fruition, however. Despite a lucrative offer from the Bears, as well as the offer of a Major League Baseball contract from the Pittsburgh Pirates, Scott decided against a career in professional sports.

While an undergrad, he had participated in the Civilian Pilot Training Program, an initiative by the United States aimed at increasing the number of qualified pilots in the event the country was drawn into World War II. Unlike many of his peers at the time, however, Scott didn't wait. He enlisted in the U.S. Army's Air Corps on March 15, 1941, more than eight months before the bombing of Pearl Harbor.

Scott immediately became a commissioned pilot and was sent to Kelly Field in San Antonio, Texas, to continue his training, eventually advancing to the rank of captain. In June of 1943, he was sent to one of several AAC airbases in Great Britain where he was placed in command of a Marauder bomber crew. Scott participated in nine successful bombing missions over the next three months and was rapidly earning the reputation as one of the Air Corps' finest pilots. Eager to enhance that reputation, Scott took advantage of a rare lull in the fighting to gain more experience in the air. Three days earlier, he had been made squadron commander and led a successful raid over France, and he wanted to make further tests of his airplane's instrumentation. He took off on October 1, 1943, accompanied by his co-pilot, Second Lieutenant Ramsey J. Toon, and Master Sergeant James R. Sutton, who was serving as mechanical engineer on the routine training flight. Approximately twenty minutes after takeoff, bad weather suddenly enveloped the area and buffeted the aircraft. Scott tried valiantly to keep the Marauder in the sky and get back to the airfield, but the plane crashed near where it had taken off, killing all three men aboard.

Colonel Carl R. Storrie, Scott's commanding officer, immediately cabled Scott's father in Canton to inform him of his son's death, saying, "Captain Scott was one of the best pilots in the Air Corps. Much was expected of him as a commanding officer, and his ability as a pilot and leader of men was outstanding. He will be difficult to replace."

Scott left behind his parents and his wife, Leone, who was pregnant with the couple's first child. Eight days later, Don Sands Scott was born at Grant Hospital in Columbus. The new mother bravely posed with her newborn son for newspaper photographers but was clearly in shock over the reports of her husband's death. "Just before he went overseas, Don told me not to give up," she said. "He said, 'If you get a report that I'm missing, don't believe it. I have a pretty good idea of what to expect and I think I can get out of most situations. Don't give up. I'll be back.'"

Scott's body was flown back to Canton where he was laid to rest with full military honors. Two weeks after his death, Ohio State officials announced they would rename the university airport in Scott's honor, and that next spring, with the fallen hero's wife and infant son participating in the ceremonies, Don Scott Airport—located just fifteen minutes northwest of Ohio Stadium—was dedicated.

LESLIE
HORVATH

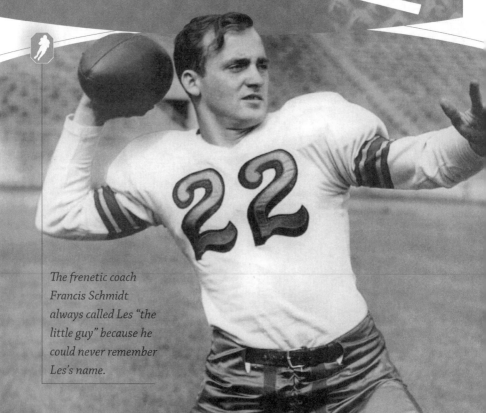

OSU HALFBACK 1940–1942, 1944

NICKNAME: Les

HOMETOWN: South Bend, Indiana

HEIGHT: 5 ft 10 in   **WEIGHT:** 173 lb

ALL-AMERICAN: 1944

NFL DRAFT: 1943, Cleveland Rams

The frenetic coach Francis Schmidt always called Les "the little guy" because he could never remember Les's name.

Ohio State wasn't expected to field much of a team in 1944 and Les Horvath's college football days were supposed to be behind him. Instead, the Buckeyes completed a perfect season, nearly won a second national championship in three years, and Horvath became the school's first winner of the prestigious Heisman Memorial Trophy.

Horvath had been a vital part of Ohio State's national championship season in 1942 as a junior halfback and had already earned three varsity letters for the Buckeyes. But with World War II raging and hundreds of thousands of college-aged young men enlisted in the military, football was a mere afterthought.

Horvath had stayed on campus in 1943 to finish his studies as part of the U.S. Army's Specialized Training Programs. The ones involved in the programs were thought of as soldiers, just the same as those overseas; therefore Horvath was barred from playing during what would have been his senior year. Following that 1943 season, during which the depleted Buckeyes had posted a 3–6 record—their first losing campaign since 1924—head coach Paul Brown

was gone, too. The 35-year-old coach was off to Great Lakes Naval Base in northern Chicago as a lieutenant junior grade in the U.S. Navy.

Brown's hand-picked successor to lead the Buckeyes was Carroll Widdoes, who had served as an assistant on Brown's staff. Similarities between Brown and Widdoes began and ended with their chosen profession, but each shared a burning desire for success, and that desire led Widdoes to seek out Horvath in the spring of 1944.

At first, the former Buckeye was content to stay just that—a former Buckeye. His commitment to the military training program had been completed, and Horvath was wrapping up his senior year in the Ohio State College of Dentistry. He had other opportunities as well, including an offer of $7,000 to play professional football for the Cleveland Rams. For the son of immigrant parents from Hungary, money like that was going to be difficult to turn down. "It was extremely tempting," Horvath said, "especially for someone who would have thought himself well-off with a fraction of that kind of money."

But then Widdoes entered the picture. He met with Horvath and told the former star that if he would come back and play for the Buckeyes, he would be their starting quarterback. Horvath listened, but politely declined the offer.

Widdoes met with Horvath several more times, each time sweetening the deal just a little. The coach explained that he felt he had a very good team but that it needed an experienced leader. Horvath could set his own practice schedule and travel to away games on his own. The university would even look into providing him with a private plane to get to away games. No matter how much Widdoes offered, Horvath refused to budge.

Finally, longtime assistant coach Ernie Godfrey asked Widdoes if he could take a shot at Horvath. "Unless you know something I don't, he's made up his mind not to play," the exasperated Widdoes said. "But go ahead. See what you can do."

Godfrey met Horvath at the student union and went over everything Widdoes had already offered, but no avail. Finally, the assistant breathed a heavy sigh, shook his head and got to his feet. He stuck out his hand and said, "Well, I guess you know best. You've been out of football for a year and you probably figure it would have been kind of hard for you to go back and get in shape. Heck, you might not even have made the team anyway. Best of luck to you, Les."

That was a challenge that Horvath simply could not refuse. Godfrey didn't make it to the door before Horvath called him back. And when the Buckeyes reported for training camp that fall, the soon-to-be 23-year-old was in uniform and ready to go.

Horvath grew up in South Bend, Indiana, dreaming of playing his college football at hometown Notre Dame—an ambitious dream for any boy, but especially one who was just over five feet tall and not even a hundred pounds soaking wet. The Horvaths moved to suburban Cleveland when Les was a youngster, and while he did show some interest in the family pharmacy business, he was more excited about basketball, football, and track. That excitement caused him to transfer out of Parma High School following his junior year because he felt his basketball teammates weren't taking the sport seriously enough.

"Before a basketball game, I heard my teammates talking about a party they were going to that night," Horvath said. "It seemed to me they just weren't taking the game seriously enough, so I told my parents and we relocated overnight."

The family rented a home in the city and Horvath enrolled for his senior year at James Ford Rhodes High School in Cleveland, one of Parma's chief rivals. He played quarterback for the Rams on a team that also featured Don McCafferty, who went on to play college football at Ohio State and later coached the Baltimore Colts to a victory in Super Bowl IV. Rhodes was a successful big-school program with several major college prospects. Still, their quarterback couldn't seem to get noticed.

"I had many offers of athletic scholarships from small colleges and universities, but my only desire was to play for a major university," Horvath said. "Having been selected all-city, my aspirations rose until the Notre Dame recruiters decided I was too small to play for Notre Dame."

Enter Godfrey, who was in charge of recruiting the Cleveland area for Ohio State. He was interested in several local players, including McCafferty, and because McCafferty and Horvath were such good friends, Godfrey figured it wouldn't hurt to let Horvath tag along whenever he treated local recruits to dinner.

"They invited me to go to dinner with them, but all the attention was paid to the other boys," Horvath said. "Surprisingly, at the end of one of the dinners, he asked me to come to Ohio State, and so my college career began with less than a whimper...I came to Ohio State as kind of an afterthought of Ernie and the other recruiters."

As a freshman, Horvath was nearly lost amid the shuffle of hundreds of young boys pursuing their dream of playing college football. He sprained his back during the first week of practice, and by the time he was able to play again a few weeks later, he was a forgotten man. After several days of not being asked to scrimmage, Horvath wandered over to a distant part of the practice field where about forty ragged walk-ons were trying their best to keep up with the coaches' demands. When someone called out for a halfback and no one stepped forward, Horvath ran into the huddle and proceeded to run circles around the less talented rabble. It didn't take long for a coach to recognize Horvath had no business practicing with the walk-ons, so he dejectedly was sent back to the scholarship scrimmage. The next day—to his surprise—he was named the starting freshman tailback.

During his sophomore season in 1940, he became something of a good luck charm for head coach Francis A. Schmidt, whom Horvath described as having "the most temper and the most vile mouth of any coach in football, but he was a genius in offensive football." Following a 40-yard punt return on a sloppy field against national championship contender Minnesota, Schmidt chided Horvath for his gamble to catch the slippery ball.

"It was a short punt," Schmidt screamed as he towered over Horvath on the sideline. "Why would you try to handle a slippery, wet football?" Horvath quietly replied, "I am sure I will never drop a football I can get my hands on." A smile crossed the coach's face as he put his hands on Horvath's shoulders and said, "You're going to play a lot of football."

For the remainder of the season, Schmidt required Horvath to sit next to him on the bench although he could never seem to remember his good-luck charm's name, simply referring to him as "the little guy."

Following the 1940 season, Schmidt was replaced by Brown, who used Horvath only sparingly. When he rode the bench for the entire Michigan game, he'd had enough, telling Brown he was going to enter dental school and would not be back for the 1942 season. However, when fall practice began in '42, Horvath got the itch to play again and asked Brown to be reinstated. The coach had only one stipulation—that Horvath move from his familiar left halfback spot to right halfback.

"Before the season started, he told me we could be national champions if I were willing to make the change," Horvath said. "I like to feel that my willingness to make that change made the difference when we were acclaimed national champions of 1942. Paul was never one to pass out compliments to individual players, but he did remark that he thought I was the best right halfback in the country in 1942."

Beginning in 1943, World War II decimated the athletic programs at most universities throughout the country and Ohio State was no different. The following year, though, the Army discharged its students in the dentistry and veterinarian programs, leaving Horvath eligible once again and susceptible to Godfrey's reverse psychology.

Horvath played brilliantly during the 1944 season for the Buckeyes, leading his team to a perfect 9–0 record and the No. 2 ranking in the nation, behind a powerful Army team that had many of the best players from across the country. Horvath logged time at quarterback, halfback, and defensive back that season, and played 402 of a possible 540 minutes. He rushed for 924 yards, threw for 344 more, scored 72 points, and earned the team's most valuable player award, an honor bestowed upon him by a vote of his teammates.

In addition, he earned first team all-conference honors, won the Big Ten's most valuable player award, and was voted a consensus All-American. To top things off, he was announced on December 1 as the tenth recipient of the Heisman Trophy.

Several years later, his wife, Shirley, who admittedly didn't know much about her husband's athletic exploits, asked him about the large bronze trophy that was prominently displayed in their living room. When Horvath tried to explain that it was the Heisman Trophy, Shirley nodded and smiled, then asked why it had to be so ugly.

Les finally convinced her of the trophy's importance, but after visiting some of their friends' homes—friends such as fellow Heisman winners Tom Harmon and Doc Blanchard —Shirley discovered that they also had the same ugly bronze trophy in their living rooms.

Horvath always loved to relate the story of what happened next.

"Les," Shirley said, "you told me that football trophy of yours was really something special, but it turns out that everyone we know has one."

PAUL BROWN

OSU COACH 1941–1943

HOMETOWN: Norwalk, Ohio

RECORD: 18-8-1

BIG TEN CHAMPIONSHIPS: 1942

NATIONAL CHAMPIONSHIPS: 1942

Paul Brown's mother wanted him to be a musician but he marched to the beat of his own drum and became a football player instead.

Success was Paul Brown's constant companion throughout a legendary football coaching career that spanned five decades. He won six consecutive Ohio high school championships at Massillon, four straight All-American Football Conference titles with the Cleveland Browns, and three more championships when the Browns moved to the National Football League.

Yet Brown, one of the foremost innovators and tacticians the game has ever known, cherished most his three seasons as a college head coach at Ohio State. He so loved the simplicity of university life and the wholesome athletic competition provided by college football that had it not been for World War II, Brown might have been content to spend his entire career with the Buckeyes.

"He always had a warm spot in his heart for Ohio State," wrote longtime *Columbus Dispatch* sportswriter Paul Hornung. "He still said that right up until a couple of weeks before he died. I talked to him about it and he said, 'Those were the happiest days of my life, the happiest days of my coaching career.'"

Overwhelming success at Massillon, where his teams fashioned an 80-8-2 record, including thirty-five consecutive victories during one stretch, convinced many observers that Brown should become Francis A. Schmidt's successor as head coach at Ohio State. University officials were less enthused, especially since the 32-year-old wunderkind had no previous coaching experience above the high school level. The age and inexperience arguments quickly melted away, however, when Brown detailed his innovative philosophy and attention to detail—the very antithesis of the wild, shoot-from-the-hip antics of Schmidt.

Brown was hired and immediately went to work overhauling every phase of the OSU program, including detailing practice schedules and assigning specific positions to be coached by his assistants, facets of today's coaching that are taken for granted.

"Complete organization in every phase of the game was the hallmark of Paul's coaching," said Heisman Trophy-winning halfback Les Horvath, who had been recruited by Schmidt. "Where Schmidt had more than three hundred plays, Paul had very few. But those few were gradually expanded into groups that required each player to know the assignments of the other players on each offensive play or defensive alignment. In addition to athletic talent, Paul demanded intelligence, courage, and dedication. The pre-practice sessions were much like a college classroom."

It was perhaps not a coincidence that Brown ran his program with the precision of a railroad. Born September 7, 1908, in Norwalk, Ohio, Paul Eugene Brown was the son of railroad dispatcher Lester Browne—somewhere along the way, the *e* at the end of his surname mysteriously disappeared. Lester's job was to make sure the trains for the Wheeling and Lake Erie Railroad ran on time, and his meticulous attention to the tiniest detail rubbed off on young Paul. So, too, did the competitive nature of his mother, Ida, who excelled at gin rummy, euchre, pinochle, and other card games in which strategy and sizing up one's opponent were the keys to victory.

When Paul was nine, the family moved to Massillon and it changed his life forever. Norwalk was a small town located just ten miles south of Lake Erie, founded by New England settlers and not unlike thousands of other communities dotting the Upper Midwest. Entertainment in Norwalk might include bluegill fishing along the Vermilion River, an afternoon hike through the woods at the edge of town, or listening to a band concert on a cool summer Saturday night.

An hour and a half to the southeast from the tranquility of Norwalk was Massillon, which would have been like any other grimy steel town with its fiery coal furnaces belching soot and smoke into a slate-gray sky—except for its football team. Massillon featured big-time high school football, a sport Washington High School first offered in 1894. The Tigers produced their first undefeated season in 1909 and their first of a record twenty-three state championships came seven years later.

Paul's father hoped his son would become a lawyer while his mother wanted him to be a musician, but the youngster loved sports. "I was just about six years old when my father bought me my first football," Brown said. "I used it until the bladder wore out, and then I stuffed it with rags and leaves and went on playing as if nothing had happened."

visioned furthering his career at Ohio State. But when he showed up for his first freshman practice in the fall of 1925, coaches took one look at his smallish frame and shuffled him aside.

"I wasn't even allowed to try out," he remembered years later.

"When you win, say nothing. When you lose, say less."
—Paul Brown

Paul entered high school in 1922, but because he weighed less than 150 pounds, he didn't even try out for the football team, joining the track team and focusing upon becoming a pole vaulter. When football coach Dave Stewart saw the youngster's analytic approach to the event, he persuaded Paul to come out for the football team. It proved a shrewd move on Stewart's part as Brown eventually became the starting quarterback for the Tigers and led them to a combined 15–3 record during his junior and senior years.

Like many high school football players from Ohio, especially those from Massillon, Paul en-

"I was too small for that caliber of football, they told me, and it was a mortal blow to my pride. I considered their refusal to give me a try-out the cruelest injustice."

Ohio State's loss wound up being Miami University's gain. Paul transferred after his freshman year at OSU and became starting quarterback for the Redskins. He led his team to fourteen victories during his final two seasons and earned second-team All-Ohio small-college honors as a senior.

Brown had every intention of following his father's wishes and pursuing a law degree upon his graduation, and considered furthering his studies abroad, applying for a Rhodes scholarship. But his football roots had grown too deeply, and he began his coaching career in 1930 at a private high school in Maryland, hired at the tender age of twenty-two. Paul's first team at Severn High School, a prep school for the United States Naval Academy, resulted in an undefeated season and the Maryland state championship. Two years later, he was back in Massillon, taking over a program that had grown fallow during the year after Stewart had left following the 1925 season.

Nine years and six state championships later, Brown was on the move again, this time to Ohio State. At thirty-three, he became the youngest coach in the history of the Big Ten, earning a salary of $6,500 per year.

"That was only about $1,500 more than I had been making at Massillon," Paul said, "but that wasn't important. I don't believe I ever discussed salary (with athletic director Lynn St. John). All my life, money had been a secondary thing. I needed it to provide the necessities for my family, but what counted was football. It was such an ob-

session for me that it never seemed like work."

Brown's first season in Columbus resulted in a 6-1-1 record in 1941, the team's best winning percentage in six years. Fans wondering what the boy coach could do for an encore quickly got their answer in 1942 when the Buckeyes produced the first national championship in school history.

Influential donors and alumni implored St. John and university president Howard Bevis to give Brown a lifetime contract, an offer Paul might have accepted had it been extended. But as World War II raged throughout Europe and the Pacific, college football was the last thing on anyone's mind. College and university presidents came close to canceling the 1943 season, but decided against that idea and allowed games to proceed. The college game began a shadow of itself, however, with most able-bodied young men in military service.

Ohio State finished with a 3-6 record that season, and a few months later Brown was commissioned as a lieutenant in the Navy, with the caveat that Ohio State would keep its head coaching job open so that he could resume his duties after the war. But that 1943 season had left a bitter taste in the coach's mouth.

"Not only were we being unfair to a group of seventeen-year-old kids, we were exposing them to serious injury whenever we played much bigger, older, and stronger opponents," Brown said years later. "My sense of justice and personal pride rebelled at these inequities, and I didn't spare Mr. St. John my feelings. His justification was that we were performing a service to intercollegiate football and saving the program at Ohio State. In reality, we were providing money for the athletic department, and while we may have kept the continuity of Ohio State's football program, it was at the personal expense of those kids.

"What made the situation worse was that no one ever appreciated what those kids went through. Actually, those Baby Bucks were a victim of the war, but I never could reconcile myself to the fact that the university never ever bothered to give them a year-end football banquet. It angered me so much that if influenced my decision to go into professional football instead of returning to Ohio State after the war."

Brown was given the honorary title of head coach in absentia with most alumni and fans believing he would return to the Buckeyes following his military service. But in February of 1945, he chose to become vice president, general manager, and head coach for the Cleveland team in the upstart All-America Football Conference. The news sent shock waves through Columbus with several university officials and influential donors claiming Brown had reneged on a promise to return to Ohio State.

The university changed coaches four times during an eight-year span between 1944 and 1951, and while Brown was always mentioned as a leading candidate, he never wavered. "I was constantly being touted as the next head coach, but I was with the Browns then and had no intentions of leaving," he said. "Every time my name came up, however, friction arose between some factions at Ohio State and among the alumni, some of whom never forgave me for my not returning as head coach after the war."

Brown coached Cleveland to four consecutive AAFC championships from 1946–49, a successful run that continued when the Browns joined the NFL for the 1950 season. The team played in the championship game in each of its first six years in the league, and took home three titles. Brown left the Browns following the 1962 season, but resurfaced six years later in Cincinnati as head coach and general manager of the expansion Bengals, leading the team to an American Football Conference Central Division championship in only its third year of existence.

Brown finally retired from coaching following the 1975 season, finishing his forty-year career with a combined high school, college, and professional record of 338-127-15. Yet for all of his success at every level, it was those three seasons at Ohio State that he cherished most.

Although he admittedly never got over how his final season in Columbus played out, Brown wrote in his 1979 autobiography, "I have warm, fond memories of my time at Ohio State. My first two years there were the happiest, most exciting and rewarding periods of my life, better in some respects than the great years in Cleveland because coaching the Buckeyes had been my ultimate dream.

"Ohio State was all that I had ever imagined, and the sweet taste of those first two years still lingers."

CHARLES CSURI

NICKNAME: Chuck

HOMETOWN: Cleveland, Ohio

HEIGHT: 6 ft 0 in   WEIGHT: 195 lb

NFL DRAFT: 1944, Chicago Cardinals

60

Csuri had two passions— football and art.

It's a long way from the dank and dirty coal mines of eastern Ohio to the glitz and glamour of Hollywood, but Chuck Csuri made the journey with stops in between as an All-America football player, decorated combat hero, and computer graphics pioneer, world-renowned as the father of digital art and computer animation.

Charles Alexander Csuri was born on Independence Day in 1922, the third son of Hungarian immigrants who had joined the mass migration of Europeans from their homelands to America. Like so many immigrants before them, the Csuris soon discovered the path to a better life in the New World was a demanding one. After scraping up enough money to afford passage aboard an overcrowded steamship and enduring the arduous often dangerous trip across the Atlantic Ocean, many former Europeans found life in America with its myriad of culture and language barriers every bit as challenging as the despair they were trying to escape in Europe.

Csuri's father was luckier than most, able to find work in the eastern Ohio coal mines that honeycombed the shores of the Ohio River. But the hours were long, the pay was minimal, and adding to the anguish of trying to feed, house, and clothe a young family, the elder Csuri was seriously injured during a mine shaft explosion and forced to have his leg amputated above the knee to save his life.

"Being crippled, along with being penniless, led to a deep depression for my father," Chuck said. "His only salvation was the close relationships he had maintained with his friends from Hungary who were living in Cleveland. They urged him to move there, and he decided that any change in the meager existence of coal mining country would have to be an improvement."

Once relocated in the Hungarian enclave on the west side of Cleveland, among friends who shared the commonality of struggling against life's hardships, Csuri and his family began to prosper. His father became an accomplished shoemaker, crafting his own special tools and equipment to compensate for his disability and displaying an ingenuity that allowed him to finally support his family. Meanwhile, Chuck's older brothers finished high school and went to work, while Chuck attended West Technical High School.

Too small by most standards to play football, Chuck experienced a growth spurt between his freshman and sophomore years and quickly began to earn acclaim as an excellent all-around player. Off the field, he was known for a dry sense of humor usually accompanied by one raised eyebrow and a wry grin. On the field, however, he was all business with squint-eyed determination and a low center of gravity that helped him control both sides of the line of scrimmage.

Unlike many of his teammates who had few interests outside sports, Chuck was a budding artist, influenced by the bright colors and thought-provoking subjects of the modern art movement. As a result, when he enrolled at Ohio State in the fall of 1940, he was much more interested in the College of Fine Arts than he was pursuing an athletic career.

Nevertheless, football provided a fun pastime and Chuck was good at it. He showed up at fall camp with more than two hundred other freshmen, and impressed coach Fritz Mackey enough to become one of sixty players to earn letterman sweaters. The following fall, the Buckeyes had undergone a coaching change with Paul Brown coming from Massillon High School and installing a new philosophy predicated on specificity and attention to detail.

"Paul Brown brought a more procedural approach to coaching," Chuck said. "He had a system. He had a methodology, playbooks, plans, and specific assignments in practice. While this seems obvious today, it was a radical notion at the time. He was also extremely organized. He set goals. That's commonplace today, but people forget that was not the case in my era."

Brown also was much more focused on winning than making friends. Csuri, who started his sophomore season in 1941 as the second-string tackle behind senior team captain Jack Stephenson, quickly supplanted his more popular teammate in the starting lineup. "It soon became apparent that Paul was only interested in bringing his best players to each position and no other factors, such as being the captain of the team, made any difference," Chuck said.

sity had scheduled one more game, against the Iowa Seahawks, as a morale booster for the World War II effort. The Buckeyes grounded the Seahawks, 41–12, and when

"In the short history of computer art, there are no Rembrandts or even Picassos. But there is Professor Charles Csuri at Ohio State University, who may be the nearest thing, in this new art form, to an Old Master."
—*Smithsonian magazine*, 1995

During the fall of 1942, Csuri was ready to devote more of his time to his art career, but football took center stage again as Ohio State won its first Big Ten championship under Brown, sewing up the title with a 21–7 victory over fourth-ranked Michigan. Csuri played a vital role during the win, blocking a punt to set up one of the Buckeyes' touchdowns. "That probably was the only punt I ever blocked in my life," he said. "It was just one of those things that you do automatically, and that day it worked."

The game against Michigan usually served as the regular-season finale for Ohio State, but the univer-

top-rated Boston College and second-ranked Georgia Tech each lost that same afternoon, Ohio State leapfrogged into the top spot in the Associated Press poll and was named national champion for the first time in program history.

It was a huge accomplishment for Brown and his players, but one achieved against the stark backdrop of world war. "It was very bizarre all the way around," Csuri said. "When we played, we didn't have the media hype about who was number one or number two. I didn't even know we were in consideration for the national championship that year. It came down to the final week of the season when we were number three and the two teams ahead of us lost while we won. Of course, it was very exciting and satisfying, but at the same time we had this whole atmosphere of war hanging over our heads. It was a different time. All we knew was this was the end of the line—that we were going into a war."

By the spring of 1943, when the Buckeyes should have been preparing to defend their national title, nearly every player had been drafted into military service. Csuri, who had been elected to serve as team captain for his senior season, was already headed to a U.S. Army engineering program in New Jersey. He enrolled in a fast-paced program designed to complete two years of engineering courses in just twelve months, but when the program was suddenly discontinued, Csuri found himself an infantry corporal and headed to Europe where the Battle of the Bulge was about to begin along the densely forested Ardennes region of Belgium, France, and Luxembourg.

Assigned to a First Army unit of engineers who were among the most advanced battalions for the division, Chuck and his unit saw almost continuous action throughout the six-week battle. At one point, the battalion had advanced so far forward through the enemy lines that it was cut off and surrounded by German army units. Chuck volunteered to attempt to reestablish contact with his unit's division by working his way back through the German lines, but the assignment involved being exposed to constant bombardment as well as agonizing small-arms fire. After several hours, Csuri finally made contact with the American lines and later received the Bronze Star for bravery in action. "My helmet was shot away, even my leather belt," he said. "It was the most harrowing experience of my life, and how I survived was way beyond my comprehension."

Csuri returned to Ohio State following the war and resumed his football career, but his heart really wasn't in it. "To be honest, I was not very motivated because I had served in combat. I was in the Battle of the Bulge and I saw some nasty stuff. I came back a very different person, and the whole no-tion of violence just didn't have the appeal to me," he said. "The reality was that I didn't want to play col-lege football anymore, but because of the social pressure, because I had been an All-American and was the team captain and that sort of thing, I felt obligated to play. But I just went through the motions."

The Buckeyes finished 4-3-2 during that 1946 season, after which Csuri left behind his athletic career for good. He had a number of offers to play professionally, including one from the Chicago Cardinals, who had selected him in absentia during the 1944 NFL draft, but Chuck was much more interested in getting on with his life. He graduated from Ohio State in 1947, and immediately became a member of the Fine Arts College faculty. Three years later, he met his wife, Lee, whom he described as "a perfect fit with my percep-tions of beauty and art."

Together, the couple pursued their love of art, Lee creating mys-tical wood carvings based upon mythological creatures while Chuck became a prolific painter, following the precepts of modern art as he conceived them. His work found its way into the private collections of several noted art enthusiasts, and he received critical acclaim for a 1957 exhibition of his paintings in New York City.

Ever eager to branch out into new media using the cutting edge methods of the day, Chuck was in-troduced to computers in the early 1960s and helped usher in a new era of expression through digital means. "The ability of computers to achieve both linear depth as well as perceptions of third-dimensional depth brought together in my mind the mathematics of my Army en-gineering courses with the infinite colors and artistry of modern art," he said. "In addition to my personal excitement in the use of a computer as the medium for artistic expres-sion, the powers of the computer could be used in a multiplicity of practical areas. Almost every field of endeavor could benefit from computer technology."

Csuri was among the first to embrace the limitless expression available through the new media, creating computer-animated films in 1965 and earning worldwide acclaim as the father of computer animations and graphics. The National Science Foundation, the U.S. Navy, and the Air Force Office of Scientific Research have supported Csuri over the years, and graduates of his programs are employees of such innovative companies as Pixar, Walt Disney Studios, and Industrial Light and Magic, and their work has been seen in such popular films as *Star Wars, Jurrasic Park,* and *Toy Story.* Additionally, he has won nearly every award available in the field of computer graphics and digital art, has been recognized all over the world by museums and research organizations, and continues to be professor emeritus at The Advanced Computing Center for the Arts and Design, the celebrated research center he founded at Ohio State.

Still active into his nineties, Csuri continues to add to a rich legacy that has intersected with history on countless occasions. Football star, war hero, educator, artist, visionary—a person with any one of those accomplishments would be considered to have led an impressive life. All of them and you become something of a legend. You become Chuck Csuri.

With his matinee idol good looks, Csuri could have also been a movie star.

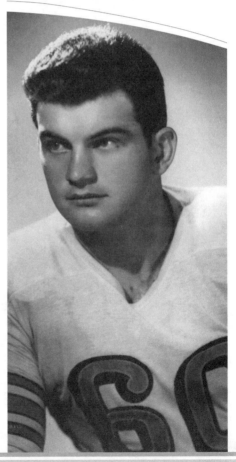

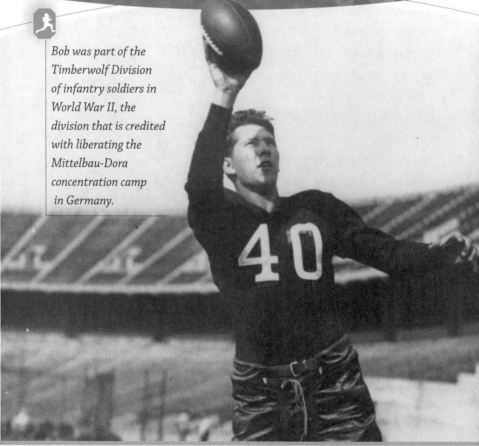

ROBERT *SHAW*

OSU TIGHT END 1941–1942

40

NICKNAME: Bob

HOMETOWN: Richwood, Ohio

HEIGHT: 6 ft 4 in **WEIGHT:** 226 lb

ALL–AMERICAN: 1942

NFL DRAFT: 1944, Cleveland Rams

Bob was part of the Timberwolf Division of infantry soldiers in World War II, the division that is credited with liberating the Mittelbau-Dora concentration camp in Germany.

Bob Shaw bore little physical resemblance to the movie character Tom Hanks made famous in the 1994 Academy Award-winning film *Forrest Gump*. Whereas Gump was slow-witted and naïve, a Deep South native who needed to wear leg braces as a youngster to correct a crooked spine, Shaw was the sharp and strapping 6-foot-4 son of a hard-working northern Ohio family who went on to earn a postgraduate degree in education.

Appearances aside, Shaw and Gump had a lot in common—superlative athletic achievements, brushes with greatness, lifelong scars carried from the horrors of war, and devotion to one woman. Perhaps that is why Shaw often said *Forrest Gump* was his favorite movie, admitting to watching it more than fifty times.

Shaw was born May 22, 1921, in tiny Richwood, Ohio, the only child of factory workers Fred and Lucy Shaw, who soon moved the family north to Fremont. It was only seventy-five miles away in terms of distance but a million miles from the sleepy one-block downtown of Richwood. In addition to being the

home of Rutherford B. Hayes, the nineteenth President of the United States, Fremont was a bustling industrial city and the site of the world's largest ketchup factory.

There young Bob began making a name for himself on the playgrounds and sandlots around Fremont. He was endowed with the physical strengths of a natural-born athlete—size, speed, strength, agility, and heart—and it wasn't long before he was gaining statewide notice in a variety of sports while at Ross High School. He established a new Ohio high school shot put record, was an All-State performer in basketball, and earned prep All-America status in football as a senior in 1939 when he led the state in scoring with 154 points.

"Not to sound cocky, but I was pretty good at about every sport I ever tried," Bob said. "My parents blessed me with a loving and stable home, not to mention some God-given abilities that allowed me to pursue any kind of athletic endeavor I chose. And I chose a lot of them."

When it came time to choose a college, Shaw was inundated with scholarship offers, many of which offered much more than just an education. "I remember my dad and I drove down to a university in North Carolina whose athletic inducement even included a job for Dad in addition to a completely financed education," Bob said. "At the time, we were just coming out of the Great Depression and some of the offers we received were very difficult not to at least consider."

But Fred Shaw was a proud man who wanted nothing to do with handouts. Moreover, he didn't want anything he didn't earn himself. Bob remembered, "While we were driving back to Fremont from North Carolina, my father said, 'Son, after listening to all of those attractive offers, I believe it would be best for you to go to Ohio State. This is your home state and where you will probably live after your graduation.' That was all I needed to hear. Ohio State it was. I enrolled in the College of Education and joined the freshman football team."

Bob arrived on campus along with about two hundred other freshmen, each of whom believed he was good enough to play football for the Buckeyes. Many of them were wide-eyed country boys from small schools who quickly fell by the wayside when their minimal skills were exposed. Others, who had been recruited by head coach Francis Schmidt and his chief lieutenant Ernie Godfrey, formed the nucleus of a freshman team that regularly scrimmaged against the varsity. Shaw had been a star quarterback and running back in high school, and those were the positions he played on the freshman squad in 1940, a team that often gave its varsity counterparts all that it could handle on the practice field.

That turned out to be a double-edged sword, however. Pushed mercilessly by the ever-driven Schmidt, the Buckeyes experienced a three-game losing streak midway through the 1940 season. It marked the first time OSU had lost three games in a row during Schmidt's seven-year tenure, and university officials who had grown increasingly tired of the head coach's antics were looking for an excuse to fire him. That opportunity presented itself when the

Buckeyes suffered a 40–0 shutout loss to Michigan on the final day of the season. Less than a month later, the announcement came: Schmidt was out.

In his place, Ohio State hired Paul Brown, the 32-year-old architect of a high school powerhouse in Massillon, Ohio, and the antithesis of the sometimes scatterbrained, often salty-tongued Schmidt. The young coach adhered to a strict practice schedule, was able to explain his philosophy in great detail, and left no doubt as to who was in charge. As a result, Shaw had no say when, during his initial meeting with the new coach, Brown told the young quarterback he was switching positions.

"My first impression wasn't a good one," Bob said. "I was taken aback a little bit because I had come down to Ohio State as a quarterback and running back. Those were the positions I had played in high school, those were the positions I had played as a freshman, and those were the positions I was comfortable playing. But one of the first things Paul said was that he was moving me to an end position—

tight end. I didn't like it, but I went along with it. As it turned out, of course, it was a very good decision."

In their first game under Brown, the Buckeyes opened the 1941 season with a 12–7 win against Missouri, but it wasn't until the following week that the OSU squad began garnering national recognition. After traveling across the country by train to face a heavily favored team from the University of Southern California in the Los Angeles Coliseum, the Buckeye dominated the Trojans during a 33–0 victory that included the first touchdown of Shaw's college career, a 48-yard scoring pass from fullback Jack Graf in the third quarter. "For an old country boy like me, that was a big thing," Bob said.

The following year, the Trojans paid a return visit to Columbus in search of revenge and jumped out to an early 6–0 lead. But that was quickly erased by a pair of Shaw touchdowns in the first quarter, the first on a 64-yard pass from halfback Paul Sarringhaus. "It was just a crossing pattern," Bob said. "It wasn't a long pass, but I ran a long way." It was a part of a

28–12 win for the Buckeyes, who marched their way to the 1942 national championship, the first in Ohio State program history. Shaw earned his second consecutive All-Big Ten honor that season and joined four teammates on the All-America team.

"Looking back on it, that was a great thrill," Bob said. "At the time, though, we didn't really realize the magnitude of what was going on. We had a bunch of young players and a young coach, and we were really just having a lot of fun. Unfortunately, we weren't able to enjoy it for very long."

Bob, who had also lettered in basketball and track at OSU, entered military service to fight in World War II and was preparing to be sent to Fort Bragg for basic training. Just before shipping out, however, Bob married his girlfriend, the former Mary Katherine Hawkins, whom he had met before a home football game at Ohio State. Team members would typically gather in downtown Columbus on a Friday night, often attending a stage show or taking in a movie at the Palace Theatre. "Mary was an usher at the Palace, and one night she showed me to my seat," Bob said. "It was love at first sight."

Following his training at Fort Bragg, Shaw was sent by the Army to engineering school at Northwestern University. The program was suddenly abandoned before the school year had ended, however, and he was supposed to have been returned to an artillery unit. However, his transfer orders were mixed up with another soldier named Shaw, and Bob found himself assigned to the Timberwolf Division of the 104th Infantry, fighting its way across Europe. Shaw's duties included serving as personal bodyguard for the regimental commander, but his unit often faced heavy combat and Bob was awarded a Bronze Star for his service.

The Timberwolf Division is also credited with liberating the Mittelbau-Dora concentration camp in Nordhausen, Germany, a gruesome camp designed for political prisoners of the Third Reich. Troops found three thousand to five thousand corpses, many stacked like cordwood under stairways, while six thousand survivors—most of them reduced to skin stretched over skeletons—were found lying among the dead.

Bob figured the best way to put the horrors of war behind him was to resume his athletic career. And what a career it was. He spent four seasons in the National Football League, during which he caught five touchdown passes in a single game

ing in 1987 to spend more time with his beloved Mary.

The couple was married sixty-three years before Mary passed away in 2007. Bob followed four years later at the age of 89, but not before several more tearful viewings of his favorite movie. He always seemed to like a line near the end of the film when Forrest asked

At one point Bob and his wife were so poor they lived in a chicken shack in Los Angeles.

for the Chicago Cardinals in 1950, an NFL record that has since been equaled twice but never surpassed. That was followed by two years as a player in the Canadian Football League, as well as a lengthy coaching career during which Shaw tutored such future Pro Football Hall of Fame players as Raymond Berry and Roger Staubach.

Somehow, he also found time to play three years of pro basketball with the Cleveland and Toledo franchises of the old National Basketball League, and he served as a scout for New York Yankees owner George Steinbrenner, finally retir-

his dying mother, "What's my destiny, Mama?" Mrs. Gump smiles at her son and says, "You're gonna have to figure that out for yourself."

Bob Shaw had no trouble figuring out his destiny. And what a wonderful one it was.

PAUL
SARRINGHAUS

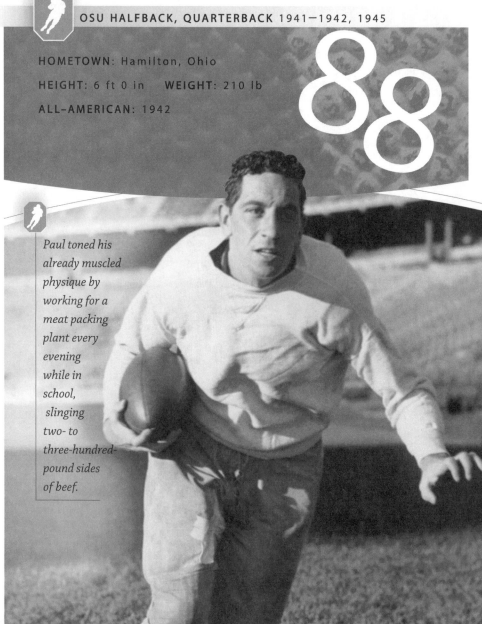

OSU HALFBACK, QUARTERBACK 1941–1942, 1945

HOMETOWN: Hamilton, Ohio

HEIGHT: 6 ft 0 in   **WEIGHT:** 210 lb

ALL–AMERICAN: 1942

88

Paul toned his already muscled physique by working for a meat packing plant every evening while in school, slinging two- to three-hundred-pound sides of beef.

College football was a rough-and-tumble enterprise during the 1940s and that suited Paul Sarringhaus almost perfectly. A rock of a young man with chiseled features, a barrel chest and long, narrow fingers perfect for gripping an oblong, leather ball, no matter the weather conditions, Sarringhaus was one of the anchors of the 1942 Ohio State team that earned the school's first national championship.

"How tough was Sarringhaus?" teammate Gene Fekete was asked. "As tough as nails. You could beat on him all day long and he'd just keep coming. Never an ounce of quit. I don't think he knew the meaning of the word."

Fekete should know. As a sophomore fullback on that 1942 team, Fekete was the Big Ten's leading rusher and scorer, often playing off lead blocks thrown by Sarringhaus. Following one of those blocks, Sarringhaus came to the sideline, his nose gushing blood. When he reached the sideline, head coach Paul Brown asked if he thought the nose was broken. When Sarringhaus said that he couldn't tell, Brown replied, "Well, we need you in the game. We'll fix your nose later." With a shrug of his shoulders, Sarringhaus ran back into the huddle.

That kind of grim determination and iron will were forged early for Sarringhaus, whose grandparents had come from Germany at the turn of the twentieth century and settled in Hamilton, Ohio, a small industrial city just north of Cincinnati. By the time Paul was born in 1920, his parents had moved just across the Indiana border into Ripley County where they were trying to make a living as farmers.

Paul's father, George, enjoyed athletics more than farming and would steal away every chance he could to play semi-pro baseball. His obsession with the game was often at odds with the family's financial situation, as George would purchase a pair of baseball cleats in lieu of paying down his credit at the feed store. Despite being born into poverty, Paul was much like any other toddler in rural Indiana until the age of two when his father fell ill and died during the post-World War I flu epidemic. Paul's mother, Marie, packed him, his four-year-old sister Ruth and their meager belongings into the family truck and moved back to her parents' house in Hamilton, where she took a job as a seamstress in a department store.

Young Paul was lively and precocious, seemingly more interested in mischief than schoolwork as he spent three years struggling through the first and second grades. Teachers simply assumed the youngster was unmotivated, mentally challenged, or both, until one casually asked Paul, from his seat at the back of the room, to read a lesson off the blackboard. While he struggled with the words, the teacher noticed the youngster squinting his eyes into tiny slits.

As Sarringhaus became more focused on his academics, he was beginning to gain an interest in athletics as a way to escape the poverty he had always known. As he began to fill into a willowy six-foot, 185-pound body, he became a football star at Hamilton High School, and during his senior year, he used a combination of powerful shoulders and swift feet to lead the state in scoring and earn All-Ohio honors as a halfback. He was heavily recruited by more than forty major college programs, but only one school had occupied his mind since the age of fifteen.

Sarringhaus and a young friend had hitchhiked their way to Colum-

"At Hamilton High School, he was a 185-pound six-footer with hula hips and the ability to send would-be tacklers into outer space."

—*Schoolboy Legends*

It wasn't that he couldn't read or understand the words; he couldn't see the blackboard. "I was fitted with eyeglasses," he said, "and soon I could read, write, and learn as well as the other children."

bus on an early November morning in 1935 and sneaked into what many college football writers later called "The Game of the Century," between undefeated Ohio State and Notre Dame. Paul found himself enthralled with the pageantry of attending his first college football game at Ohio Stadium and immediately began rooting for the Buckeyes as they raced out to 13–0 at halftime. But his friend, a Notre Dame fan, had the last laugh when the Fighting Irish scored three second-half touchdowns to squeeze out an 18–13 victory.

Distraught that his team had blown what seemed to be an insurmountable lead—as well as being needled mercilessly by his friend on the trip back to Hamilton—Sarringhaus secretly made a vow that he would play for the Buckeyes one day and exact his own measure of revenge on Notre Dame. He didn't realize it at the time, but his chance against the Irish would never come. Ohio State and Notre Dame played the following season, with the Fighting Irish scoring a 7–2 triumph in South Bend, but that game ended a two-year contract between the schools. They would not meet again on the gridiron until 1995.

Sarringhaus earned his scholarship to Ohio State in a number of ways—first by his excellence in high school football and later by working a part-time job at a meat processing plant. "There were no athletic scholarships as we know them today," he said. "The athletic department had part-time state jobs for us or part-time jobs in private companies in Columbus where owners were devoted Ohio State alumni. Besides waiting on tables at the fraternity house to earn my keep, I worked at the David Davies Baby Beef Company. The only thing 'baby' about the sides of beef was on the company labels. The evenings were spent throwing two- to three-hundred-pound sides of beef to be loaded or unloaded."

Sarringhaus spent his freshman year of 1940 acclimating himself to campus life, then broke into the starting lineup and earned his first varsity letter as a sophomore during Brown's first season as head coach. The following year, with Sarringhaus and Fekete in a backfield that included future Heisman Trophy winner Les Horvath, the Buckeyes won the school's first national championship. Brown, who would later win seven professional championships with the Cleveland Browns, was an inventive young coach fresh from a successful run of high school titles in Massillon, Ohio. Several of Ohio State's victories in 1942 could be traced directly to innovative plays Brown had devised, including a special one he cooked up for the traditional rivalry game against Michigan.

Tailback Tommy James, the fastest running back on the team outside of Horvath, was forced out of the previous week's game against Illinois with an injury. As the week went on, the medical reports weren't good, and less than forty-eight hours before the game, Brown announced it was doubtful James would play at all against the Wolverines. It was all a ploy, though. James was on the mend, but Brown wanted an excuse to unveil a new play he had been working on all season. His intent was to spring it on an unsuspecting opponent at just the right time.

The play was designed for George Slusser, the second-string tailback behind James, to take a handoff and begin sweeping to his left, and then hand the ball to Sar-ringhaus on a delayed reverse—at least that was how Brown drew it on the chalkboard. On a bleak and rainy November afternoon on the swampy practice field just outside Ohio Stadium, the play was finally put into use for the first time against a live defense. As the 165-pound Slusser streaked to his left with the slippery pigskin, Sarringhaus—now a strapping 210 pounds—came running full speed to his right from the left wingback position. Just as the exchange was to be made, Slusser's foot slipped on the muddy turf, resulting in a head-on collision between the two players. The ball popped loose and squirted away in the slop.

Slusser had played the part of guinea pig before for Brown, playing under the coach's tutelage for three years at Massillon. Then when Brown was hired at Ohio State, Slusser sacrificed a year of his college eligibility and transferred to OSU from Ivy League member Dartmouth so he could play for Brown again. As Slusser picked himself up and wiped the mud from his face, he obviously was having second thoughts about that decision. He looked at Brown and shouted, "P.B., you can take that play and stick it up your ass!"

As raindrops continued to make ripples in the mud puddles on the practice field, you could have heard the proverbial pin drop. "Those of us who were grouped behind Coach Brown were incredulous," said Robin Priday, a backup quarterback on the 1942 team. "No one ever talked to a coach like that, what's more, Coach Brown. I fully expected the clouds to part and a bolt of lightning to strike George down before our eyes." Before Mother Nature could intervene, however, a huge smile crossed Brown's face and he doubled over in laughter before finally managing to say, "Let's try it again."

The play worked perfectly several times against the Michigan defense, which never seemed to know exactly where Sarringhaus was. As a result, he caught a 35-yard pass from Horvath for the game's first touchdown and heaved a 60-yard touchdown pass of his own to teammate Bob Shaw, who made a leaping catch against three defenders, then barely kept his bal-ance along the sideline on his way to the end zone. The Wolverines cut Ohio State's lead to 14–7 in the second half, then were driving in the fourth quarter when they fumbled on their side of the field. Sarringhaus followed with the game-clinching play, a 32-yard touchdown pass to Horvath, giving the Buckeyes a 21–7 victory.

Brown and Horvath get most of the credit for that 1942 championship season, and deservedly so. But the Buckeyes would likely not have been nearly as successful without the contributions of Sarringhaus, who earned first-team all-conference and All-America honors that year.

WILLIAM WILLIS

OSU MIDDLE GUARD 1942–1944

NICKNAME: Bill

HOMETOWN: Columbus, Ohio

HEIGHT: 6 ft 2 in   WEIGHT: 210 lb

99

Bill was the first African-American to receive All-America honors in football.

Bill Willis never intended to become a trailblazer. He just wanted to escape his big brother's shadow.

William Karnet Willis was born October 5, 1921, into pre-Depression poverty on the east side of Columbus. His father, Clement, died when he was only four years old, and the tragedy left his mother alone to raise him and older brother Claude. A bright, honest woman whose strong principles and deep faith were the bonds that kept her family together, Willana Willis performed household chores six days a week for families all over Columbus to support her family, then spent each Sunday laying a spiritual foundation for her two boys that included gospel music, Biblical teachings, and church socials.

Claude, nicknamed "Deacon" because his friends thought he spent too much time at church, captivated the entire black community of Columbus with his play on the football field, earning comparisons to former East High School and Ohio State superstar Chic Harley while providing a heavy dose of mixed emotions to his younger brother. On one hand, Bill was ex-tremely proud of Claude, who was an All-City selection in football and basketball before playing college football at Claflin College in South Carolina. At the same time, the youngster had already had a bellyful of "Deacon did this" and "Deacon did that," and was eager to forge his own path.

"One day, some of my friends and I were playing in the park, throwing a ball back and forth, when one of the people watching shouted, 'Let's see if you are as good as your brother,'" Bill remembered years later. "The ball came sailing through the air, I jumped to catch it, and I dropped it. 'Well, you ain't no Deacon Willis, that's for sure.'"

By the time Bill arrived at East High, his muscular 6-foot-2, 200-pound frame coupled with the speed of a greyhound would have made him one of the most formidable high school running backs in the nation. But since his older brother had played fullback, Bill decided he wanted to play another position. It was a decision he would never regret, becoming every bit the dominating player as a lineman that Claude had been at fullback. Unlike his brother, however, Bill longed to stay closer to home to continue his education.

Wanting to go to Ohio State and being accepted at Ohio State were altogether different matters, however. Black players had worn the Scarlet and Gray periodically over the years, but the program's record of racial equality was spotty at best. Fredrick D. Patterson, the light-skinned son of a Greenfield, Ohio, businessman was the first black football player at Ohio State in 1891, and a handful of others followed a few years later. But African-Americans had all but disappeared from the OSU roster for thirty-five years until William Bell earned three varsity letters from 1929 to '31.

A few years later, Howard Gentry, who would find success as head coach at Tennessee State, was an All-City performer at West High School in Columbus, but when he inquired about playing at Ohio State, he found a very real color barrier. "The athletic director (Lynn St. John) refused to talk to me, the head coach (Francis A. Schmidt) refused to talk to me," Gentry said. "Ernie Godfrey, the freshman coach, finally told me they had all the blacks they could handle at the time and that they weren't very good students. He said I was wasting my time."

That sentiment didn't change until Willis was in his last semester of high school and Ohio State hired successful high school coach Paul Brown to succeed Schmidt. Brown, who had earned the reputation for playing black athletes while he was at Massillon High School, recruited Willis hard for the Buckeyes, and there was no question Bill wanted to play for his hometown college team. But he also wanted to run track, and told Brown he would not play for him if he couldn't be a member of the Ohio State track team as well. Brown, who once described Willis "as quick as a snake's fang," remembered years later that was an easy compromise to make. "I didn't care what else Bill wanted to do," the legendary coach said, "as long as he wanted to play football."

As a result, Brown and Willis got to Ohio State in the fall of 1941 and helped change the face of the program. Over the course of the next four seasons, the Buckeyes posted a 27-8-1 record, captured their first national championship, won two Big Ten titles, celebrated the first Heisman Trophy winner in program history, and solidified themselves as a perennial college football powerhouse. Willis was unquestionably one of the team's stars during that time, often playing every minute of every game each season as a bulldozing blocker on the offensive line and a punishing tackler on defense.

"He had the whole package, and I never saw a more dedicated, genuine person than Bill Willis and I'm proud to be one of his teammates," said Gene Fekete, an All-American in 1942 when he led the Big Ten with 910 rushing yards and set an OSU single-season scoring record that would stand for nearly three decades. "I would say Bill's biggest asset playing football was his initial thrust when the ball was snapped. He had the greatest uncoil that I've ever seen in football. He almost got to the ball before the center snapped it to the quarterback."

Willis was more than deserving of making the All-America team as a sophomore in 1942, but he was passed over in favor of older (and whiter) players. As a junior, however, voters could no longer overlook his accomplishments, and he became the first African-American at Ohio State to earn All-America honors. It was an achievement he repeated following his senior season in 1944, but an achievement that paled in comparison to what he and Brown were able to accomplish in terms of the segregation of college football.

"I am a very fortunate person in that I came along the same time that Paul Brown came along," Willis once said. "Paul made the difference. There were only two or three other blacks in the whole league at the time, but I hardly noticed. Paul treated me the same as everyone else, and by the time I left, there were several blacks on the roster. But more than that, I cannot really give enough credit to that guy because he afforded me the opportunity. People would have never known about a fellow by the name of Bill Willis if it hadn't been for Paul Brown."

Following his graduation at Ohio State, a player with Willis's impressive résumé would normally have enjoyed a seamless transition to the National Football League. However, an agreement among NFL owners had kept black players out of the league since 1933. With few other options, Bill became head coach at Kentucky State University for one season before agreeing to resume his playing career in the Canadian Football League with the Montreal Alouettes.

He never made it north of the border, however. Brown, by then head coach of the Cleveland Browns in the fledgling All-American Football Conference, summoned Willis to join him for the 1946 season, and Bill became a mainstay in the middle of the Browns defensive line for the better part of the next decade. When the NFL absorbed All-American Football Conference teams, including the Browns, for the 1950 season, Willis became one of a handful of black players who broke professional football's color barrier for good.

For his part, a humble Willis was simply happy to be afforded the luxury of playing the game he loved so much. "It's strange, but it just happened," he said. "I mean, I was happy to play football and happy to be associated with a championship team, but I never thought of it as something that was historical in nature."

Not only did Willis make history, he became one of pro football's finest players. During the eight years he played for the Browns, Willis was a first-team All-League selection seven times. He played on four championship teams in the AAFC, then earned All-Pro honors three consecutive years after Cleveland joined the NFL.

Willis retired after the 1953 season and embarked upon a new challenge, returning to the Columbus area to work for the Ohio Youth Commission. He became that group's director in 1963 and took charge of the state's juvenile institutions. His work was so outstanding through the next twenty-five years that when the Ohio Department of Youth Services built its own high school in Delaware, it was named William K. Willis High School in his honor.

Because of Bill's success counseling troubled youths throughout central Ohio, Woody Hayes asked if he would be willing to use his advisory skills and unique experiences to mentor some of the African-American players on the Ohio State football team. Bill eagerly agreed, helping with the development of myriad players including two-time All-America lineman Jim Parker and All-America defensive end Jim Marshall, like Willis a product of Columbus East High School.

Another Willis disciple was Ben Espy, a tailback at Ohio State in 1962 and '63, who later became an attorney and a Columbus City Councilman before holding the title of minority leader in the Ohio Senate from 1996 to 2000. Espy credits Willis as a trusted advisor for many years, saying, "Throughout the years, I always looked upon him for advice. He was a mentor and a role model and everything you could be. He was a second father, quite frankly."

Willis became one of only a handful of former Ohio State players to earn enshrinement in both the Pro and College Football Halls of Fame, but one of his favorite moments came each year when he was invited back to hand out the Bill Willis Award to the Buckeye voted the most outstanding defensive player of the year.

He received one final tribute on November 3, 2007, when Ohio State formally retired his No. 99 jersey. A frail Willis rode in a golf cart to midfield of Ohio Stadium and basked in the glow of another thunderous ovation from appreciative fans, many of them born long after his playing days were over. It was clear, however, how much he still meant to the university and game he loved so much.

A little more than three weeks later, Bill Willis died at the age of 86, his legacy intact as a legendary football player, courageous racial pioneer, selfless community leader, and trusted mentor to those less fortunate.

FRED
MORRISON

OSU RUNNING BACK 1947–1949

NICKNAME: Curly

HOMETOWN: Columbus, Ohio

HEIGHT: 6 ft 2 in   WEIGHT: 215 lb

NFL DRAFT: 1950, Chicago Bears

33

*Fred played in one
of the very first
televised Rose
Bowl games.*

There is no one quite like Fred "Curly" Morrison. Jovial, emotional, loyal, opinionated, and straightforward on a wide-ranging variety of topics, Morrison parlayed a successful college and professional football career into lucrative business opportunities that included sales and marketing for CBS television as well as a cutting-edge video company. Now well into his 80s, Morrison remains a much sought-after speaker on the banquet circuit because he is truly a one-of-a-kind guy with a 24-carat heart and a reputation to match.

"I've had a wonderful life," Morrison said recently. "I played football at Ohio State and was fortunate enough to be on a team that won a Rose Bowl. I played seven years in the NFL, and played on two world championship teams with the Cleveland Browns. I've been successful in business, I have a beautiful wife, a wonderful family... I have really been a very lucky guy."

Luck likely had very little to do with the success of Fred and Ruth Morrison's only son, a bundle of mop-topped energy whose wavy locks earned him his nickname

at an early age. Curly's father was manager of a business supply company, and the family's Northwest Boulevard home in the tony Columbus suburb of Upper Arlington was just a stone's throw from the Ohio State campus.

As with most of boys in his neighborhood, he played a lot of sports, but football was his passion and he dreamed of one day playing in Ohio Stadium for head coach Paul Brown, who had led the Buckeyes to the national championship in 1942. "There's just something special about football," Curly said. "In football, it's *we*, not *me*. It's eleven guys on offense and eleven guys on defense who just want to win a game. Football is vital to me, and it always has been."

Morrison had grown up only about a mile from the stadium where the Buckeyes played each autumn Saturday, but the stately Horseshoe with its soaring concrete columns and cheering throngs might just as well have been a million miles away. Nearly every healthy young man was expected to join the armed forces fighting in World War II, and Morrison was no different. Upon his graduation from Upper Arlington High School, he packed away his ribbons and trophies and traded his black and gold football jersey for the olive green BDUs of the U.S. Marine Corps and reported to Parris Island, South Carolina, for basic training in October of 1945. Fortunately, the war in Europe had already come to an end while hostilities had ceased September 2 in the Pacific when Japan signed surrender documents.

With the war over, Morrison served only a brief stint with the Marines and was already back home by the fall of 1946, anticipating a warm welcome from the Buckeyes. But the program had undergone radical changes during the war. Brown had enlisted in the Navy after the 1943 season, and his reluctant hand-picked successor, the soft-spoken Carroll Widdoes, had resigned after only two years. Taking Widdoes's place as head coach was Paul Bixler, another former assistant who wasn't any keener on being head coach than Widdoes had been.

Into that unstable environment, Morrison stepped as a fresh-faced nineteen-year-old, barely 180 pounds and contending for playing time against grizzled older men, many of whom had been fighting Germans, Italians, and Japanese for the better part of the last four years. Bixler wasn't any help, seemingly ill-equipped to be the leader of his own program, and that showed as the Buckeyes finished the 1946 season with four victories, three losses, and two ties. Morrison had difficulty getting noticed as a freshman, but he finally began to get more and more playing time at offensive and defensive end as the season progressed. He even wound up the team's leading receiver for the year with seven receptions for 113 yards.

Less than three months after the '46 season ended, Bixler tendered his resignation, but that was a blessing in disguise for Ohio State and for Morrison. The Buckeyes hired three-time All-American end Wesley Fesler, who returned to his alma mater as a conquering hero. And when Fesler overhauled the OSU offense, Morrison was moved back to the fullback position he had played as a prep star. Eventually, that curly hair was perched atop a

6-foot-2-inch, 215-pound slab of muscle, and Morrison hit full stride during his senior season in 1949 when he led the Big Ten champion Buckeyes with nine rushing touchdowns, and finished second on the team with 606 yards.

Morrison punctuated his senior year with an MVP performance in Ohio State's 17–14 win against the University of California at the Rose Bowl. Following a week of festivities that had such movie stars as Elizabeth Taylor, Bob Hope, and Bing Crosby visiting their practice sessions, the Buckeyes secured the victory in front of a record crowd of 100,963 when Jimmy Hague kicked a 27-yard field goal with 1:55 remaining in the game. Morrison was the star of the game, rushing for 127 yards and one touchdown, and had two other TDs scored by Curly not been wiped out because of penalties, the Buckeyes would likely have never needed Hague's game-winner.

"We didn't realize it at the time, but I believe that was the very first Rose Bowl game that was televised (on a regional basis)," Morrison said. "If you go back to 1949, a lot of people didn't even have a television set, and the ones that did probably didn't know the Rose Bowl game would be televised. I remember coming home a week later and seeing it on the newsreel. I didn't even know it was televised until after the game. We only found out because we got telegrams about it. At the time, while we knew this was one of the big bowl games, I don't think we really realized the magnitude of it. We just knew it was the Rose Bowl and it was important, and to us it was a matter of pride. We weren't going to get beat by some guys from California."

Morrison parlayed his Rose Bowl MVP performance into a first-round selection in the 1950 NFL draft, going to the Chicago Bears with the tenth overall pick. He played four seasons in Chicago for legendary head coach George Halas before being traded to the Cleveland Browns prior to the 1954 season. In Cleveland, he finally achieved his boyhood dream of playing for Brown, and he earned two NFL championship rings in three seasons with the Browns.

He retired from the game following the 1956 season, but his outgoing personality, overall football acumen, and key contacts he had made throughout his career led CBS Sports to hire him in 1958 as the network's first former NFL star to provide color commentary for professional football games. He joined veteran sportscaster Bob Wolff for analysis during Browns games, and the duo also became part of the original "CBS Sunday Sports Spectacular" show in 1960.

During the NFL's offseason, Curly became a network salesman for CBS, and in late 1959, the network moved him to New York to join the network's sales team on a full-time basis. He called on major advertising agencies and clients, with his main responsibility to see that all available advertising slots were sold for the network's signature sports programs such as The Masters, the Triple Crown, and the Major League Baseball Game of the Week. Morrison later branched out past sports telecasts, selling sponsorships for many of the network's top shows.

In 1962, a production company showed him the pilot episode of a new show it was trying to sell to CBS. Curly liked what he saw, and sent a copy of the pilot to executives of the Toni hair care company, recommending they buy at least a weekly one-half interest in the show. The company's executives turned both Curly and CBS down, pronouncing the show as too silly, saying they didn't know anyone would watch such a farce. The show was *The Beverly Hillbillies*, the number one-rated show on television during the first two years of its eventual ten-year run. The next year, when Curly called the company pitching another unsold pilot, the company agreed to sponsor the show sight unseen. That was *My Favorite Martian*, which finished its first season as a top-ten rated series.

Morrison's connection in network television led him in 1969 to help found a company that pioneered videotape production. The company, known as Trans-American Video Inc., transformed the television and movie industry from using conventional black-

and-white and color film to the use of more inexpensive videotape. In addition to the business venture, which he and his partners even-

lar Monterey Peninsula in northern California. The event features live and silent auctions with proceeds benefitting the Boys and

> "Fred played in the leather helmet era. You ask him now about face masks and he giggles. He broke his nose so many times that he couldn't breathe out of it until he was 50, when he had surgery."
> —*Bill Dwyre,* The LA Times

tually sold to entertainer Sammy Davis Jr. and a group of investors, Morrison went on to several other successful ventures, including serving in 1974 and '75 as general manager of the Southern California Sun of the upstart World Football League, and as chief executive officer and general manager of the USFL's Los Angeles Express from 1983 to 1985.

Meanwhile, Morrison has remained an advocate for retired NFL players, launching in 1990, along with his wife Sophie, the NFL Legends Invitational Golf Tournament played at the Pebble Beach, Spanish Bay, and Spyglass Hill golf courses on the spectacu-

Girls Clubs of Monterey County as well as funding a college scholarship for a worthy member of the clubs. The golf tournament and its accompanying events have raised nearly one million dollars since its inception, thanks mostly to Fred "Curly" Morrison, the man with a modern-day Midas touch.

VICTOR JANOWICZ

OSU HALFBACK, DEFENSIVE BACK, KICKER 1949–1951

NICKNAME: Vic the Quick

HOMETOWN: Elyria, Ohio

HEIGHT: 5 ft 9 in   **WEIGHT:** 181 lb

NFL DRAFT: 1954, Washington Redskins

31

Vic was the first of two Heisman winners to play both professional football and major league baseball, the other being 1985 winner Bo Jackson.

On the football field, there was nothing Vic Janowicz could not do. He could run like a gazelle, throw with pinpoint accuracy, punt the ball in any direction, play defense with finesse and power, and alter the outcome of any game with an uncanny ability to return kicks. But while Janowicz is arguably the best all-around player Ohio State has ever produced, he might also be one of the program's most tragic heroes.

"I wasted a lot of years feeling sorry for myself," Janowicz said in 1992. "If things didn't go my way, someone else was always to blame. It took me a long time to realize that I was the one who was responsible for the way things were. Until I understood that, nothing would change. That's about the time I took control of my life."

Self-introspection was never the strongest character trait for Victor Felix Janowicz as he was growing up in a large Polish family in Elyria, a small city fixed squarely in the steel country of northeastern Ohio. Vic's father, Felix, worked as a welder in the steel mills while his mother Veronica stayed home and cared for the couple's nine children.

Young Vic seemed always in a hurry, quickly growing into a sinewy young man with fast feet. Fifteenth Street neighbors remembered the youngster as a blur, always running to get where he wanted to go. He would challenge all comers to foot races and win easily. He would wait almost until the school bell was ringing before sprinting off to class. And he constantly asked his mother if there was anything she needed from the corner market just so he could run there to get it for her.

Mostly, though, Vic figured he had to run to escape a life in the steel mills. That was fine for his father and his older brothers, but Vic wanted something more, and he thought he had found it on the playing fields of Elyria High School.

In addition to being a star baseball player, Janowicz was a triple threat in football, starring for the Pioneers on offense, defense, and special teams. His blazing speed made him a threat to score anytime he touched the ball as a halfback or kick returner, and he played safety on defense with reckless abandon. His athletic talents were so great that he was also his team's punter and placekicker. Although recruiting was not the specialized industry it is today, Vic's exploits in high school made him one of the most highly sought-after prospects in the nation, and more than sixty colleges and universities offered full scholarships, many of them promising to build their entire programs around him.

The Buckeyes, however, had a little something extra going for them as they pursued the services of the prospect now known as "Vic the Quick." The year before Janowicz became a high school senior, an organization known as the Frontliners was formed to help recruit top talent for the Ohio State football program. Alumni Association field secretary J. Edward Weaver—who from 1970–1977 served as the school's director of athletics—joined with longtime assistant coach Ernie Godfrey to form the group composed of prominent alumni, top businessmen, and well-heeled program supporters. The group's main purpose was to help steer top high school talent to Columbus. One of the group's founding members was property developer, thoroughbred horse breeder, and Pittsburgh Pirates owner John W. Galbreath, an influential man who took an immediate liking to Janowicz. The feeling was evidently mutual and the Buckeyes were able to land one of the most prized high school recruits in the nation.

Janowicz arrived at Ohio State in the fall of 1948 and immediately made a name for himself on the freshman squad. The following season, he was one of several talented sophomores that helped the Buckeyes win a share of the Western Conference championship as well as a 17–14 Rose Bowl victory over the University of California. It marked OSU's first-ever Rose Bowl win, and Janowicz helped the cause with a return of forty-five yards with an interception early in the third quarter when the Buckeyes were facing a 7–0 deficit. But Vic wanted to do more. Despite his obvious talents with the ball in his hands, he was used primarily as a blocking back on offense during his sophomore year. As a result, the highly-prized prospect who had scored more than fifty touchdowns in high school wound up his first varsity season with only 112 yards on thirty carries. Vic secretly sulked while head coach Wesley Fesler drew heated scrutiny for not fully utilizing his most lethal weapon.

"Vic Janowicz came here as one of the most highly recruited players ever at Ohio State," said longtime *Columbus Dispatch* sportswriter Paul Hornung. "He was nationally publicized before he ever played, and everybody in the world knew he should be the starting tailback. But Fesler played him on defense, and it infuriated people that Fesler didn't play him on offense."

Fesler, who had been a three-time All-America end at Ohio State in 1928–1930, should have known better, but he apparently didn't care. After only three years as head coach of the Buckeyes, a queasy stomach had turned into a full-fledged ulcer and Fesler was ready to resign following the 1949 season. He was persuaded by university officials to finish the term of his contract and return for another year, but only after agreeing to feature Janowicz prominently in the 1950 offense.

The rest is history as Janowicz had a season for the ages. During his junior season, he rushed for 314 yards and five touchdowns, threw for 557 yards and twelve TDs, and added countless other big plays on defense and special teams. He won the 1950 Heisman Trophy in a landslide vote in December but in reality sewed up the award six weeks earlier with his performance during an 83–21 victory against Iowa. Janowicz was a one-man wrecking crew during that cool, crisp late October afternoon at Ohio Stadium as he scored two touchdowns, threw for four other scores, recovered two fumbles—each of which led to Ohio State touchdowns—and was responsible for kicking ten extra points.

"It was like a dream," Janowicz said. "Everything we tried just seemed to work. It seemed like every time we got the ball, we scored." Not exactly, but close. After the Buckeyes' eighth touchdown of the day made the score 55–0, Vic pushed his point-after kick attempt wide to the right. An account the next day in *The Columbus Dispatch* characterized the missed kick as "just to show the guy is human—perhaps."

That wasn't the only superhuman-like effort Janowicz turned in during his Heisman Trophy year. During the final game of the season, the infamous "Snow Bowl" against Michigan, he booted a 38-yard field goal into the teeth of a 35-mph Arctic wind, providing the Buckeyes their only points in a 9–3 defeat. "The greatest singular play I ever saw in football was that field goal," longtime OSU assistant coach Esco Sarkkinen said. "He drilled that baby into a howling gale, and honestly I don't know how he did it."

Janowicz also punted 21 times that day—a single-game school record that still stands—but two of the kicks were blocked, one for a safety and the other for a touchdown, providing the winning points for Michigan.

Although Janowicz was named college football's finest player the next month, the loss to Michigan sealed the fate of his head coach. Fesler made good on his threat to resign, and successor Woody Hayes brought with him an offensive attack that scrapped the single-wing formation in which Vic had flourished. Instead, the Buckeyes switched to the Wing-T and Janowicz spent a nondescript senior season at wingback. As the team stumbled to a fifth-place finish in the conference race, Janowicz failed to finish among the top ten in the 1951 Heisman voting.

Years later, Vic would explain, "Woody and I always got along well, but I didn't like his technique of coaching. He was a believer in three yards and a cloud of dust, but I felt you had to have a little finesse with that." The truth was that his senior season soured him on football, an attitude further cemented when the Washington Redskins offered a contract he thought was unworthy of the seventh overall selection in the 1952 NFL draft. He spurned the Redskins and instead accepted an offer from Galbreath to play major league baseball with the Pirates. Unfortunately, Pittsburgh wasn't very good in those days and manager Fred Haney didn't much care for an owner-selected bonus baby rammed down his throat. As a result, Vic appeared in only eighty-three games over two seasons, hitting .214 with two homers and ten RBI.

Following the 1954 baseball season, Janowicz decided to return to football and signed a contract with the Redskins. After easing his way back into the game in '54 primarily as the team's kicker, Vic appeared to be back in form the following year when he rushed for 397 yards and four touchdowns, caught eleven passes for 149 yards and two more TDs, and booted six field goals and twenty-eight PATs.

The following summer, Janowicz was primed for a breakout season and was eager to get to training camp. He caught a ride with a teammate, but while he was asleep in the backseat, the car went off the road and struck a bridge abutment. Vic suffered severe head injuries and was in a coma for nearly a month. He wound up spending six weeks in the hospital and was partially paralyzed, ending his athletic career. Around the same time, Janowicz's daughter Diana was diagnosed with cerebral palsy. She died in 1965 at the age of nine, leaving the family buried beneath an avalanche of medical bills.

Miraculously, Janowicz refused to give up. After years of rehabilita-tion, he overcame the paralysis, and through therapy learned how to deal with the death of his daughter. "It's pretty easy to feel sorry for yourself," he said. "The hard part is to get your head on straight. It took me a long time to figure things out, but boy when I did, man, what a life I've had."

Janowicz spent the next several years as administrative assistant to the Ohio state auditor and ex-perienced a rebirth of sorts at his alma mater. Admittedly bitter for many years about what had hap-pened during his senior year, Vic decided to return to Ohio State in the mid-1970s and was hailed as a returning hero. He was elected to the College Football Hall of Fame in 1976, spent time as a radio analyst on Ohio State football broadcasts, and was a member of the inaugural class of inductees into the univer-sity's athletic hall of fame.

Much in demand as a public speaker, especially at schools where he would cheerfully display his Heisman Trophy for youngsters, he continued to tour the state as a goodwill ambassador for the uni-versity until his death from cancer on February 27, 1996.

WOODY
HAYES

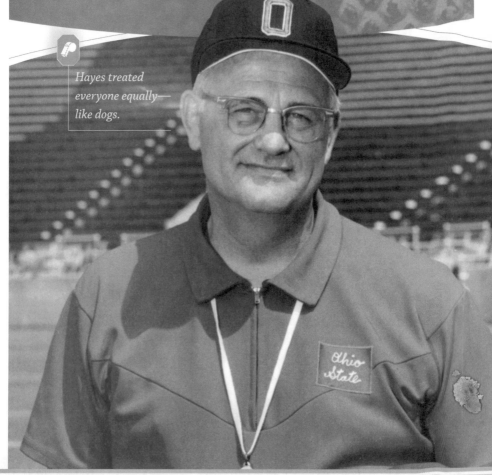

OSU COACH 1951–1978

HOMETOWN: Clifton, Ohio

RECORD: 205-61-10

BIG TEN CHAMPIONSHIPS: 1954-55, 1957, 1961, 1968-70, 1972-77

NATIONAL CHAMPIONSHIPS: 1954, 1957, 1961, 1968, 1970

Hayes treated everyone equally— like dogs.

So much has been said and written about Wayne Woodrow Hayes that details of his life tend to become colored pieces of glass in a kaleidoscope. If you listen enough, read enough, and turn them over enough, they fall into a pattern. The husky scrapper of a country boy who wanted nothing more than to become a teacher like his father. The driven bull of a man who believed anything could be accomplished through hard work. The military historian whose coaching philosophy was steeping in military battlefield tactics. The master of psychology. The maniacal motivator. The loyal friend. The mentor. The father figure. The saint. The sinner. The very devil himself.

"Most people believe Woody Hayes had a total dedication to coaching, and that is true—but only to a point," said former longtime Ohio State sports information director Marv Homan, himself a member of the university's athletic hall of fame. "I have always believed Woody worked so hard because of his total dedication to the university. He had tremendous loyalty to the university, and total dedication to making the university a better place.

"I know that sounds terribly idealistic, but it was true," Homan continued. "Woody wanted to make the college experience a lasting one for each of the players he coached, intent that they would look back at their college years as a memorable experience, not just one of playing on the football team. He was demanding, of course, and difficult to deal with at times. But if you take time to look at the total picture of the man, take time to really get to know and understand what Woody Hayes was about, some of that bluff and bluster begins to melt away."

Once asked to describe the legendary coach, his longtime assistant Esco Sarkkinen replied with a question of his own. "How much time do I have?" he asked. "Thirty seconds," came the reply. Sarkkinen laughed the entire half-minute, later remarking, "You don't describe Woody Hayes in one sentence or one paragraph, and certainly not in thirty seconds. It takes chapter after chapter after chapter after chapter."

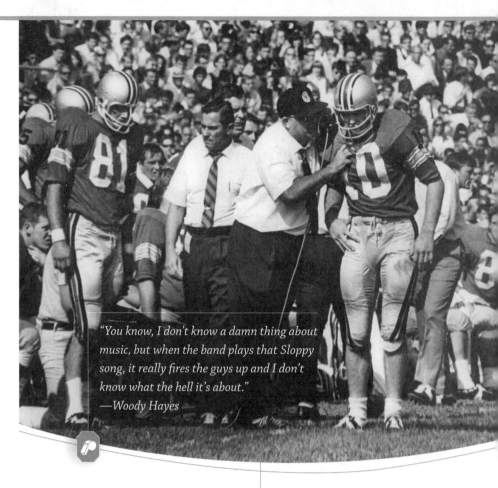

"You know, I don't know a damn thing about music, but when the band plays that Sloppy song, it really fires the guys up and I don't know what the hell it's about."
—Woody Hayes

Although there are many who remember Hayes as blinded to almost every other facet of his being by an intrinsic drive to win, he was a multifaceted man with a variety of interests on a wide array of topics. Born February 14, 1913, in tiny Clifton, Ohio, it is worth remembering the sum of Hayes's life was more than just football. He was a U.S. Navy officer in World War II, a tireless fundraiser for countless charitable causes, and a goodwill ambassador for the Ohio State University around the world.

Still, it would be extremely difficult to separate Woody Hayes and college football. The two are, after all, synonymous. "The name Woody Hayes will forever be intertwined with the game of college football—and rightfully so," said longtime OSU football historian Jack Park said. "The championships, the great players, the Rose Bowls...You think of all of those things, and as great as those things are, it barely scratches the surface for a man who accomplished nearly everything there was to accomplish in his chosen profession."

In twenty-eight seasons as head coach of the Buckeyes, Hayes won 205 games, coached fifty-eight All-Americans, captured five national championships and thirteen Big Ten crowns, and according to at least one biographer, "was the subject of more varied and colorful anecdotal material than any other coach past or present, including fabled Knute Rockne."

The coach's pearls of wisdom read like scripture for anyone who fancies himself a member of Buckeye Nation. There was the philosophical: *You win with people.* The pragmatic: *There's nothing that cleanses your soul like getting the hell knocked out of you.* And the just plain Woody: *Show me a good guy that the players love all the time and I'll show you a loser.*

There are also the many legendary stories, some of which are so steeped in Scarlet and Gray lore

that whether they are fact or fiction seems meaningless.

One often-told story among former players is the way the coach with his bare hands would destroy his trademark black ball cap or stomp on his wristwatch when things weren't going well during practice. Only years later was it discovered those fits of pique were only for show. The coach not only stocked up during the summer on dime-store watches, he instructed equipment managers to use razor blades to slice strategic parts of his cap, making it easier for the coach to rip it to shreds.

Other stories deal with Hayes's legendary temper. Wooden chairs were apparently no match for him, as a handful of players learned during one afternoon practice session in the Horseshoe. After the coach became displeased with a particular drill, he trained his focus on several Buckeyes sitting on chairs around the track. As Hayes stomped toward the group, the players scattered for their lives while the coach turned the chairs into kindling.

Then there was the day Hayes split his pants trying to show to a kicker what he thought was proper form. Or the time he instructed groundskeepers to turn hoses on the practice field to prepare for less than ideal weather conditions and wound up with a muddy quagmire nicknamed "Lake Hayes" that forced practice indoors on an otherwise perfect afternoon.

Not all of the stories portray the brusque side of the coach, however.

All-America quarterback Rex Kern has often repeated the story of Hayes being stopped one day while shopping in Upper Arlington. A man came up to him and told him how much he and his wife loved the Buckeyes and how he just wanted to shake the coach's hand. "Well, where is your wife?" Woody asked. "I'd like to meet her." The man told him she was dying of cancer in Riverside Hospital. That evening, when the man went to visit his wife, Woody was sitting by her bedside.

"I've heard all of those stories and a lot more just like them," Homan said. "Some of those things have maybe taken on a life of their own over the years. But most of the stories you hear, there is a lot of truth in them. Coach Hayes was such a larger-than-life figure, so it stands to reason most of the stories about him would also seem larger than life."

One of the coach's final public appearances occurred March 14, 1986, when Ohio State awarded him with an honorary Doctorate of Humanities degree. During commencement ceremonies, a frail Hayes gave a heartfelt speech that stressed the value of education, the worth of a diploma, and the need for good acts in the community. It resonated with even his harshest critics. "Today," he began, "is the greatest day of my life. I appreciate so much being able to come here and talk to a graduating class at The Ohio State University— a great, great university."

A year later, almost to the day, the coach was gone, dead at the age of 74. Woody's heart, described by Earle Bruce as "as big or bigger than his chest," had finally given out.

"That news just hit me like a bomb," two-time Heisman Trophy winner Archie Griffin said. "Everyone knew he had been sick, but it was still a shock. I remember it like it was yesterday. I was driving to work that morning, and I had to turn around and go back home. I had to collect my thoughts and just get myself together."

Some fifteen thousand people attended a memorial service at Ohio Stadium in his honor, and among the mourners at the funeral was former U.S. President Richard Nixon, who gave a touching eulogy.

"God, I miss that man," Kern said. "The day he died was the saddest day of my life. Even now, it brings great sorrow to me."

More than a quarter-century after his death, Hayes remains the iconic figure he was in life. And he continues to inspire debate, especially when those who knew him best discuss how he might fare in today's game. Several of his former players espouse the view that Hayes could not or would not conform to the socially-driven media of the modern age. Others believe the coach's strengths would transcend any era.

"I think he would be even better today than when I played by virtue of his organization and discipline," All-America offensive tackle John Hicks said. "I think the kids would love him even more. I find today

that people want that kind of discipline and leadership."

Hicks is definitely not alone in that assessment.

"Coach Hayes was about the old-fashioned values of education, hard work, and paying forward," said Walter Adamkosky, writer and director of the one-man play *Woody: His Life, Times and Teachings.* "It's about how to be a success in life—on and off the field. And if that sounds corny today, the undeniable fact is it still works. His messages never go out of style. And they may be more relevant—and needed—today than ever."

THURLOW WEED

NICKNAME: Tad

HOMETOWN: Grandview Heights, Ohio

HEIGHT: 5 ft 5 in   **WEIGHT:** 148 lb

24

Tad was a bit like Forrest Gump—world traveler, entrepreneur, adventurer, and avid sportsman.

*T*ad Weed was an entrepreneur, raconteur, innovator, inventor, war correspondent, skilled sportsman and starry-eyed revolutionary, an outside-the-box thinker who overcame more obstacles and counted more successes than most people could in three lifetimes.

Barely five-foot-five and 130 pounds, Weed was a three-year letterman for the Ohio State football team, helped the Buckeyes win the 1954 national championship, and later became the first OSU kicking specialist to play in the National Football League.

He was an avid sportsman, adept at golf, tennis, skiing, basketball, track, swimming, and even figure skating. He climbed Mount Kilimanjaro—at 19,341 feet, the tallest peak in Africa and highest freestanding mountain in the world—by himself on a whim. He swapped stories with Ernest Hemingway at the Pulitzer Prize-winning author's home in Cuba. He filed news reports from the war-torn Middle East, patented and manufactured the first oversized tennis rackets in the United States, and even tried to form his own independent country.

"You know, whenever you have any kind of success, you get in your head that almost anything is possible," Weed said. "If you get that firmly in your head as part of something that you've seen demonstrated, it lets you do a whole lot of things in life that you might not otherwise have thought you might be able to do."

Thurlow Weed was born January 18, 1933, a diminutive baby whom his father Roy quickly dubbed "Tadpole." Young Tad seemed athletically challenged by his small stature, but that didn't seem to deter his steadfastness of mind. As a youngster, he played just about every sport offered at Grandview High School in suburban Columbus, but he didn't exactly look the part of a football star—and admittedly, he wasn't one. "I was probably the worst halfback Grandview ever had," he said. "I didn't go 130 (pounds) and I was slow."

Having grown up just a few minutes from the Ohio State campus, Weed had always dreamed of playing football for the Buckeyes. He knew, however, that head coach Woody Hayes would have little use for a pint-sized running back, so he began spending countless hours teaching himself how to kick a football. Still, during the first freshman practice in 1951, Weed took his place among the dozens of halfbacks on the field. "I was so small, it was just ridiculous," he said. "After one day of running at halfback, Woody's eyes just sort of rolled back in his head, and he said, 'Here, don't try running any more plays. Just take this bag of balls and go over on that field and kick.'"

Like all freshman players, Weed was not eligible to play in 1951—not that there would have been a spot for him anyway—but the rules of college football changed for the 1952 season, allowing for unlimited substitutions and a chance for punting and kicking specialists to contribute. "Up until that time—especially on Woody's teams—you had been expected to make the team as a player before you'd ever get a look as a kicker," Weed said.

As the '52 season approached, however, it appeared the rule change would have no direct effect on Weed. Throughout fall camp, he was buried on the depth as a third-string kicker, a position Weed described as roughly on par with the water boy and a stadium hotdog vendor. On the eve of the season opener against Indiana, though, his status suddenly changed. During a final walkthrough at Ohio Stadium, the team's top two kickers missed attempt after attempt. In desperation, Hayes signaled for the "little guy" to give it a try. By the time the walkthrough had ended, Weed had earned the job as the team's primary kicker, a position he would retain for the next three years.

Following the 1954 season, Weed had earned three varsity letters—a first in Ohio State history for a kicking specialist—but he was far from satisfied. The Buckeyes had won the 1954 national championship, finishing the season with a 20–7 win over the University of Southern California in the Rose Bowl. It hadn't been a very good day for Weed, however. A heavy rain that fell throughout the afternoon turned the field into a quagmire, and the OSU kicker missed his only field-goal attempt, as well as an extra point.

On the way back from Pasadena, Weed set an individual goal to make 10,000 consecutive PAT attempts. Alone in Ohio Stadium, he kicked night after night, knocking several hundred balls through the uprights and into a net. He lined up five balls at one time, knocked them through, retrieved them, and began the process again. He was more than halfway toward his goal when Mother Nature intervened.

"There was this loud clap of thunder, a bolt of lightning, and I choked," Weed said with a laugh. "I missed one at five thousand-and-something, turned around, and started over like an idiot." When he reached 9,999, he threw in an extra challenge for himself—kicking the final one blindfolded. Attempt No. 10,000, caught by a Columbus-area photographer, sailed through the uprights just like all the ones before it. And had he missed? "I guess I would have started all over again," he said.

While their careers in college football defined the lives of many young men who played the game,

Weed was just getting started. During spring break of his senior year, he joined teammate Dick Brubaker and fraternity brother John Miller, who was captain of the OSU basketball team, for a weekend trip to Fort Lauderdale, Florida. The trio soon found themselves in Key West and then on a flight to Havana, Cuba, where they took a taxi to Hemingway's house, a well-known spot in the suburb of San Francisco de Paulo. Standing outside the gate, they were spotted by one of the writer's assistants, who was told who they were and why they were there. A few minutes later, they were ushered into the house where they shared drinks and swapped stories with the famed writer, much to his wife's chagrin.

Once he graduated from Ohio State, Weed's life became a whirlwind of activity as he went from one endeavor to another. He appeared in six games with the Pittsburgh Steelers during the 1955 NFL season, converting all twelve of his extra point attempts and three of six field goals. He later joined the U.S. Marine Corps where he organized teams in various sports to compete throughout the Far East. When Weed was discharged, he decided to take a year to travel abroad, a decision that soon found him in Tanzania, determined to make it to the summit of Kilimanjaro. The problem was that it cost money to climb the mountain and Weed was broke. "So, when nobody was looking, I took off up the trail and didn't tell anyone where I was going," he said. He followed a worn path up the mountain, resting each night in makeshift huts along the trail, until reaching the top after three days.

From there, Weed's adventures took him to Lebanon, where the United States had sent Marines to help monitor a burgeoning civil war. Curious and eager to continue traveling, Weed secured a media credential by telling the defense department he was a reporter for *The Columbus Dispatch*. He later called his hometown newspaper and said the Pentagon would be calling, and if the publication vouched for him, he would send back exclusive reports from the war-torn region.

Once he returned home to the Columbus area, Weed started to work in the family oil business and took up skiing and tennis to remain active. Skiing came easily, but he became increasingly frustrated with tennis and his inability to hit the ball consistently. While tinkering one day in his garage, he wondered what would happen if he could increase the size of a racket's hitting area. After sketching a few prototypes, he applied for and received a patent—and thus was born a business manufacturing the first oversized tennis rackets in the United States.

Success in business, however, came at a price. Becoming increasingly disillusioned with the country's tax laws, Weed became part of a group that sought to start a new country as a form of demonstration. That group was unable to gain any traction, but Weed later met a man at an economic conference who had a similar idea and had located a pair of uninhabited coral reefs in the South Pacific to serve as their new country. Unfortunately, the king of Tonga took exception to the idea and threatened to have Weed or any of his cohorts executed if they set foot on the reefs. That signaled the end of Weed's days as a revolutionary.

The only thing that finally slowed Weed was a freak accident in 1999. During an annual skiing trip with Brubaker, an out-of-control skier collided with Weed, who was later diagnosed with a rare neurological disorder that scars the part of the nervous system that allows the spinal cord to interact with the rest of the body. Weed, who had led such an active life, was suddenly confined to a wheelchair with a bleak prognosis. While that would have devastated most people, Weed met the new challenge with the same kind of verve he had exhibited all his life.

"Head-on is the only way to take this because the alternatives are all much worse," he said. "I get angry when I'm frustrated, and I'm frustrated every day trying to live in a wheelchair. But I've been so lucky my whole life, so I can't complain about how this happened to me or whatever brought it on."

Weed remained as active as possible for the remainder of his life. He continued playing golf from a specially-made cart, and he even rejoined Brubaker on the ski slopes, moving through the snow on a special chair mounted on runners with an instructor guiding him from behind. He always believed he would eventually regain the use of his legs, but his health gradually worsened and he died in November of 2006 at the age of 73. His friends and family knew that his health had been on the decline, but his passing still came as something of a shock.

"He had done so many things and overcome so much in his life," Brubaker said. "It never entered our minds that he wouldn't beat this, too. Tad was such a special person. I've never met anyone quite like him in my life, but I never really expected to, either."

HOWARD CASSADY

OSU HALFBACK 1952–1955

NICKNAME: Hopalong

HOMETOWN: Columbus, Ohio

HEIGHT: 5 ft 10 in   WEIGHT: 172 lb

ALL-AMERICAN: 1954, 1955

NFL DRAFT: 1956, Detroit Lions

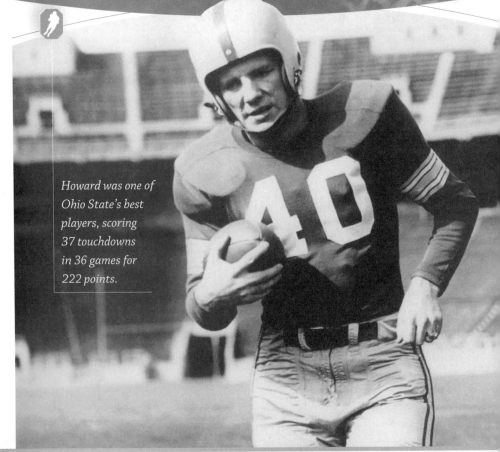

Howard was one of Ohio State's best players, scoring 37 touchdowns in 36 games for 222 points.

*H*oward "Hopalong" Cassady has truly lived a sporting life in full. How many other men can claim close relationships with two of the twentieth century's most polarizing American sports figures while altering the history of both college football and Major League Baseball in the process? Yet the little freckle-faced kid with the funny nickname is credited with saving Woody Hayes's job as Ohio State head coach, as well as transforming George Steinbrenner's New York Yankees from contenders to World Series champions.

Named for his paternal grandfather, Howard Albert Cassady made his debut March 2, 1934, in Columbus to parents Pearl and Vivian Cassady. Pearl Cassady worked as a carpenter and wallpaper hanger and on weekends was an avid bowler. His son, however, wasn't content to stay indoors for any length of time, and he quickly became adept at nearly every sport he tried. Despite a lack of size and a shock of fire-engine red hair perched atop a dappled face that made him look even younger than he was, Cassady soon became a multisport star at Central High School in downtown Columbus. When thoughts turned to his future, however, Cassady thought he would just follow in his father's footsteps.

"I never figured I would go to college because nobody in my family ever went to college. Why would I go?" Cassady said. "But I played football, basketball, and baseball, and I pole-vaulted on the track team at Central, and suddenly I realized I had a chance to go someplace. I knew I wanted to play baseball in college as well as football, but there were times when I didn't figure I was good enough for football because I was never that big. I weighed about 155 pounds, and everybody in college football was so much bigger than me."

Enter Hayes, who was looking for something to help turn the tide of criticism after his first year as head coach at Ohio State. Hayes had been a compromise candidate in February of 1951 for university officials looking to replace Wes Fesler, who had resigned after four seasons, and the Buckeyes hadn't exactly distinguished themselves in their first year under new management. The team capped a 4-3-2 season with a 7–0 loss at Michigan, marking the seventh straight year Ohio State fans had been unable to celebrate a victory over their hated archrivals to the north. Eager for something—anything—to breathe some life into the program, boosters and alumni turned against Hayes in the fervent hope the university could somehow coax former coach Paul Brown into returning from the pro ranks. They even rewrote the first verse of *Carmen Ohio*, the school's alma mater, and loudly sang, "Oh, come let's sing Ohio's praise, and say goodbye to Woody Hayes!"

Hayes seemed unfazed, although he knew recruiting and signing Columbus born-and-bred Cassady would at least help stem some of the local criticism. Not that Cassady was all that interested in the Buckeyes. Growing up in the shadow of Ohio Stadium, he knew all about Ohio State, sneaking with friends into the Horseshoe a few hours before kickoff and then staying on the move, fearful of getting caught without a ticket. But there were other programs that had caught his attention, most spe-

cifically Notre Dame and Kentucky. Cassady also took notice of the fact those two schools had long-established head coaches—Frank Leahy with the Fighting Irish and Paul "Bear" Bryant at Kentucky.

In the end, it wasn't Hayes's sales pitch that sold Cassady on the Scarlet and Gray. It was a lack of confidence. "I wasn't sure at all that I could play college football," Cassady said, "but I figured if I didn't make it at Ohio State, at least I was home."

Changes in college football rules implemented with the 1952 season meant Cassady would be eligible to play as a freshman, but Hayes had already formulated his starting backfield and little rookie halfbacks weren't part of the equation. So the future Heisman Trophy winner donned a ragged practice jersey for his first fall camp as a collegiate player and began work on the scout team. As two-a-day practices gave way to game-week drills in preparation for the season opener against Indiana, Cassady copied the style of the Hoosier running backs so well that Hayes decided he could dress for the opener.

"I never had a uniform until two days before that game, and by that time, 13 and 40 were all that was left," Cassady remembered. "Well, I sure as hell didn't want 13, and I knew Route 40 ran right through Columbus, so that was how I got my number."

In that first game against Indiana, Cassady might have been in uniform but he was as far from the field as he could get, relegated to a seat on the end of the bench as the Buckeyes trailed 7–6 after the first quarter. With nothing going right and precious little to lose, Hayes finally yelled, "Get the little red-head up here." Cassady responded by spearheading a come-from-behind 33–13 victory during which he scored three touchdowns. Suddenly, the little kid from Columbus known simply as "Red" had a new nickname. Columbus sportswriters wrote that he "hopped all over the field like the performing cowboy," a reference to radio, television, and movie star Hopalong Cassidy.

More important, Hayes had a go-to player upon which he could build his program around the next four years. Behind an offensive line anchored by future College and Pro Football Hall of Fame guard Jim Parker, Cassady terrorized opposing defenses with a mixture of slashing moves and blazing speed. The Buckeyes won six games in both '52 and '53, and then captured the 1954 national championship with a perfect 10-0 record that included a 21–7 victory over Michigan as well as a 20–7 win against the University of Southern California in the Rose Bowl.

The team would not repeat as national champs in 1955, but Cassady still had a superlative senior season by leading Ohio State to another Big Ten championship, the program's first back-to-back titles in thirty-six years. His final home game was an emotional one with a record crowd of 82,701 filling the Horseshoe to bid farewell. Cassady, who ran onto the field in front of the Dads' Day crowd, accompanied by his proud father, electrified the crowd the first time he touched the ball with a 45-yard touchdown run early in the first quarter. The touchdown erased an early 3–0 Iowa lead, and the Buckeyes went on to a 20–10 victory.

Cassady, who accounted for two more touchdowns in the game, was hoisted onto the shoulders of his teammates as the final gun sounded. In the gathering dusk, the huge throng surged toward the field to catch one last glimpse of their hometown hero while those who couldn't get close simply stood where they were and cheered as Cassady—his redhead bare, his rugged face flushed, and squinting back the mist in his eyes—was borne toward the sideline one final time.

The following week, Cassady completed his college career with 146 yards during a 17–0 win at Michigan, moving his career rushing total to a school-record 2,466 yards. He also scored 222 points as a Buckeye, a school mark that stood for more than two decades. He was named on every All-America team, won the Heisman Trophy by a vote total higher than the next three nominees combined, and was voted Male Athlete of the Year for 1955 by the Associated Press, beating such luminaries as heavyweight boxing champion Rocky Marciano and Cleveland Browns quarterback Otto Graham.

Cassady went on to a seven-year NFL career after the Detroit Lions made him the third overall pick in the first round of the 1956 player draft. He played primarily as a defensive back, but still finished his career with 1,229 rushing yards, 1,601 receiving yards, and twenty-four touchdowns. Upon his retirement from pro football, Cassady became a manufacturer's representative who sold steel to Steinbrenner's American Shipbuilding Co.

The two had originally met at Rickenbacker Air Force base in Columbus, where Cassady was in ROTC and Steinbrenner was a lieutenant. "He was doing some graduate work at Ohio State when I was there," Cassady said. "But my sophomore year, he went to Northwestern to coach under Lou Saban, so I'd see him on the sidelines." Steinbrenner remembered that encounter in 2005. "We went to play Ohio State and thought we had a pretty good chance," he said. "I tried to act standoffish, and when he came over to shake my hand, I said, 'Get outta here you little (bleep)! You're on the other team!' First thing I know, he fumbles at his three, picks up the ball in his end zone, and is suddenly running past me. He was a great, great player."

It was a relationship that eventually paved the way to Steinbrenner hiring Cassady, whose various duties with the Yankees included a stint as conditioning coach for the big-league club beginning in 1976. That year, the team reached the World Series for the first time in a dozen years, and then won back-to-back series championships in '77 and '78. "We had a lot of fun with Hop, but he got people in shape," said former Yankees outfielder Lou Piniella. "He got our attention and made everybody work. He used his knowledge of training from his football exploits to help people get ready to play baseball."

In recent years, Cassady has been content to stay close to his home in Tampa, Florida, surrounded by memorabilia that includes the last Ohio State jersey he wore, family pictures (including son Craig, who played defensive back at OSU as well as five NFL seasons in New Orleans), a framed letter from Steinbrenner, and of course the Heisman Trophy.

Cassady nearly lost the trophy in the mid-1980s when his home was burglarized and many of his awards were stolen. Fortunately, the thieves didn't realize what they had and discarded the twenty-five-pound bronze statue in a trash bin where it was found a few days later by an alert garbage collector.

"Apparently the guy who took the trophy didn't think it measured up to the other stuff he took, so he kept the silver and dumped the rest," Cassady said. "The price of silver was way up back then, and they just didn't realize the value of the Heisman."

It was quickly returned to him where it remains the centerpiece of the Cassady home, keeping watch over a lifetime of memories.

JIM
PARKER

OSU GUARD 1954–1956

NICKNAME: Big Jim

HOMETOWN: Macon, Georgia

HEIGHT: 6 ft 3 in   **WEIGHT:** 273 lb

ALL–AMERICAN: 1955, 1956

NFL DRAFT: 1957, Baltimore Colts

62

In Parker's first ten seasons playing in the NFL, he did not miss a single game.

Whenever legendary Ohio State head coach Woody Hayes was asked about Jim Parker, the words flowed easily. "Jim Parker was the greatest lineman I've ever coached," Hayes said. "Big, strong, tough, disciplined—he was everything an offensive lineman should be. Quality—that's what Parker has. I'd trust him with everything I own."

Such high praise from Hayes, who tutored countless All-America linemen throughout a career that spanned more than three decades, speaks for itself. After all, the College Football Hall of Fame coach knew brilliance when he saw it—he just wouldn't pay for it.

"Back in 1952 when I first met Woody, I had fifteen or twenty college offers to play football," Parker once said. "Everyone came with a bag of money. One Big Ten school came with a car, and I had never had a car. Then there was Woody. He came with nothing—nothing but his word that I would get a first-class education and have a chance to play football. In that order."

Hayes must have made a whale of an impression on the youngster, who was born in ramshackle sur-roundings near Macon, Georgia, one of six children born to a railroad track gang laborer. Long before he filled out into a 6-3, 275-pound All-America lineman at Ohio State and perennial All-Pro for the NFL's Baltimore Colts, Parker was a gangly youngster at the age of 15, sickly from a burst appendix and subsequent peritonitis.

"I had no means, no ends, no physical ability, six feet tall, weighing about 110, 120 pounds," Parker remembered. "So my daddy bought a case of oatmeal and a case of grits, and had me eat it three times a day."

The steady diet of whole grain and carbs seemed to be a magical elixir for Parker. He went out for the football team at Macon High School and spent two seasons on the junior varsity. Despite failing to gain a spot on the varsity team, Parker was still better at football than he was in the classroom. He was described by his principal as an average student. That was being generous, and Jim decided what was best for him was to join the Army.

In preparation for that move, Parker relocated to Toledo to live with an aunt and spend his final two years of high school. In addition to schoolwork and playing football at Scott High School, he worked three jobs to support himself and his aunt. But he found himself miserable, barely scraping by.

"It was hellish for that year trying to go to school and work all those jobs," Parker said. "I didn't even go to the prom because I couldn't afford a suit."

ing gifts and monetary incentives to get Jim to join their programs. But there was something else Parker's father fed him back in Macon, something that stuck with him even more than thick oatmeal or creamy grits. Integrity was something a price could not be put on, and Hayes had an abundance of it. As a result, Parker decided Ohio State was the place for him despite the fact Hayes warned him that only a fixed num-

"My wife and I were in G.M. Don Kellett's office negotiating. I wouldn't sign. We broke for lunch, and he sent someone to the bank to get 1,500 ones. When we came back they were all stacked on the desk. 'That's yours,' he told me. My wife pinched the hell out of my leg. It still hurts. 'Sign it,' she said. So I signed. When we got back to the hotel room I put all those one-dollar bills in the bathtub. 'Let's take a bath in money,' I said. Hell, that wasn't any damn money....'"
—*Parker,* on signing with the Colts

Somehow, though, he persevered. Despite the fact he remained a raw prospect as far as football was concerned, his size attracted a number of the finest college coaches in the Midwest, many of them bear-

ber of African-Americans could play at any one time, and they would be banned from segregated hotels while the team was on the road.

While Parker took an instant liking to Hayes, the feeling was mutual. The youngster was invited to live with the Hayes family in their Upper Arlington home at the beginning of his freshman year, and Parker remembered years later what it was like to live under the same roof with the legendary head coach.

"It was like a father-son relationship," he said. "He treated me just like I was his son. He was real good to me. If Woody had told me, 'Go out there and move that stadium two inches to the right or four inches forward,' I would do it."

Being part of the Hayes family meant Parker had his share of household chores. One was picking up prospective recruits at the Columbus airport or train station to take them on a tour of the campus or to a local restaurant to meet with the Ohio State coaching staff. Most days, he was also assigned the duty of driving a neighborhood youngster to the OSU golf course. The youngster's name was Jack Nicklaus.

Even staying with the Hayes family, Parker never really escaped his modest upbringing—he and teammate Bill Cummins used to steal milk off a local milk truck—

but Parker also benefited from his coach's generosity.

"I was one of his favorites," Parker said. "I knew it, but I never took advantage of that. I think he liked me because I was really honest with him. He'd give me his credit card, and I'd go (downtown) and order two shirts and a pair of pants. I don't even charge $10 on his credit card. Anybody I know would have taken that card, and he would have at least got fifty or sixty dollars charged on it... When it came time to travel, he said, 'Here, go get you some clothes.' "

Parker repaid Hayes' kindness by becoming arguably the finest lineman in program history.

He spent the 1953 season on Ohio State's freshman team but often made his mark when the frosh scrimmaged against the varsity. The following year, Hayes inserted him into the lineup and Parker became the only sophomore starter for the Buckeyes, playing guard on offense and rotating between the middle guard and linebacker spots on defense.

He quickly became a mainstay of both units as well as special teams, and his legend continued to grow as the Buckeyes won the 1954 national championship and back-to-back Big Ten titles in his sophomore and junior seasons.

Parker was named to the All-America team in 1955 and again in '56, a senior season that produced a multitude of individual honors. He was selected as his team's most valuable player in a vote by his teammates—an achievement most rare among linemen—and he became Ohio State's first-ever winner of the prestigious Outland Trophy, awarded annually to the top college football lineman. Parker also finished eighth in the balloting for the 1956 Heisman Trophy, finishing just behind such luminaries as Syracuse running back Jim Brown, Stanford quarterback John Brodie, Tennessee running back Johnny Majors, and eventual winner Notre Dame halfback Paul Hornung.

But mere accolades and trophies could not come close to describing exactly what Parker meant to the Buckeyes. His ferocious blocking was credited with helping to spawn what would later become Hayes' notorious three-yards-and-a-cloud-of-dust offense.

Howard "Hopalong" Cassady became Ohio State's second Heisman Trophy winner in 1955, and Parker was a primary reason why.

"Hop's quick hitters were run over by Jim's outside hip, and Jim could always create a hole at that position," Hayes said. "On the quick trap play, on which Hop was an expert, Jim quickly trapped anybody who came into the area. On the sweep, Jim would pull and lead Hop downfield, and Jim's the only player I've seen who could consistently run through a defensive man, knock him down, and keep right on going for the next man."

When Parker achieved all he could at the collegiate level, he became one of the finest offensive linemen the NFL has ever seen. After being selected eighth overall by the Colts in the 1957 NFL draft, Baltimore head coach Weeb Ewbank pulled Parker aside during his first professional practice session.

"See that guy right there," Ewbank said, motioning toward quarterback Johnny Unitas. "Your primary job is to make sure there aren't any grass stains on his ass. You follow me?"

Parker nodded and then went about his business. During an eleven-year career with the Colts, he picked up a variety of nicknames including "Unitas' Bodyguard," "The Den Mother," and "The Guardian."

With Unitas at the controls, Parker anchoring the offensive line, and such future Pro Football Hall of Fame performers as running back Lenny Moore, wide receiver Raymond Berry and tight end John Mackey, the Colts won back-to-back NFL championships in 1958 and '59. If Unitas was the heart and soul of those Baltimore teams, Parker was the guts. He played guard for four years and made the Pro Bowl each season, then switched to tackle and made the Pro Bowl four more years in a row.

Along the way, he became the prototypical offensive lineman—275 pounds of snarling speed and strength, a runaway freight train bearing down on opposing defensive backs who had the choice of either sacrificing their bodies or simply getting the hell out of the way. And when Parker wasn't in the open field, lowering his shoulder on unsuspecting 180-pound safeties, he was an impenetrable wall as Unitas picked apart rival secondaries.

"When I walked on that field on Sunday and I looked at you," Parker said, "it wasn't if I was gonna whup your ass. It was how bad I was gonna whup your ass."

How good was Parker? For his 1984 book, *The New Thinking Man's Guide to Pro Football*, longtime *Sports Illustrated* football writer Paul Zimmerman polled twenty-five former players and asked them to name their candidates for best-ever offensive linemen. The consensus: Parker was described as "the best pure pass blocker who ever lived."

Parker played 139 consecutive games for the Colts between 1958 and 1965, but a nagging knee injury limited him to only three games in 1967 and he decided to retire at the age of 33. The team tried to convince him to rehab the injury and return the following season, but Parker refused. "If I can't help the team, I won't deprive forty (other) guys of their big chance," he said.

Head coach Don Shula, whose Colts were undefeated at the time, called it "one of the most unselfish moves ever made in sports. Jim has stepped aside strictly to help the team. He will be remembered as one of the greatest offensive linemen in pro football history."

Parker's jersey number 77 was later retired by the Colts, and in 1974 he became the first full-time offensive lineman to become enshrined in the Pro Football Hall of Fame, inducted in his first year of eligibility. That same year, he was inducted into the College Football Hall of Fame, joining his boyhood idol Bill Willis as the only Ohio State players enshrined in both the pro and college football halls of fame. In 1977, Parker joined Willis again, this time as a member of the Ohio State Athletics Hall of Fame.

Following his retirement from the NFL, Parker settled in the Baltimore area and ran his own business. He rarely made it back to Columbus, but planned to celebrate with his teammates on the fiftieth anniversary of their national championship. Unfortunately, it was not to be.

Parker, who suffered a series of strokes in the late 1990s and lived in an assisted care facility, was un-able to join the 1954 team reunion, held in October of 2004. Nine months later, he passed away at the age of 71 from congestive heart failure and kidney disease.

Despite last appearing in a Scarlet and Gray uniform more than a half-century ago, many Ohio State historians believe a player of Parker's stature comes along only once in a lifetime.

"I would say Jim was among the top players—regardless of position—that Ohio State has ever had," said Marv Homan, a member of the university's sports information department for nearly forty years and its director from 1973–'87. "His role was a little different than you might see these days because he played both offense and defense. But if anything, I'd say that probably enhances his stature even more.

"Woody Hayes often said that Jim was the greatest lineman he had ever coached, and that's good enough for me."

DICK
SCHAFRATH

NICKNAME: The Mule

HOMETOWN: Wooster, Ohio

HEIGHT: 6 ft 3 in **WEIGHT:** 253 lb

NFL DRAFT: 1959, Cleveland Browns

In June of 1971, on a dare from a friend, Dick agreed to run the 62 miles from Cleveland Stadium to his old high school field in Wooster. It took him 14 hours.

More colorful than a box of crayons, more driven to excellence than a Fortune 500 executive and more self-confident than a fox in a henhouse, Dick Schafrath could be described in any number of ways, but boring wouldn't be one of them. Growing up on a dairy farm in northeastern Ohio, he never saw a football game until he played in one. He locked horns with a bull at the age of two and took forty stitches in the back of head. He wrestled bears, won competitive eating contests all over the state, once ran sixty-two miles nonstop on a dare, and paddled a canoe across Lake Erie just to see if it could be done. And somehow he found time to anchor the offensive and defensive lines for Ohio State from 1956–'58, win a national championship with the Buckeyes in 1957 and go on to earn six Pro Bowl appearances with the Cleveland Browns.

Not bad for an overachieving farm boy known so much for his stubborn determination that teammates and opponents alike call him "The Mule."

"Dick is one of most extraordinary human beings I have ever met,"
said Pro Football Hall of Fame running back Jim Brown, who spent seven seasons as Schafrath's teammate in Cleveland. "As a teammate, he displayed an impeccable work ethic. He drove himself tirelessly to excellence. He is probably the greatest overachiever I ever met."

Schafrath didn't have to go far to earn those admirable personality traits. He was practically bathed in them every day by his parents Norman and Mary, a hard-working Catholic couple of German and Irish descent who raised their children on two basic principles—love one another and take nothing for granted. They also liked big families. Each was the oldest of eleven children, and by the time they died they had twenty-nine grandchildren and fifteen great-grandchildren.

Norm enjoyed music and was a champion euchre player and part-time community barber, but what he loved most was working his dairy farm and invoking one of his favorite sayings, "No one ever died from their own sweat." Mary, also known affectionately as "Gabby," was allergic to animals, strange from someone who lived her entire life on a farm. But she never complained and enjoyed her fulltime duties as a housewife, mother, nurse, accountant, taxi driver, cook, baker, gardener, canner, washer, disciplinarian, and counselor.

Richard Philip Schafrath was born March 21, 1937, in a farmhouse just east of Wooster, Ohio, a small college town nestled about halfway between Cleveland and Akron. Dick apparently wasn't ready for the world, and birth complications forced his hospitalization in nearby Canton for the first few weeks of his life. By the time he was released, however, he seemed more than ready. "By that time, I was king of the nursery," he said. "I weighed nearly twenty pounds!"

As the first-born of five boys and two girls, Dick was expected to be his father's right-hand man on the farm and he eagerly accepted those duties. He was up every day before the sun to help milk the family's black-and-white Holstein cows by hand, then just before midnight—after a day filled with plowing, planting, cutting wood, loading hay, shocking wheat, and/or husking corn—he would crawl back into one of two attic beds he shared with his four brothers.

"Hard work? Sure it was," Dick said. "But to get to work with my dad all day, every day? I loved it."

He loved it so much he never thought much about a formal education. Norm had dropped out of school after the eighth grade, but Gabby had graduated from Wooster High School and was determined her children would do the same. Dick packed a sizable lunch inside a Roy Rogers lunchbox and dutifully shuffled off to a two-room schoolhouse each morning. By the time he reached high school, Dick had only 175 pounds spread over a spidery 6-foot-1-inch frame, but he was adept at every sport he tried, including boxing, basketball, and baseball. He was good enough in baseball to earn the interest of the Cincinnati Reds, but by the time he was a senior, football was beginning to take over his life. He had sprouted up an additional two inches, and thanks to a prodigious appetite, he had gained thirty-five pounds and was now one of the most sought-after fullback and middle linebacker prospects in the Midwest.

There was just one problem. Dick wasn't the least bit interested in going to college. "I was never a very good student because I wasn't that interested," he said. "I liked playing football, but I didn't want to go to college. When I was done with the eighth grade, I thought I was done with school. But Mom and Dad talked me into going to high school. After that, the Reds drafted me and I was going to go to their training camp. Then Woody Hayes showed up in the driveway."

Fresh off his 1954 national championship season at Ohio State, the 42-year-old Hayes had enjoyed the two-hour Sunday drive from Columbus to Wooster and stepped out of his car to introduce himself to the large brood of Schafraths. Nearly everywhere else in Ohio, such an introduction would not have been necessary.

"But we didn't know him. Had never heard of him," Dick said. "He came one Sunday morning as we were getting ready to go to church, and he asked if he could join us. So we all got in the car with him and we all went to church together. When we came back, he put an apron on and helped cook lunch with my mom, and after that he went down to the barn and talked to my dad for a couple of hours. When he left, he shook my dad's hand, kissed my mom on the cheek, and went back to Columbus. Never even said goodbye to me.

"I went back into the house about an hour later and told my mom that I wasn't very impressed with that Woody Hayes, and she said, "Well, I'll tell you what, Son. You'd better get impressed because you're going to Ohio State.'"

As always, Woody had worked his charm on a prospect's parents. But he wasn't the only coach who could play that game. Blanton Collier was head coach at Kentucky, and he had dispatched an assistant to Wooster, telling him not to return to Lexington without Schafrath. The assistant coach checked into a hotel a few miles away, and every day he drove to the Schafrath farm and asked Norm if he could help with the chores.

"Finally my mother told him that if he was going to spend so much time there he should move into the house," Dick said. "We had a bedroom for him, and so he did. He stayed about a week. Well, I started to feel obligated about that and told my mother I was going to call Blanton and tell him I was coming to Kentucky. She said I couldn't make that call until I called Woody and told him first. I couldn't do that, so I went to Ohio State."

When he got to Columbus, Schafrath didn't want to stay. He showed up for his first freshman practice and was immediately told he'd be switching positions. After starring at fullback and middle linebacker in high school, he became an interior lineman, listed as both a right and left tackle—tenth-string to boot—and was quickly lost in the shuffle. He disliked his classes and had no social life on campus, driving home on weekends and waiting until the last possible second on Sunday night to go back to Columbus. Slowly but surely, however, Woody began to take a personal liking to Schafrath, inviting him to spend some time at the coach's Upper Arlington home, especially on weekends.

Hayes had an ulterior motive, of course. "Every time I'd want to leave school," Dick said, "Woody would barricade me in his house."

After that rocky freshman year, Schafrath's competitiveness began to show itself again. He quickly moved from fourth-string tackle at the beginning of his sophomore season to the starting left tackle midway through the season, playing next to All-America guard Jim Parker on both offense and defense. He remained at tackle throughout his junior season, helping the Buckeyes to a Big Ten title, a Rose Bowl victory over Oregon, and the national championship.

He was primed for an All-American senior season in 1958 until Hayes approached him with a dilemma. The Buckeyes were loaded with talented tackles but deficient at the end position, and the coach asked Schafrath—by then a team co-captain—for a recommendation. Dick thought for a few moments and then offered to move to an end position, where he flourished.

In addition to catching the only touchdown pass of his career, Schafrath matched athleticism with his experience as an interior lineman and turned in a standout senior campaign. In his final game in the Scarlet and Gray, he preserved an 18–14 victory over Michigan by causing a fumble near the goal line inside the final minute.

"I have often thought about what Dick sacrificed when he volunteered to change positions," Hayes said years later. "He could have been an All-American, but he wanted to help his team. I can't begin to tell you the satisfaction a coach gets from that kind of unselfish athlete."

For his part, Dick has always shrugged off those kinds of accolades with the assertion that "you don't have to be an All-American to be a team player. I was never that talented and everything I did was probably overachieving. I never looked at stats and I never looked at press clippings. I played the hardest I could play, and if that was good enough, so be it. I give all the credit to my teammates."

Schafrath went on to a successful professional career with the Browns, then spent three seasons as offensive line coach for the Washington Redskins before getting involved in politics, even-

tually serving several terms in the Ohio State Senate.

In 2006, at the age of 69, he followed through on a longstanding promise to his parents and Hayes and returned to Ohio State to receive his bachelor's degree in sports and leisure studies. On graduation day, Dick happily strode onstage to accept his diploma, wearing a huge smile as well as something else that helped epitomize his unusual personality.

To each side of his mortarboard, Schafrath had attached a large pair of mule ears.

ROBERT FERGUSON

OSU RUNNING BACK 1959–1961

NICKNAME: Bob

HOMETOWN: Troy, Ohio

HEIGHT: 6 ft 0 in   WEIGHT: 227 lb

ALL–AMERICAN: 1960, 1961

NFL DRAFT: 1962, Pittsburgh Steelers

46

Bob was a powerhouse. He carried the ball more than four hundred times in his college career.

*B*ob Ferguson's running style was once described by an opponent as "a cross between a runaway locomotive and a rolling ball of butcher knives. You really don't want to be in the path of either one."

Barely six feet tall and a 227-pound mass of muscle, the Ohio State fullback was built like a tree stump and almost as difficult to move. He pounded through opposing defenses, bruising the bodies of would-be tacklers—as well as their egos—with thighs roughly the same circumference as an average man's waist. He was as reliable as a Swiss watch, carrying the ball more than four hundred times during his college career and losing yardage on only four occasions.

Still, none of those attributes endeared him to his head coach as much as his no-frills, straight-ahead rushing style. When asked what made Ferguson his prototypical fullback, Woody Hayes replied, "He gives us what we like, and we like the ball-carrier pointed toward the goalposts."

Ferguson fit perfectly into Hayes's three-yards-and-a-cloud-of-dust mentality, creating the necessary yards, taking time off the clock, and scoring touchdowns, which slowly but steadily wore opponents down over the course of a game. For a three-year period from 1959 to 1961, Ferguson was regarded among the finest college football players in the country and lauded by Hayes and Ohio State fans as one of the best Buckeyes in history.

More than a half-century later, however, his name is barely mentioned when the Scarlet and Gray faithful gather to discuss their favorite running backs of all-time. Perhaps that is because the sensitive, soft-spoken Ferguson had a learning disorder and refused to draw attention to himself. Maybe it was because an injury-riddled body wouldn't allow him to live up to what was expected of a first-round draft choice in the National Football League. Perhaps it is because he voluntarily dropped out of society for a four-year period during the 1970s, leaving a wife and four children to fend for themselves.

"I think Bob gets shortchanged a little bit when people talk about the greatest Buckeye running backs, and it's really too bad because he was certainly one of the best and most productive running backs Ohio State has ever had," Ohio State football historian Jack Park said. "He was just so powerful up the middle—had a very low center of gravity—and he seemed to get better as his career went along."

Born August 29, 1939, in Troy, Ohio, Robert Eugene Ferguson was the third child of Wade and Irma Ferguson, a family of modest means. Wade, who had dropped out of school after the eighth grade, was a member of a local road construction crew while Irma cared for Bob and his siblings, Sallie and Wade Jr., in their small rented house on Sherman Street. Bob was pretty much like every other young boy—he liked to play and he liked to eat, but when it came to studying, he was nowhere to be found.

Once he began playing football at Troy High School, however, Bob was everywhere. During his three seasons of varsity football, the Trojans rolled to three consecutive undefeated seasons as opponent after opponent was flattened beneath the Ferguson steamroller.

Some of his high school exploits bordered on superhuman. He rushed for 529 yards in a single game, a state record that stood until 2001. He rushed for 2,089 yards as a junior in 1956, averaging an eye-popping 232.1 yards per game. And he established national high school records with 5,521 career rushing yards and 578 points scored. It was little wonder why every major college football coach in the nation wanted Ferguson in their backfield.

There was just one minor problem. It wasn't going to be easy to get Ferguson admitted and just as difficult to keep him eligible. "Bob was considered to be someone who wasn't very smart, but Bob and I basically had the same problems," said teammate Billy Joe Armstrong, a three-year starting center from 1960–1962. "I never thought I was stupid; I didn't know what I was. Bob was pretty much the same way. Everybody tried to help us, but they tried to help us in the wrong way—by letting us get by with our weaknesses."

Hayes steadfastly denied any circumvention of academic eligibility standards regarding any of his players, but there was always the "don't ask, don't tell" atmosphere on campus during much of the coach's tenure. As a result, players such as Armstrong—whose studies improved dramatically following surgery to repair a shattered eardrum—and Ferguson were always in uniform and ready to play on Saturday afternoon.

When Ferguson arrived at Ohio State in the fall of 1958, freshmen were not eligible to play varsity football. The following year, Ferguson led the team in rushing, albeit with a modest total of 371 yards, and handled defensive halfback duties as well. But the Buckeyes weren't very good in 1959 as they stumbled to a 3-5-1 record, one of only two losing seasons Hayes had in twenty-eight years as head of the program. During the offseason, the coach began to formulate a play that was so simple, it could be run again and again with opposing defenses never knowing what hit them.

"Woody's favorite play was called '26,' and Bob was a master at running that play," said Paul Warfield, a Ferguson teammate in '61 before embarking upon a Pro Football Hall of Fame career with the Cleveland Browns and Miami Dolphins. "It was just a basic fullback off-tackle play, and the way it was designed, Bob was to run toward the tackle and read his block. He could then break the play back over the guard or the tackle. He had those heavy thighs and a low center of gravity, and he could really run up in there and create movement. They talk about moving the pile? Bob moved the pile and then some."

Ferguson ground out 853 yards as a junior, and then bettered that mark with 938 yards as a senior, leading the Buckeyes to an 8-0-1 overall mark and the national championship from the Football Writers Association of America. He also saved his best for last, totaling 152 yards and four touchdowns during the team's 50–20 rout of Michigan. That victory sewed up the Buckeyes' first Big Ten championship in four years and earned them the right to represent the conference in the Rose Bowl. However, the Ohio State

Faculty Council, fearing that athletics was overtaking academics on the campus, voted to deny the trip to Pasadena. It was a bitter pill for the players on the 1961 team to take.

"The whole team was hurt," Ferguson said years later. "The administration voted not to send us and we had to live with it. That was probably the one regret I had about my time at Ohio State—not ever getting to play in a Rose Bowl."

Somewhat softening the blow was the fact that Ferguson won the Maxwell Award as college football's outstanding offensive player. A short time later, Ferguson finished a close second to Syracuse running back Ernie Davis in the Heisman Trophy voting. Davis edged Ferguson by an 824–771 margin in what remains one of the closest votes in Heisman history.

Following his college career, Ferguson was rated a surefire professional football star, and he was a first-round selection in both the NFL and upstart American Football League drafts. The San Diego Chargers offered more money, but he decided to stay with the more established league and signed with the NFL's Pittsburgh Steelers. He spent two seasons there backing up future Hall of Fame running back John Henry Johnson, but a chronic knee injury was never properly treated and Ferguson was unceremoniously traded to Minnesota during the 1963 season. He played only two games for the Vikings before being forced to retire with only 209 yards and one touchdown to show for eighteen NFL games.

Following a professional career that was regarded as a failure, Ferguson's life began to spiral downward. He tried a comeback in 1966 with the Washington Redskins, but the team let him go after just one day. Ferguson then bounced from job to job, trying his hand at social work and as a factory foreman before a brush with the law as a suspect on gambling and narcotics charges. At one point, he simply disappeared for four years, resurfacing in late 1975 only because of serious health problems. His family found him in a Washington, D.C., hospital following a stroke at the age of 35.

"Bobby had a lot of problems and he was embarrassed by them," Armstrong said. "They just destroyed him in Pittsburgh, and then he got sickle cell anemia and went into a coma. He was down and out and using a phony name, but he didn't want anyone to know about it." However, when Hayes got wind of his former player's problems, he contacted Armstrong to begin fund-raising on Ferguson's behalf. "In a little over five days, we put together about $22,000," Armstrong said. "We paid off his bills and got him back on his feet."

Buoyed by the caring efforts of his former coach and teammates, Ferguson rallied and returned to Columbus. He took classes at Ohio State to finish his undergraduate degree, and later worked hard to obtain a Master's degree in sociology. He worked for the Westinghouse Corp. for several years and then took a job with the Columbus Parks and Recreation Department, a job he held until health problems in 1990 forced his early retirement. He suffered another stroke in 1993 and battled diabetes for the last several years of his life, ultimately succumbing to its complications in 2004 at the age of 65.

Ferguson did, however, have one final hurrah on the gridiron when he was inducted into the College Football Hall of Fame in 1996. "What a great honor," he said at the time while dabbing at reddened eyes with a handkerchief. "It's hard to believe someone thinks I'm one of the best players in college football history."

Former OSU sports information director Marv Homan believes it was an honor long overdue. "I've always thought of Bob as a semi-tragic figure at Ohio State," he said. "I think he was always troubled and felt maybe he didn't measure up to other people's expectations. That's why I felt really good when he was inducted into the college hall of fame. It showed that a lot of other people around the country recognized his abilities and accomplishments. It was an honor richly deserved."

ARNOLD CHONKO

NICKNAME: Arnie

HOMETOWN: Parma, Ohio

HEIGHT: 6 ft 2 in **WEIGHT:** 204 lb

23

Arnie played so hard that once he knocked himself unconscious during practice and had to be sent to the hospital.

Woody Hayes was used to making deals with no intention of following through on promises. Countless times along the recruiting trail, the Ohio State head coach had encountered prospective football players who thought they were good enough to pursue other sports in college. The persuasive Hayes would nod his head in agreement, but once the ink had dried on a national letter of intent his memory of any prior commitment seemed to fade.

Then Woody met Arnold Chonko, who kept the legendary coach's feet to the fire.

A shy, pug-nosed kid with broad shoulders, an omnipresent crewcut, and a keen interest in progressive jazz, Arnold Mathew Chonko was born May 17, 1943, in Parma, Ohio, to hard-working parents of Slovakian descent. Because they grew up during the Great Depression, Andrew and Agnes Kathryn Roth Chonko were exposed to little formal education, but they were a bright, intelligent couple who raised three athletic boys in a quiet, tree-lined suburb located just south of Cleveland's soot-belching smokestacks and ca-

cophony of traffic congestion and noise pollution.

Arnie's older brothers, Andy and Allan, parlayed outstanding football and baseball talents at Parma Senior High School into college careers, playing both sports at Ohio University and Notre Dame, respectively, but the brothers knew how difficult it had been for them to play both sports on the college level and warned their younger sibling not to take a coach at his word on any promise. As a result, whenever a football coach went for the close while recruiting Arnie, he turned the tables on them, requesting a written agreement stating he would be able to play baseball as well as football. He had no problem asking such mild-mannered coaches as Michigan's Bump Elliott or Ara Parseghian of Northwestern, but Arnie was admittedly worried about getting such an agreement from Hayes.

The relationship between the legendary coach and his prospective player had already gotten to a somewhat rocky start, anyway. "My dad worked in a slaughterhouse in those days and had forearms like Popeye," Arnie remembered. "When

Woody first met him and stuck out his hand to shake my father's hand, my dad put a grip on there, and Woody said, 'Gee, I should be recruiting you!' I thought we'd blown it right there. Woody comes all the way from Columbus to meet us and gets his hand squashed."

Later, when the subject was broached about Arnie playing baseball as well as football for the Buckeyes, Hayes smiled, nodded his head, and quickly changed the subject. He was well into a detailed presentation of the academic benefits of Ohio State when the subject was revisited. Again, the coach nodded and smiled—this time the grin seemed a little more forced—and resumed his sales pitch. When baseball was brought up a third time, Hayes knew he wasn't going to get away without giving the youngster and his father some kind of assurance. That still didn't make things any easier.

"I was concerned about Woody's notorious temper, but I decided to ask for the letter anyway," Arnie said. "Woody was only mildly irked and pointed out to me that his word was his honor. I thanked him for his interest but pointed out that other coaches had agreed to my baseball-in-the-spring request in writing. Woody's reaction was swift and measured. He wrote a very nice letter to me, asking me to attend spring football practice during my freshman year but allowing me to pursue baseball in the spring of the last three of my undergraduate years."

It wasn't difficult to figure out why college coaches, long established in their careers, would accede to a teenager's demands. Chonko was simply that good. With a muscular 6-foot-2, 192-pound frame that seemed the very definition of a football player, Arnie had starred as a quarterback and defensive back for Parma Senior and won nearly every conceivable award, including MVP accolades in the Lake Erie League and player of the year honors by the Cleveland Touchdown Club. Best of all, Arnie was a winner. From grades eight through twelve, he helped lead his team to a league championship every year, including as a senior when he intercepted a pass with less than three minutes remaining against rival Euclid and returned it 61 yards for a touchdown to preserve another unbeaten season for the Redmen. As accomplished as he was as a football player, Arnie was even better at baseball, earning All-Ohio honors and a host of scholarship offers from diamond programs around the nation. "I was an All-American in football and baseball," he once said, "but baseball was my better sport."

In addition to his athletic exploits, Arnie had a keen interest in becoming a doctor. "I was thrilled to play and represent the university," he said, "but I was truly a student-athlete. I went to school to learn and get an education." Within a half-hour of arriving on the OSU campus for his official recruiting visit, Hayes asked the dean of the medical school to show him around the medical school campus and Arnie was awestruck. "Ohio State had everything I wanted in a school—a great football team and an excellent medical school," he said. "Woody was a master recruiter. He sold the whole tradition thing because he knew it would work with a recruit. It worked with me."

Arnie got another up-close look at the university's hospital services during his freshman year on campus, albeit not the kind he might have wanted. After tackling teammate Bo Scott during a full-scale scrimmage in the stadium on a fall afternoon in 1961, the youngster was knocked unconscious. After being helped to the locker room, a dazed Chonko sat on the end of a trainer's table when Woody walked in. "Do you know who I am, son?" the coach asked. When a glaze-eyed stare was the only answer Arnie could provide, Hayes said, "Better get him to the hospital."

"I awakened in the OSU neurosurgery observation ward thirty hours later in the middle of a conversation with my brother Al," Arnie remembered. "The next two weeks were without serious contact for me, and it led me to wonder if I should forget football and play only baseball."

The following fall, Chonko suffered a separated shoulder, a painful injury that required rest and repeated whirlpool treatments. But just when his collegiate football career seemed derailed because of injuries, defensive back Ed Ulmer was forced to leave school due to academic problems. That gave Arnie his first real chance at playing time and he seized upon the opportunity. He won a starting job as a sophomore in 1962 and didn't relinquish it for the next three seasons.

Along the way, he became one of the top defensive backs in college football, earning the nickname "Old Reliable" from his teammates. During his senior season, he earned first-team All-America honors alongside such future Pro Football Hall of Fame

with only fourteen seconds to play—to preserve a 17–9 victory against Indiana.

Armed with his written agreement from Hayes, Arnie also earned three varsity letters in baseball and became one of only a handful of Ohio State players ever to win All-America honors in football as well as baseball. He hit .355 as sophomore and .371 as junior before helping to lead the baseball Buckeyes to a Big Ten championship and second-place finish at the 1965 College World Series during his senior year. A stellar first base-

"We were never allowed to go onto the field without our mouth guards, but I hated wearing mine, so I stuck it in my jock. I had been running and had my mouth open when I got hit, shattering my molars. I had white pieces of my tooth in my hand as I was walking off the field."
—*Arnie Chonko*

stars as Fred Biletnikoff, Tommy Nobis, Dick Butkus, and Gale Sayers. Also that year, he tied a school record with three interceptions in a single game, picking off three fourth-quarter passes—the last

man and solid hitter near the top of head coach Marty Karow's lineup, Arnie joined teammates Bo Rein, Chuck Brinkman, and Steve Arlin on the CWS All-Tournament Team, a roster that included such future major league stars as Sal Bando and Rick Monday.

Along with his athletic accomplishments, scholastic honors came Arnie's way. He was an Academic All-Big Ten selection as a senior, the same year he was the first Ohio State football player to be named a National Scholar-Athlete, which was accompanied by a monetary grant for postgraduate studies.

Upon completion of his undergraduate work at Ohio State, Arnie was faced with the choice between playing professional football or Major League Baseball, and while it seems difficult to believe anyone would turn their back on such lucrative opportunities, he decided to stick with his studies and pursue a career in medicine. "Who knows?" he said. "If I had gone to play professionally somewhere, I might never have gotten back into school. I finally decided, 'Nah, if you're going to do this, you'd better do it right now.' So I went back to school."

And when the going got rough, Arnie received motivation from a reliable source. "I was exhausted and depressed during my sophomore year in medical school when I got a phone call," he said. "It was Woody. 'Chonko, you damned fool,' he said. 'You need to learn that you can't know everything about medicine as a young doctor—that's why they call it the *practice* of medicine.'"

Chonko went on to graduate summa cum laude from the Ohio State College of Medicine and embarked upon a long and distinguished medical career, specializing in the treatment of kidney disease and becoming a professor of medicine and nephrologist at the University of Kansas School of Medicine.

All-American in two sports, Phi Beta Kappa member, decorated medical practitioner, educator, Arnold Chonko is a man who has accomplished much during his life. He also turned out to be a pretty good judge of popular music.

"When I was at Ohio State, I loved the band," he said. "My junior or senior year, they started playing a new song just before the beginning of the fourth quarter, and I remember telling my teammate Jim Nein in the huddle, 'Hey, that's a catchy tune.'"

The song? *Hang On Sloopy*.

DONALD
UNVERFERTH

OSU QUARTERBACK 1963–1965

NICKNAME: Don

HOMETOWN: Dayton, Ohio

HEIGHT: 6 ft 3 in   **WEIGHT:** 208 lb

26

Don was the school's leader in career passing yardage before Art Schlichter broke his record of 2,518 yards in 1979.

*H*undreds of heart patients and their families stay rent-free each year in a building near the Ohio State campus named for the doctor who in 1986 oversaw the University Medical Center's first heart transplant. About a mile and a half away from that building sits Ohio Stadium where an athletic, handsome youngster from Dayton encouraged Woody Hayes to embrace the passing game and rewrote the university's record books in the process.

The cardiologist whose quiet, charismatic bedside manner put countless patients at ease, and the strapping young lad who convinced a legendary coach to modify his three-yards-and-a-cloud-of-dust philosophy were one and the same. Unfortunately, Don Unverferth has largely been relegated to the back pages of history, partly because his life was cut tragically short by cancer and partly because his football exploits have been surpassed many times over since his playing days in the mid-1960s.

Still, those who knew him best say he didn't mind toiling in the shadows of others, and would likely be comfortable in allowing his many accomplishments speak for themselves.

"Don was clearly a leader," said Dr. Charles Bush, a cardiologist and colleague of Unverferth at Ohio State. "You'd never hear him talking about his achievements. He was not somebody who would go around tooting his own horn."

Donald V. Unverferth was born April 21, 1944, in Dayton, the second son to Louis and Beatrice Unverferth. Don's father was a payroll accountant at the huge Frigidaire plant in Dayton that once employed as many as twenty-two thousand workers manufacturing refrigerators, ranges, air conditioners, and other household goods, while his mother was a professional stenographer. The couple provided a loving and stable home for Don and his older brother, Jack, both of whom became star quarterbacks at Chaminade High School, the Catholic boys school located on South Ludlow Street near midtown Dayton.

Not surprisingly—given how innovative he would become in later life—Don, as a youngster, developed a unique way of throwing the football. Most quarterbacks at the time cradled the football in the palm of their throwing hand with the fingers spread out over the laces, but Don began placing his index finger on the rear tip of the ball to gain more accuracy with his throws. Today, putting the forefinger at the tip of the ball is the preferred method of delivery for nearly every college and National Football League quarterback, but Don refused to take any credit for the innovation. It was a style borne from necessity, a method employed by a little boy who simply couldn't grip the football properly.

"My brother was a quarterback," Don said, "and when we were just kids, we'd play catch. He'd always pass the ball to me, and I'd just throw it back to him any way I could. Finally, I started putting my index finger on the tip of the ball—kind of throwing it like a dart—and that way I found I could get the ball to go where I wanted it to go."

Don followed Jack to Chaminade and became an All-State quarterback, then he followed him to Ohio State. Jack, however, had decided not to continue his football career, opting to concentrate on becoming a doctor. Don enjoyed the game so much that he figured he could do both, and joined the Buckeyes as a freshman in the fall of 1962.

The mid-1960s represented a transitional period for the Ohio State football team and its head coach. A power struggle between Hayes and Alumni Association founder and secretary Jack Fullen was being waged with battle lines drawn between the burgeoning athletic department and officials such as Fullen who believed athletics were taking over academics in terms of on-campus importance. Fullen scored a major victory when the Faculty Council voted against sending the Buckeyes to the Rose Bowl following the 1961 season, a decision that had far-reaching ramifications.

"One of the things that is hardly discussed is the adverse effect the (Rose Bowl) decision had upon recruiting," said former Ohio State sports information director Marv Homan. "We lost some very good prospects who thought of Ohio State as sort of anti-Rose Bowl. That wasn't the case, of course, but it was something Woody had a tough time overcoming for a couple of years. It wasn't that the program went downhill, but it wasn't as good as it might have been."

Further complicating matters for Hayes was his avowed offensive philosophy of ground control. When the Buckeyes won the national championship in 1954, the team threw 125 times during the ten-game season. The following year, Hayes called for only fifty passes all season. The team total didn't rise much over the next several years, and when the 1961 team won the Big Ten title, as well as the national championship from the Football Writers Association of America, it attempted only ninety passes while running the ball 522 times. Perhaps as a result, Hayes was unable to sign one of the nation's top high school quarterbacks at the time—Tommy Myers of Troy, Ohio, who passed on an offer to attend Ohio State, heading instead to Northwestern to play for Ara Parseghian.

With Unverferth, Hayes was able to rectify two problems with one player. Don was eager to get into pre-med at Ohio State, so he didn't need much recruiting. And his strong-armed skills as a quarterback would help bring Hayes and his offense out of the dark ages. Substitution rules were also changing in college football, and Hayes embraced them. Players forced to play both offense and defense began to disappear in favor of the platoon system, paving the way for specialists on either side of the ball. Practice time could now be divided between separate offensive and defensive units, and Hayes began to tutor his offensive linemen in the fine art of pass protection.

Unverferth had come along at just the right time. Blessed with a strong right arm and a solid 6-foot-3, 205-pound frame, Don began his sophomore season as the Buckeyes' starting quarterback and he never relinquished the position. He sometimes shared duties with Tom Barrington, who was a more accomplished runner, but Unverferth was clearly the better thrower and became one of the first classic drop-back quarterbacks in Ohio State history.

His coming-out party occurred in late October 1963 at Wisconsin. With the Buckeyes trailing the second-ranked Badgers late in the game, the sophomore calmly completed four passes during an eighty-yard drive that gave Ohio State a 13–10 victory and knocked Wisconsin from the ranks of the unbeaten. Four weeks later during the season finale in Ann Arbor, Don threw for one touchdown and ran for another as the Buckeyes took a 14–10 win over Michigan.

"I coached some fine passers," said OSU offensive backfield coach Lou McCullough, whose Southern drawl was as thick as the molasses his father used to produce in his northwestern Alabama hometown. "But Unverferth had the best arm of them all. Plus, he was tall enough to see and throw over towering linemen charging at him."

Perhaps Don's best attribute was his intelligence. He learned quickly and never made the same mistake twice. As a result, his numbers increased every season until he threw for 1,061 yards and four touchdowns as a senior in 1965. When his career had finished, Don owned nearly every career passing record at Ohio State, including 2,518 yards through the air. It was a mark that would last for fourteen years, until Art Schlichter broke it in 1979. Off

the field, Don's performance was every bit as outstanding as it was on it. He was a member of the Phi Delta Theta fraternity as well as an honor student in pre-med, and he was named the most outstanding cadet in a class of more than 3,900 in the ROTC program at Ohio State. Once his playing days were over, Don was offered a tryout by Green Bay Packers head coach Vince Lombardi. Don turned Lombardi down, however, deciding to pursue his dream of becoming a doctor, rising to the top of his class during his freshman year in medical school.

After graduating from medical school, he joined the Army and served as a military physician. He later returned to Ohio State to complete training in internal medicine, specializing in cardiology. He joined the faculty at University Medical Center, and in 1986 laid the foundation for the center's heart transplant program. Eventually becoming a world-renowned expert in the areas of cardiomyopathy and the treatment of congestive heart failure, Unverferth published countless articles and several books, and occupied the first chair of the James Hay and Ruth Jansson Wilson professorship in cardiology at Ohio State, all the while retaining the charisma and steady pulse of a successful college quarterback.

"He was impressive," said renowned plastic surgeon Dr. Jan Adams, who was treated in 1978 by Unverferth for cardiomyopathy. "He was 6-feet-3-inches tall, still about 210 pounds, prematurely gray hair but still looking all the part of the athlete. All the secretaries and all the nurses loved him. It was amazing to watch them all swoon as he walked by, oblivious to all of it. He simply loved taking care of people. I envied him that. He was just so happy to be doing it. The process was his reward."

Don's brother, Jack, director of orthopedic education at Riverside Methodist Hospital in Columbus, echoed those sentiments when Don died in January of 1988 at the age of forty-three, the victim of a malignant brain tumor. "He was a leading researcher, not only in Columbus, but in the nation," Jack said. "He really didn't make much money; he was so much like Woody in that way. His research was what was important to him, and unlike so many of those in our profession, it far outweighed the financial considerations. His work was what was important to him."

Seventeen months after Don's passing, the Unverferth House was established in his memory, a building containing nine fully-furnished apartments to house patients and their families during treatment at the Richard M. Ross Heart Hospital, just five blocks away. The project was spearheaded by Don's widow, Barbara, who was struck by the outpouring of affection for her husband whose life touched so many others. "The idea (for Unverferth House) really came from his patients because they loved him dearly," she said. "He would have so loved something like that."

A framed letter hangs in each apartment of the house, detailing Don's life as well as his legacy of paying forward, a legacy of which Woody would be so proud.

JOHN
BROCKINGTON

OSU RUNNING BACK 1968–1970

NICKNAME: Brock

HOMETOWN: Brooklyn, New York

HEIGHT: 6 ft 1 in   **WEIGHT:** 222 lb

NFL DRAFT: 1971, Green Bay Packers

42

It has been said that John was one of the first players to combine elite speed with power and brute.

*J*ohn Brockington always seems to have a smile on his face, and it's no run-of-the-mill, I-know-something-you-don't-know smirk. It is a gleaming, high-voltage, ear-to-ear, full-of-life grin that would make the Cheshire cat envious. It is also a smile that belies the iron-willed toughness of a man who overcame the initial doubts of his head coach to become a star at Ohio State and in the National Football League.

"There was no tougher son of a bitch on the football field than Brock," said former OSU teammate Jack Tatum, a man who knew something about tough sons of bitches. "He would have made a great linebacker because Brock always gave as good as he ever got. He would lower his shoulder, run over you, and just keep going. You'd get up with cleat marks on your chest."

Brockington admits his easygoing personality of today belies the persona he left behind years ago on the gridiron. Still, he gleefully recalls the time when his Green Bay Packers were playing the Dolphins in Miami, and he took on blitzing All-Pro safety Jake Scott. "Scott comes in on a blitz, and I hit him in the head with my forearm. Knocked him clean out. I had to carry him to the sidelines because I didn't want him lying on the field. Several years later, I was at an autograph show and Jim Langer, who played center on that Dolphins team, looked at me and said, 'Hey, you're the guy who knocked out Jake Scott.' I said, 'How'd you remember that? That was in 1972.' And Langer said, 'Everyone in the stadium heard that hit.'"

Most Ohio State fans remember Brockington as a hulking steamroller of a fullback who helped the Buckeyes to the 1968 national championship and two years later won first-team All-Conference and All-America honors as a senior. The truth is that Brockington wasn't oversized at all, standing only 6-foot-1 and weighing a modest 216 pounds. But his speed, leverage, and power made him a punishing blocker, and he struck terror in opposing defenses during his sophomore and junior seasons as a halfback running interference for quarterback Rex Kern and fullback Jim Otis. When Otis graduated following the 1969 season, Brock moved seamlessly into the fullback spot where his methodical, piston-like running style helped establish a new school rushing record with 1,142 yards.

That Brock wound up wearing the Scarlet and Gray was something of a fluke. Woody Hayes, who prided himself on taking young men from a wide range of environments, meshing their disparate personalities and molding them into a team with single-minded unity, wasn't sure he wanted to take a chance on an inner-city kid with questionable academics.

John Stanley Brockington was born September 7, 1948, in New York City, and he spent most of his youth across the East River, growing up in a housing complex in the heart of the Brooklyn melting pot. The Bayview Projects were predominantly white and Jewish, with only six black families scattered among the thirteen-building cluster, but everyone seemed to get along well enough, and the Brockingtons were just another typical middle-class family in a typical middle-class neighborhood. John's father was a civil servant who worked at the local post office, while his son earned money delivering newspapers, a job that led to his introduction into the divergent cultures around him.

"More than once when I was on my paper route, I lit a stove on the Sabbath when someone was having trouble," John said. "But I never minded doing that. Never minded it at all."

As John grew from adolescence to young adulthood, his body grew with him. Broad shoulders were anchored atop a barrel chest, while sinewy thighs and calves gave him power to go along with speed. He became something of a local legend after winning All-City and All-America honors while playing for the legendary Moe Finkelstein under less-than-ideal conditions at Thomas Jefferson High School in Brooklyn.

To say the playing conditions at Jefferson were sparse would be an understatement. The football field contained only a few blades of grass and had to be watered down in the fall to make sure the players didn't choke from the dust. When the weather got cold, the barren surface was as slippery as ice and harder than concrete. The locker room—if you could call it that—was located inside an old cinder block building that shook to its foundation every fifteen minutes when subway trains passed overhead.

Still, Finkelstein managed to win more than two hundred games, five city league championships, and eighteen division titles at Jefferson, and he produced National League Football players such as Brockington and Chicago Bears linebacker Otis Wilson.

"John was a big youngster who could run very fast, and it was obvious he was going places," Finkelstein said. "I will never forget this: We had a history teacher by the name of Bob Shane, and he used to do the announcing at the games. On the Monday after the first game that John played for us, Bob came over to me and said, 'This youngster's going to play in the NFL someday.' Obviously, that was true. Everyone could see the talent."

Syracuse University seemed a logical choice for any New York high school running back with an eye toward college football. The Orange had a rich tradition of producing some of the best running backs in history, beginning with Jim Brown in the late 1950s and 1961

Heisman Trophy winner Ernie Davis, continuing into the middle 1960s with Jim Nance and Floyd Little. But Brockington had drawn interest from other schools as well, including Ohio State.

Larry Catuzzi, a young assistant on Hayes's staff in 1967, was assigned to recruit the New Jersey and New York City areas—fertile recruiting grounds for eastern colleges and universities but largely neglected by Midwestern powers such as Ohio State. However, Catuzzi faced a huge hurdle when he wanted Hayes to include Brockington in the star-studded recruiting class of 1967 that included Kern, Tatum, Mike Sensibaugh, Jim Stillwagon, Leo Hayden, and Jan White.

With his electric smile and bona fide football pedigree, Brock was an easy prospect to like. Digging a little deeper, however, found a youngster not much interested in the student part of the student-athlete equation. He had begun studies at a New York prep school in order to improve his grades, but the schooling was being paid for by Syracuse, and it only stood to reason that school's football program would likely want something in return—like John's signature on a national letter of intent.

After an official trip to Columbus, however, Brockington was sold on the Buckeyes, but Catuzzi still had to sell his head coach on Brockington. The prospect's grades remained shaky, Hayes argued, and there was the matter of Syracuse paying for his prep school classes. And Brockington had another issue. By then, John had become a father, and Hayes wondered if it wouldn't be better for all concerned if the New York native stayed closer to home to care for his young family. But Catuzzi was unwavering. For every point raised by Hayes against signing Brockington, his young assistant offered a counterpoint. Finally, as the May 17 signing deadline neared, Hayes relented. Brockington would become a Buckeye, a decision neither man would regret.

"If it wasn't for Larry Catuzzi," Brock later said, "I would never have gone to Ohio State. That little guy changed my life."

Still, there was some tough sledding ahead. John got lost on campus during his first day of school at Ohio State, and when he finally stumbled his way into an American history class, he drew the stares of some five hundred others in the lecture hall. Later, he looked on as several fellow students around him began scribbling in notebooks. Finally, curiosity got the better of him. "What are you doing?" he asked a pretty girl seated next to him. "Taking notes," she whispered back.

"Taking notes? I didn't have any idea about taking notes," said John, who enlisted the help of academic advisors to help him learn what notes to take and how to take them.

On the football field, things weren't going much better. On one of Brock's first practice carries, he started up the middle before bouncing outside and using his speed to get to the edge for a long gain. As he returned to the huddle wearing that huge smile of his, Woody came running over in a rage.

"That play goes off-tackle," the coach screamed, "and by God, you'll run off-tackle or you'll never carry the football here again!" Brock got the message that there were two ways to do things at Ohio State: Woody's way and the wrong way.

Nevertheless, Brockington had arrived. Freshman coach Glenn "Tiger" Ellison took to calling him "Wild Horse" for his knee-pumping gallop. Meanwhile, Kern was forced to perfect his skills at handing off the ball after he got too close to Brock during a practice drill one afternoon and was knocked head over heels in the powerful running back's wake.

When the 1967 freshman team joined the varsity the following season, they helped lead the Buckeyes to a Big Ten championship and the program's first Rose Bowl appearance in eleven years. Ohio State took care of business in Pasadena, too, scoring a 27–16 victory over the University of Southern California to secure a national championship. Brockington got only two carries for six yards in the game, but his devastating blocks sprung Kern, Otis, and Hayden on countless occasions and helped the OSU running game pile up 270 yards against the Trojans.

The Buckeyes won another Big Ten championship and Rose Bowl berth two years later, and this time Brockington made his own holes, rumbling for 102 yards and a pair of touchdowns despite a 27–17 loss to Stanford. After college, Brock was an instant star in the National Football League, becoming the first player in league history to rush for at least 1,000 yards in each of his first three seasons after Green Bay made him the ninth overall selection in the 1971 draft.

Following a seven-year pro career, Brockington went into private business. Today, he is a financial advisor in the San Diego area, as well as a tireless fundraiser for kidney disease awareness. Brock was a 2003 kidney transplant recipient from his wife, Diane, and together they partner in assisting kidney disease patients with expenses not covered by other sources, relying upon dialysis clinics and social workers to identify those in greatest need of help.

"I'm just doing what Woody taught us," John said. "Pay forward, he used to say. You can never pay back, so you should always pay forward."

And doing it with a big, warm smile certainly doesn't hurt.

REX
KERN

NICKNAME: Rex

HOMETOWN: Lancaster, Ohio

HEIGHT: 6 ft 0 in   WEIGHT: 184 lb

ALL–AMERICAN: 1969

NFL DRAFT: 1971, Baltimore Colts

Rex was part of the sophomore football class at OSU that had 11 high school All-Americans.

A cold snap had invaded Columbus in early December of 1968, but the mercury dipping below freezing did little to darken the mood of Rex Kern as the sophomore made his way across the Ohio State campus. Two weeks earlier, the fresh-faced redhead—who looked more like he belonged in a Norman Rockwell portrait than on a football field—had helped lead the Buckeyes to a 50–14 win over archrival Michigan, and Kern was eager to begin preparations for the team's first Rose Bowl appearance in eleven years.

The initial practice session was supposed to be little more than a light workout designed to shed some of the excess pounds gained during the Thanksgiving break, but Woody Hayes had other ideas that had nothing to do with turkey or mom's apple pie. After about thirty minutes of watching his team lollygag its way through drills, the legendary coach exploded.

"We're going to the Rose Bowl and we're going to goddamn act like it!" Woody bellowed. With that, he turned the French Fieldhouse thermostat as high as it would go, creating a greenhouse effect inside the old wooden and cinderblock structure, and players who had merely been going through the motions a few minutes before had broken off into position groups and were swimming in their own perspiration.

"I don't think it really mattered, though," Kern said. "Everyone was pumped up. We knew we were good, we knew we would be ready to play. We were going to the Rose Bowl to play the University of Southern California, the defending national champions. They had what we wanted and we were going out there to get it."

While Kern and the rest of the quarterbacks took to one end of the indoor practice field to begin passing drills, there was a buzz in the middle of the field where Woody was presiding over a tackling drill with one position group and then another. Before long, he decided to school his quarterbacks in the art of bringing down an opposing ball-carrier.

"We weren't really paying any attention," Kern said, "and in fact, when he called for us to come over and hit the tackling dummy, we thought maybe he was really joking. Then we saw the look on his face and we knew. He wasn't joking. So, fired up and not knowing any better, we ran over toward Woody and got ready to hit the tackling dummy."

Kern was the starter, so he was first in line. He ran the few yards and flung himself headlong into the dummy before falling to the ground with a shriek of pain. "Oh, shit!" the coach yelled as he ran toward his fallen quarterback.

"What the hell happened?" the coach asked.

"I think I dislocated my shoulder," Kern answered through gritted teeth.

What followed was classic Woody as he shouted, "Shit! Shit!! Shit!!!" his voice rising at least an octave with every expletive. Longtime trainer Ernie Biggs quickly confirmed Kern's diagnosis, putting a swift end to the tackling drills for the day. As Woody stood up, shook his head, and pondered his team's future without its starting quarterback, Kern looked up and said, "Don't worry, Coach. I'll be ready for Pasadena."

Such was the competitive nature of Rex William Kern, the younger of two sons of a barber and housewife from Lancaster, Ohio, a town nestled in the middle of the picturesque Hocking Hills. Rex's father, Trenton, operated a two-chair shop on Sixth Avenue where he cut hair, dispensed advice, listened to his customers' troubles, and opined on baseball, football, and basketball. His younger boy wanted to be a major league baseball player almost from the time he could wrap his tiny fingers around a bat, but it really didn't matter which sport Rex was playing just as long as he was playing.

"It gave me a real adrenaline surge to make that basket or hit the ball or throw the pass, but it was the competition more than the winning," Kern said. "That's what I really enjoyed—physically competing. It fit my personality. I had a little more aggressiveness than some kids. Probably being the younger one in the family—second-born, last-born—made me more aggressive. And being the smallest kid in the neighborhood. They beat up on you all the time. And probably having red hair. They always made fun of my hair. I think that tempers your personality. 'Wait a minute. I'm tired of this stuff.' If I got a chance to hit you, I hit you. If you can do that within the confines of an athletic contest, that's great."

Rex was a multi-sport star at Lancaster High School, equally adept at baseball, basketball, and football. He was offered a major league baseball contract from the Kansas City Athletics, wishing instead to pursue a collegiate basketball career. Kern was good enough to earn scholarship offers from the likes of such coaches as John Wooden of UCLA and Dean Smith of North Carolina, but he wanted to stay closer to home to play at Ohio State for Fred Taylor. Once Woody got wind that Kern was interested in becoming a Buckeye, he inquired if Rex wanted to play both sports in college. Kern certainly did and accepted a football scholarship so he wouldn't count against Taylor's smaller quota of grants-in-aid. But the youngster made it clear to Hayes that basketball would take precedence if a choice had to be made in the fu-

ture. Woody agreed, but he needn't ever have worried.

"Rex looked around a little, talked to some other people, but he had his mind made up all along," his father said. "Ever since the fourth grade, he dreamed of the day he could play for Ohio State. Woody didn't have any trouble getting him at all."

Kern quarterbacked the 1967 freshman team for Hayes, and once his football duties had ended, Rex made a seamless transition to the freshman basketball team. Toward the end of the season, however, he felt a twinge in the back of one of his legs. Shrugging it off as a slight hamstring pull, Kern finished the basketball season and began spring football drills a few months later. The nagging injury never seemed to go away and it got so bad that Rex could barely get out of bed one day. An examination by Ohio State team doctors diagnosed a ruptured disk in Kern's back, and surgery in June of 1968 repaired the problem.

Only 45 days later, Rex was under center for the Buckeyes as they embarked upon their 1968 national championship season.

Rex giving a group of OSU football players a pep talk.

What transpired over the next three years featured some of the most exciting quarterback play in Ohio State history. Hayes ceded control of his offense to the untested youngster, despite once swearing never to place his job in the hands of a teenager. But with Kern checking plays and ad-libbing, the Buckeyes began winning and never stopped. He helped lead the Buckeyes to the national title as a sophomore, coming back from the shoulder injury suffered in bowl practice to earn game MVP honors following a 27–16 triumph against USC in the Rose Bowl. The following season, he earned first-team All-America honors as Ohio State extended its school-record winning streak to twenty-two games, and he topped off his college career by leading the team to another undefeated regular season, Big Ten championship, and a trip to the Rose Bowl.

Kern's style of play seemed an odd mixture of ballet and demolition derby. He had the grace and skill to masterfully extricate himself from an oncoming rush, but also enough grit and determination to lower his shoulder against bigger and stronger defenders. He wasn't the fastest player and his arm wasn't the strongest, but what he lacked in raw athleticism he made up for by improvising with his head. "When somebody starts in with that bullshit about football

Kern in 1970. "Certainly he made his contributions on the field, but aside from the tangibles, there were so many things he did in the locker room and everywhere else that you couldn't find in the stats. He had intuitiveness than everyone recognized and respected."

That respect served Kern especially well during the turbulent times while he was at Ohio State. Many of his teammates were testing, with long hair and wild clothing, the boundaries of new societal mores while Rex was tradition's answer to the Age of Aquarius.

Sometimes Kern actually meets someone who has trouble placing the name. They seem to remember that a Rex Kern once played in the Rose Bowl. "They'll ask if we're related," says Kern, "and I tell them, 'It depends upon whether you're from Michigan or Ohio State.'"

players being dumb jocks and animals," Hayes once said, "I have just two words for them: Rex Kern."

Then, there was his leadership. "We wouldn't have been the team we were without Rex," said All-America tight end Jan White, who served as team co-captain with

He kept his hair closely cropped, his face cleanly shaven, and was more apt to be seen leaving Ohio Stadium on the arm of his mother than any mini-skirted blonde. Nevertheless, what he said in the locker room was gospel, and when he suggested White—a quiet black player from Harrisburg, Pennsylvania—to be one of the team captains in 1970, it helped diffuse any possibility of racial tension on the team. "Here is one man," a normally taciturn Jack Tatum said, "who treats everybody right."

By the time he finished his career at Ohio State, Kern had reigned over one of the most prosperous three-year periods in program history. The team had a three-year record of 27–2 with two Big Ten championships and one national title, and Rex wound up with 2,444 yards passing and 19 TDs to go along with 1,714 yards and sixteen touchdowns rushing.

Despite all of those numbers, his leadership skills, and other intangibles that brought so much success to the Buckeyes, questions about Kern's smallish frame and arm strength caused him to fall all the way to the tenth round of the 1971 NFL draft when the Baltimore Colts selected him to play defensive back. Nevertheless, Rex became a starter for the Colts in his rookie season at the right cornerback position, and he spent three seasons with the Colts, appearing in thirty-three games from 1971–73, registering two interceptions and two fumble recoveries. He then played one season in Buffalo before a back injury forced him to retire after the 1974 season.

Since then, Kern—who earned a Master's degree and Ph.D. from Ohio State—has lived mostly in the Ventura, California, area with his wife, Nancy, a former Rose Bowl princess. Off the field, Rex has been as accomplished as he was on it, earning success as an investment banker, counselor, and fundraiser. In 1994, he briefly considered returning to his alma mater as director of athletics, but bowed out of the running shortly before the university named Andy Geiger as its seventh athletic director.

Kern often returns to Columbus to participate in team reunions and charity functions, and he has been honored often for his playing career, including induction into the Ohio State, Rose Bowl, and College Football Halls of Fame.

And if there was a Hall of Fame for winners who have lived their lives in exemplary fashion, Rex Kern would be a member of that one, too.

JACK TATUM

OSU DEFENSIVE BACK 1968–1970

NICKNAME: The Assassin

HOMETOWN: Cherryville, North Carolina

HEIGHT: 5 ft 10 in   **WEIGHT:** 200 lb

ALL-AMERICAN: 1969, 1970

NFL DRAFT: 1971, Oakland Raiders

32

Jack was so intimidating he even terrified his own teammates.

*J*ack Tatum grew up on the mean streets of Passaic, New Jersey, where looking at someone the wrong way could become a flashpoint to violence. Despite his grim surroundings and a seemingly omnipresent scowl on his face, however, Tatum realized at an early age that he could use that kind of bleak upbringing to his advantage—as fuel toward becoming one of the most feared defensive players in college and professional football history.

"I saw how the ghetto could reach up and grab you by the throat, but then again, all the losers I knew actually wanted to lose," Tatum once said. "Sure, it was a tough lifestyle and there isn't anything pretty about garbage rotting in the streets and ten people living together in a three-room apartment. But just about everyone in the ghetto stays there because they want to spend their days feeling sorry for themselves instead of working their way out.

"It probably would have been easier to give in to the screams of the ghetto, start running in the streets with the gangs, and take trips on drugs, but my highs came from football and doing well in school. Even though I grew up in the ghetto, I always believed that I was the luckiest guy in the world. Someday, I was going to work my way from the hell of this broken, cluttered world out into that area where the sun would shine a little brighter. I wasn't going to let the ghetto own my soul."

Passaic's maze of chipped concrete, broken glass, and mass of towers belching black smoke and despair that rained down on row after row of crowded tenement houses wasn't Tatum's first childhood memory.

John David Tatum's first six years were spent in the pastoral countryside of west-central North Carolina where he entered the world November 19, 1948, the youngest of five children born to Lewis and Annie Mae Tatum. Young J.D., as his mother affectionately called him, spent his earliest days reveling in his grandfather's tales about fighting alongside General Grant in the Civil War, almost singlehandedly sending regiments of gray-clad Confederate troops fleeing for their lives.

Only later—after the old man also insisted he helped row George Washington to destiny across the Delaware River on Christmas night in 1776—did the youngster realize his grandfather had a slight fondness for exaggeration.

Nearing six years old, young John David was suddenly uprooted when his father decided to move to New Jersey in pursuit of higher paying jobs for himself and a better education system for his children. Expansive white fields of cotton and starry, moonlit summer nights spent running barefoot in the cool grass were traded for a steamy asphalt jungle and red skies faded by streams of soot.

The family moved several times during the next few years and Jack—as he was now known—had difficulty keeping friendships. Slowly, the once gregarious, outgoing child became an introverted young teenager. His introspection never manifested itself into a chip on his shoulder, though, and Jack found himself often calling upon his Bible studies whenever trouble showed itself, trying to turn the other cheek to avoid confrontation.

It might seem difficult to believe for someone who grew up to earn the nickname "Assassin," but Tatum participated in only two fights during his childhood—winning both, of course. One came when he and several friends were confronted one night by a gang called the Crackers. When someone made a boast that he could beat up anyone in Tatum's gang, and then punctuated the dare with the N-word, Tatum stepped to the front of the pack.

"In all probability, the fight was over after my first punch…but I was riled up and decided to give (him) a serious whipping," Jack remembered years later. "By the time my friends and the Crackers had finished adding to the story and developing my reputation as a ferocious fighter, I would have backed down from myself."

During his eighth-grade year, the family moved again, this time from what Tatum described as the "classy area of Paterson's ghetto to the bottom of Passaic's ghetto." Most of his friends were thieves or worse, while many others had turned to selling or using hard drugs—sometimes both. By this time, Jack had begun filling out with 185 pounds on a 5-foot-10-inch frame that featured rippling muscular arms and catlike reflexes. Many youngsters his age and with his athletic ability found sweaty boxing gyms to escape the ghetto, but the sport that really appealed to Jack was football. He had played the game on sandlots and in the streets almost from the time he had moved to New Jersey but had never played organized football until he was a sophomore in high school.

Jack's brand of football was a form of controlled terror—light on the control and heavy on the terror. He earned All-State honors both as a running back and defensive back, and by the time his senior year rolled around, he was one of the most sought-after recruits in the United States. He received inquiries from some three hundred colleges and universities seeking his services, but he quickly tired of the recruiting wars, saying, "I almost got to the point where I was ready to say to hell with it all and go work on a garbage truck."

But that was before Tatum was introduced to Woody Hayes. The old coach was blunt and made no promises other than to mold the youngster into a better football player and a better man. Jack wasn't completely sold, but his mother was. Her son was headed to Columbus.

Once there, Tatum began to realize his potential. As a member of the Super Sophomores, he helped spark the Buckeyes to the 1968 national championship and a three-year run as one of the top football teams in college football.

The youthful Buckeyes filed notice of their potential during week three of the '68 season against top-ranked Purdue, defending Big Ten champions and a team that had administered a 41–6 beating to Ohio State the year before. The Boilermakers had a potent offense with All-America performers Mike Phipps at quarterback and Leroy Keyes at halfback, and Purdue entered the game as thirteen-point favorites. But they never got untracked, eventually losing a 13–0 decision to the Buckeyes.

Keyes, who had accounted for nearly 400 yards of offense the week before during a 43–6 win at Northwestern, totaled only 19 yards rushing against the Buckeyes, and in Tatum's words, "was all but carried off the field on a stretcher as I pounded him and blasted him every chance I had."

Phipps fared no better, completing 10 of 28 passes for 120 yards and two interceptions. Much of that performance was also attributed to Tatum's harassment.

"Early in the game, Phipps was about three feet in the air throwing a pass when Tatum hit him," OSU defensive coordinator Lou McCullough remembered. "I mean, Jack just ripped him. Phipps went out of the game, and when he came back there were four or five times when he could have run for ten or fifteen yards. But he never did because he was always looking for Tatum."

Jack made his presence known more than a few other times during that 1968 campaign, including the Rose Bowl when he seemingly came out of nowhere to knock USC running back O.J. Simpson out of bounds at the three-yard line during an early drive, a play that forced the Trojans to settle for a field goal. Had the Heisman Trophy-winning Simpson scored on the play, USC's lead would have been 14–0 rather than 10–0, and perhaps the Buckeyes would not have found the wherewithal to come back for a 27–16 victory that sealed the 1968 national championship.

Tatum was a first-team All-Big Ten selection three times and a two-time consensus All-American for the Buckeyes. Following his college career, he was a first-round selection by the Oakland Raiders in the 1971 NFL draft and made three Pro Bowls during a decade-long professional career highlighted by the Raiders' 32–14 victory over Minnesota in Super Bowl XI. During a 2006 poll conducted by *Sports Illustrated* on the NFL's best defensive backs of the twentieth century, Tatum was named on 80 percent of the ballots.

Unfortunately, his career in the NFL was marred by a devastating hit made on New England Patriots receiver Darryl Stingley during a 1978 exhibition game. Stingley lowered his head when he saw Tatum coming, absorbing the hit on the crown of his helmet. Although the tackle was well within the rules and no penalty was called on the play, Stingley broke two cervical vertebrae and wound up paralyzed from the chest down. Meanwhile, Tatum became a poster child of sorts for violence in the game, and to this day, many of his former teammates believe the incident is why Tatum is not a member of the Pro Football Hall of Fame.

Tatum, who never apologized for his self-described "affinity for controlled violence," faced more than his share of adversity following his playing days, including diabetes that cost him all five toes on his left foot in 2003 and amputation of his entire right leg a few years later. Yet he faced that adversity with the same quiet determination that led him out of the New Jersey ghetto and into the football spotlight.

He wrote several books, including the 1979 bestseller *They Call Me Assassin*, and he created the Ohio-based Jack Tatum Fund for Youthful Diabetes while lending his name to several other fundraisers to help finance diabetes research.

Tatum often returned to Columbus on a biannual basis to watch the Ohio State-Michigan game from a perch in the Ohio Stadium press box. One of his final visits came in 2008, less than two years before his death of a heart attack at the age of 61. He was sitting alone, hands cupped around a steaming cup of hot coffee, when someone approached, stuck out his hand and said, "It's a pleasure to meet you, Mr. Tatum."

Jack, his hair and beard now dappled with gray, squinted through those famous narrow slits, offering that same hardened look that had struck fear in countless opponents.

"You know who I am?" Tatum said, shaking the man's hand with a vise-like grip. "You remember me?"

"Are you kidding?" came the reply from the individual.

What followed was something unexpected—an appreciative nod, the faintest of smiles and what appeared to be a small tear in the corner of one eye.

"I appreciate that," Jack said softly. "You don't know how much that warms the ol' Assassin's heart."

JAMES STILLWAGON

NICKNAME: Jim, Wagon

HOMETOWN: Mount Vernon, Ohio

HEIGHT: 6 ft 0 in   **WEIGHT:** 220 lb

ALL–AMERICAN: 1969, 1970

NFL DRAFT: 1971, Green Bay Packers

68

Jim, who was arrested recently for a road rage incident, does not operate at a level of low intensity even in his sixties.

*R*ebellious, sardonic and very much his own man, Jim Stillwagon didn't exactly fit into Woody Hayes's crafted mold of what an Ohio State football player should be. But after three years of patrolling the middle of Hayes's defense as equal parts lineman, linebacker, and bone-crushing man-eater, Stillwagon earned a national championship ring, a host of individual honors, and perhaps most important, the respect of his head coach.

"Jim Stillwagon was our best defensive lineman," Hayes said. "He was strong, had an extremely quick charge, and was fiercely competitive. He never gave us a bad practice, and although he was an outstanding star, no one would question his dedication to the team."

High praise from a man who never seriously recruited Stillwagon, then threw him off the team after his first varsity practice.

During the spring of 1967, Hayes was amassing what many college football analysts believe was the finest recruiting class in the history of the sport. Hayes had reloaded his roster with the best high school talent the nation had to offer, seven of whom would become first-team All-Americans, five more who would be selected in the first round of the NFL draft. Hayes had little use for an underweight defensive lineman who had been sent away to military school.

Stillwagon might have been undersized but that never stopped him from trying to intimidate nearly everyone he met—from opponents on the football field to the nuns at the Catholic school in his hometown of Mount Vernon, Ohio, about thirty miles northeast of Columbus. His football days began in earnest when he organized his own team in the fifth and sixth grades, but he sometimes had trouble convincing his classmates to play. Stillwagon liked contact even then, as evidenced by the three helmets of opposing players he broke during one game.

By the time he reached St. Vincent's High School, Jim already had something of a reputation as well as a legacy to uphold. His father, ironically named Woody, had been a student manager at Notre Dame, while older brother Tommy had been a star at St. Vincent's who played center at Miami University for Bo Schembechler. The reputation superseded the legacy.

"I didn't get along with the nuns too well," Stillwagon said. "I was a little more free-spirited than Tommy. The nuns told my parents that I'd never go to college. They told them I'd probably go to the penitentiary."

At the age of 15, he was transferred to Augusta Military Academy in Fort Defiance, Virginia, the same school his brother had attended before moving on to Miami. At first glance, Stillwagon thought the nuns had been correct in their prophecy. "It was sort of like prison," he admitted.

His attitude didn't change much with his surroundings. After his first year at Augusta, he found himself inside the office of one of the academy's administrators. "Your brother," the officer said, "was voted the top cadet among the six hundred we have here. You have just been voted the second-worst cadet. What are we going to do with you?"

Athletics was the answer. Stillwagon went out for practically every sport Augusta offered, starring on the football, lacrosse, and baseball teams. During his time at the military school, he was also introduced to weightlifting. His roommate had his own set of weights, and soon Jim had his own as well. While other students spent what little free time they had watching TV, going to movies, or lazing around the campus, Stillwagon and his roommate hit the weights. "You didn't get to do much there," he said, "so we lifted weights."

The result was a chiseled, rock-hard body and a mind to match. Unfortunately, most college coaches still valued sheer size and brawn over the relatively new concept of weight training—Hayes famously said, "We don't need weightlifters. We need athletes." Thus Stillwagon didn't attract much attention from college recruiters. He initially wanted to go to Notre Dame, his father's alma mater, but during an unofficial visit to South Bend, he heard and saw some things he didn't like. That led him to a meeting late in the recruiting season with Hayes. When the short-cropped Stillwagon met with Hayes, the coach said, "You're the boy from the military school. I like your haircut." Jim replied, "Yes, sir," and got a smile. Then Hayes asked "What's the last novel you read?" The cadet quickly racked his brain before blurting out *Moby Dick*. It was a lie.

"I had never read *Moby Dick* or any other novel for that matter," Stillwagon said. "But I had just watched *Moby Dick* on TV, and we wound up talking about it for about forty-five minutes."

Hayes might have been impressed with the youngster's knowledge of Herman Melville's classic tale of Captain Ahab's obsession with a great white whale, but the coach's obsession was with great football players and short, stocky linemen were a dime a dozen. Still, when another player who had been offered a scholarship decided to go elsewhere, Hayes gave the final spot in the 1967 class to Stillwagon, on the recommendation of defensive coordinator Lou McCullough.

"Not many people knew about Jim, but I certainly did," McCullough said. "I got him off a little eight-millimeter film. He was in prep school and I wouldn't let anyone else have the film."

Stillwagon was initially positioned as an offensive center on the OSU freshman team until an assistant coach asked him if he had ever played middle guard. Stillwagon thought back to his *Moby Dick* ploy and replied in the affirmative. "Up until then," he said, "I'd never played middle guard in my life."

Stillwagon didn't take long to get noticed after switching to defense. A constant thorn in the side of varsity players during his freshman year, Jim was eager for the 1968 season to begin. Penciled in as a bench player, he figured the only way to impress his coaches was to be himself and level whoever had the football. Unfortunately, the first practice was a no-contact drill and future starting quarterback Rex Kern—only two months removed from back surgery—was the guy with the ball.

"Wagon came through the line and knocked me on my rear end," Kern remembered. "I mean, he really clobbered me. I thought my world was going to end. I had a yellow jersey on, which meant you couldn't hit me, but Wagon, with his intensity, man, he just leveled me."

What happened next was a blur as Hayes exploded from his spot behind the offensive huddle, a volcanic eruption that threatened to shake the foundation of Ohio Stadium. In between obscenities, the coach screamed for armed sheriff's deputies to remove Stillwagon from the field. "You're gone!" Hayes shouted. "Your scholarship's gone! Get this guy out of here!"

Stillwagon's reaction? "Nobody talks like that to me, so I had a few choice words for him as I was leaving. I went in the locker room, showered and dressed, and packed my stuff. (Defensive line coach) Bill Mallory came into the locker room, and I told him, 'I've had enough of this place. I'm going to West Virginia.' I wasn't that impressed with Ohio State anyway. Bill kept telling me, 'Jim, that's OK. You did the right thing. Woody will cool off.' Well, I didn't care. I wasn't going to cool off. I was leaving."

Just as Stillwagon was about to leave, a contrite Hayes appeared. His argument for staying fell upon deaf ears until he mentioned how disappointed Jim's mom and dad would be if he left campus and never appeared in the Scarlet and Gray. "He always recruited the moms and dads as much as the players," Stillwagon said. "He already had me reconsidering, and then kind of whispered, 'You did the right thing out there today.'"

Stillwagon rejoined the Buckeyes and became one of the defensive stalwarts on a 1968 team that won all nine regular-season games before rolling to a 27–16 victory over defending national champion USC in the Rose Bowl. The season resulted in a national championship for Ohio State and began one of the most successful three-year spans in program history. Along the way, Stillwagon was one of the most consistent players on the roster. He was twice a consensus first-team All-American, won the Outland Trophy as college football's outstanding interior lineman of the year, and earned the inaugural Lombardi Award, symbolic of the finest lineman or linebacker.

Following his college career, NFL scouts couldn't decide where Stillwagon fit into most defensive schemes, and he fell to Green Bay in the fifth round of the 1971 draft.

The Packers, their glory days of six league championships in eight years behind them, were coming off a 6–8 record and were in rebuilding mode. One of the team's assistant general managers showed up one day to sign Stillwagon to a relatively small salary and was quickly introduced to the Stillwagon charm. "He came into town and threw a contract in my face," Stillwagon said. "He said, 'We're getting rid of Ray Nitschke. He's a bum. We're getting rid of all the old guys.' Well, Ray Nitschke was the middle linebacker for Vince Lombardi during the Packers' championship years and he was kind of my idol. So I told the guy, 'Don't ever come back here and waste my time again.'"

Stillwagon eventually signed with the Toronto Argonauts of the Canadian Football League and played five seasons before injuries ended his career. The absence of NFL acclaim does little, however, to diminish Stillwagon's stature among his former teammates.

Bill Urbanik lined up at defensive tackle alongside Stillwagon at Ohio State, and went on to coach the likes of Pro Football Hall of Fame lineman Howie Long at Oakland and All-Pro nose guard Tim Krumrie at Cincinnati. According to Urbanik, Stillwagon was the toughest lineman he ever saw. Likewise with All-America offensive tackle John Hicks, who went against Stillwagon in practice every day during the 1970 season. "Wagon was a monster," Hicks said. "He's the best football player I've ever played against. And I'm talking about (Hall of Fame defensive tackle) Joe Greene and all of them. Wagon was the best."

JOHN HICKS

HOMETOWN: Cleveland, Ohio

HEIGHT: 6 ft 2 in   WEIGHT: 258 lb

ALL–AMERICAN: 1972, 1973

NFL DRAFT: 1974, New York Giants

74

Hicks was the first player to ever start in three Rose Bowls.

*T*he spring of 1970 was cool in Columbus, but John Hicks was hot. Hotter than two Julys wrapped inside an August.

Ohio State's talented young offensive tackle had spent much of the 1969 season—his freshman year as a Buckeye—being ground into the dirt of the practice field outside Ohio Stadium, serving as cannon fodder for a powerful varsity team. As he nursed his bruises, Hicks could at least soothe his wounded pride by knowing he played a small role in what he figured was the Buckeyes' march to a second consecutive national championship.

And then November 22 came. Under the guidance of first-year head coach Bo Schembechler, who played for Woody Hayes at Miami University and then served five years as an assistant on Hayes's staff at Ohio State, upstart Michigan engineered one of college football's most historic upsets, pulling off a 24–12 shocker against the top-ranked Buckeyes.

"My freshman year, we sat home and listened to the loss to Michigan. It was a huge shock," Hicks said. "As freshmen, we didn't think anyone— and I mean *anyone*—could beat our varsity. We practiced against them day after day. Kern, Tatum, Brockington...they were household names. When we lost up there, that's when I really understood what it meant to be a Buckeye. They took away our honor."

Schembechler had fired the first shot in what would become known as the Ten-Year War with Hayes, but the old master was intent upon gaining revenge against his coaching protégé.

"Revenge isn't a strong enough word," Hicks said. "As soon as the team got back to town, we started preparing. All the (winter conditioning) workouts were more intense—way more. All twenty-five practices in the spring were about Michigan. Woody was, and I guess we were, too, obsessed with paying them back. I kind of had an advantage because I was quick enough to handle their slant tackles on defense. The year before, they manhandled us, and I worked and worked that spring, determined not to let that happen again. It was my first shot, and I wanted to make sure they remembered me."

It was an unusual mind-set for a youngster who grew up in a loving, middle-class neighborhood on the east side of Cleveland. John Charles Hicks Jr. was born March 21, 1951, the eldest of three children to John and Charity Hicks. "We were a close family, and there was always something fun going on at the house," Hicks said. "My parents worked hard and provided for us. My dad was a mechanic for the state, and my mom was a nurse. We were a middle-class family with no hardships, no peril—my parents saw to that. There was a lot of love."

There was also a lot to do in the neighborhood. Amid the two-story brick homes and tree-lined streets were plenty of backyards and driveways where football, baseball, and basketball games were routinely played. Several members of the Cleveland Browns professional football team also made their homes in the area, and young John's first impressions of the game were molded by such future Hall of Fame players as Jim Brown and Paul Warfield. "It was cool to hang out with them," Hicks

said. "They were all my friends and my role models."

John played football all day and dreamed of football all night, pretending to emulate his gridiron heroes. But the fluid moves displayed by Brown or Warfield's catlike quickness simply were not in his DNA. From the time he first picked up a football on a playground at the age of six, Hicks was already too big to be considered anything other than a lineman. "I guess they didn't see my talent," he said with a laugh.

By the time he was a senior at John Hay High School, John had managed to put only 225 pounds onto his wiry 6-foot-3-inch frame, and despite earning All-Ohio honors as a guard, he wasn't garnering much interest from major college programs. Michigan was always eager to steal talent away from Ohio State, especially in the Cleveland area, but the Wolverines didn't seem interested. Meanwhile, the Buckeyes provided only token interest until a couple of other offensive line prospects decided to sign elsewhere. Hayes, unsure if Hicks was big enough to withstand the rigors of what was demanded of him as an offensive lineman at OSU, decided to make a visit to the prospect's home only as a courtesy. And then the coach made a gut decision—literally.

"He came up to see me, took a shot at my mom's sweet potato pie, and it was a done deal," John said. "He had about six pieces. After that, he said, 'I don't know if he'll play, but we'll get him an education.'"

Hicks still wasn't convinced major college football was for him until he took his official visit to Ohio State on November 23, 1968. That happened to be the day when the Buckeyes rolled to a 50–14 rout of Michigan on their way to the national championship. "Seeing the band, the crowd, the team in those Scarlet and Gray uniforms running onto the field—it was the greatest experience of my life," John said. "Coach Hayes later met me and asked, 'How would you like to be a Buckeye?' I thought I was living a dream."

Hicks showed up for his first camp in the fall of 1969 as a guard, serving as little more than a live tackling dummy for defensive tack-les Paul Schmidlin and Bill Urbanik, as well as All-America middle guard Jim Stillwagon. "They killed us," he said. "Every day, they just killed us. The stuff they did to us then, you couldn't get away with it today. It was boot camp."

Still, he persevered as the Buckeyes won their first eight games of the 1969 season, running rough-shod over opponents as they strung together a school-record winning streak of twenty-two games. After the Michigan loss, however, everything changed. "From day one of spring ball, I started working on the slant tackle and I never let up," Hicks said. "I think that's why I started (as a sophomore in 1970)—because I could block Michigan's slant tackle."

The rematch was decidedly one-sided as Hayes and Ohio State exacted their revenge, topping off another undefeated regular season with a 20–9 vanquish of their hated archrivals. The final score was misleading, however, as the Buckeyes physically punished the Wolverines from the opening kick-off to the final gun. "We wouldn't even look at them," Hicks said.

"There was a lot of animosity on our side. We wanted it more than Michigan—for nearly a whole year—and we were still going fullbore on the last drive of the game. We beat 'em up pretty good. Actually, we manhandled them."

The celebration didn't last long unfortunately. With next to nothing left in their emotional tank, the Buckeyes lost a 27–17 decision to Stanford in the Rose Bowl and missed a chance to win the 1970 national championship. The following fall, during a scrimmage the week before the 1971 opener against Iowa, Hicks tore the medial collateral and anterior cruciate ligaments in his left knee and was lost for the entire season. But he returned in 1972 to help spearhead another Big Ten championship and a return to the Rose Bowl, the first of four consecutive trips to Pasadena for the team.

Hicks earned All-America honors in 1972 and '73, took home the Outland Trophy and Lombardi Awards as a senior, then finished second in the Heisman Trophy balloting behind Penn State running back John Cappelletti, representing the highest Heisman finish ever for an offensive lineman. Hicks added to his trophy case, being named college football's lineman of the year by *United Press International* and College Football Player of the Year by *The Sporting News*. But each of those awards paled in comparison to the praise Hicks received from his teammates.

"John was big and super strong," said OSU defensive lineman Ernie Helms, who usually went before against Hicks in practice. "On top of that, he was fast and quick. He was into you before you could push back. He was good on straight-ahead blocking, pulling, and pass-blocking. He was a clean player, too. He never engaged in cheap shots. He was also a quality person. I never saw or heard anything negative about his character on or off the field."

Following his college career, Hicks was set to embark upon what should have been a stellar professional career. The New York Giants selected him third overall during the first round of the 1974 NFL draft, and he made an immediate impact, winning NFC Offensive Rookie of the Year honors his first year in the league. He started each of his first four NFL seasons, but he suffered another serious knee injury that robbed him of his mobility, and the Giants traded him to Pittsburgh in 1978. Hicks tried to come back from the injury but never played a game for the Steelers before officially retiring in 1979 and returning to Columbus to enter the real estate business. Since then, he has become a regular fixture at various charity functions as well as at Ohio State home games, always eager to swap football stories during tailgate parties in and around Ohio Stadium.

Since his playing days ended, Hicks has been honored many times, with induction into the Ohio State Athletics Hall of Fame as well as the College Football and Rose Bowl halls of fame. But he received his highest honor from Hayes, who called the two-time All-American "the greatest interior lineman I have ever coached." The legendary coach made a highlight reel of Hicks in action and used it as a teaching tool for the remainder of his coaching career.

Hicks was so proficient that he often told opponents what was coming, something that drove his teammates crazy. "John was the key to our offensive line, the leader of everything up front to us," said two-time Heisman Trophy winner Archie Griffin, still the all-time leading rusher in Ohio State history with 5,589 yards. "Still, I'll always wonder how many yards we could have gained if Big John hadn't told them where we were going to run."

ARCHIE GRIFFIN

OSU RUNNING BACK 1972–1975

HOMETOWN: Columbus, Ohio

HEIGHT: 5 ft 8 in   **WEIGHT:** 180 lb

ALL–AMERICAN: 1974, 1975

NFL DRAFT: 1976, Cincinnati Bengals

45

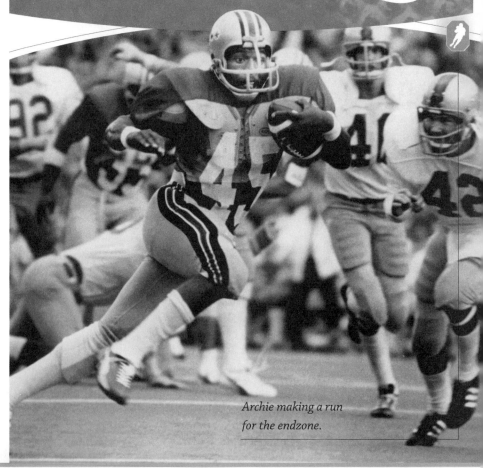

Archie making a run for the endzone.

Archie Griffin has become such a mythical figure in the pantheon of Ohio State football history that the mere mention of his name continues to stir emotion throughout the Buckeye Nation, despite the fact nearly forty years have passed since he played his final game in Scarlet and Gray.

Most fans can rattle off Griffin's on-the-field accomplishments like a country preacher reciting scripture from the pulpit: the all-time leading rusher in school history; thirty-one consecutive games with at least 100 yards rushing, an NCAA record that remains on the books; the first player ever to start in four straight Rose Bowl games; college football's only two-time winner of the Heisman Trophy.

Each of those accomplishments, as well as more just like them, came from a quietly confident young man who was molded by hard-working, God-fearing parents who provided a nurturing environment for their large family. Still, under different circumstances, Archie Griffin might have spent his life toiling away in the coal mines of Logan, West Virginia, a tiny dot on the map tucked along the Allegheny Plateau in the southwestern part of the state.

Archie was named for his grandfather, a stern-willed rock of a man who left the family home at five each morning to work in the mines, sometimes not coming back until well after midnight. The life of a West Virginia coal miner near the turn of the twentieth century was a bleak existence featuring thick smoke billowing from nearly every ramshackle house in town and an army of soot-covered faces marching in and out of the mines to the shrill sound of a steam whistle every time there was a shift change.

In that environment, A.M. Griffin and his wife Elizabeth brought six children into the world—at least they tried to bring them into the world. Only three of them survived childhood. One was Archie's father, James, who was just four years old when he stood helplessly by his mother's bed, watching her die trying to give birth to another child.

With his mother gone, and his father often working double shifts in the mines, little James quickly came to the conclusion that he wanted no part of coal mining. Escaping that toxic environment would not be easy, however. He did his best to concentrate on academics and athletics, and became an all-state lineman in high school. But at only 120 pounds, James realized football wasn't going to be his ticket out of Logan. He joined the service, working in the shipyards in Norfolk, Virginia, then returned to Logan where he began to start a family with his young wife, Margaret, who had just finished high school.

That better life included twenty-hour workdays with two fulltime jobs, as well as a part-time position five nights a week as a high school janitor. Later, he somehow found time to run a small neighborhood grocery store. On weekends, James rested—only ten hours per day with two part-time janitorial jobs. The days were long and the money barely kept food on the Griffin table and a roof over the burgeoning family's head, but it sure beat coughing up coal dust every night and gave James the peace of mind

"Being young, I thought at the time, 'Maybe I need to go ahead and win that Heisman Trophy again.'"
—*Archie Griffin,* Woody's Boys

Upon his return to West Virginia, James reluctantly worked for the mining company, first above ground on a tipple that sorted the extracted coal by size before loading it onto railroad cars, and later underground as a miner. But as his family grew—eventually to seven boys and one girl—he longed for a better life and set out for Columbus, Ohio.

he was doing something to better his family.

That family started to grow quickly, and Archie Mason Griffin arrived August 21, 1954—fittingly at University Hospital on the Ohio State campus—the fourth child of the family, and with his gap-toothed smile and easy-going nature, he quickly fit in. He was also a perpetual motion machine, always active, always playing, always doing something. "He never could just sit," Margaret Griffin once told a friend. "He was forever on the go. He loved to sleep, though. I guess he was worn out from playing so hard."

Archie spent most of his waking hours at Blackburn Park, a small expanse of barren land kept so because grass never had a chance to take root under the busy feet of the area children. When Archie wasn't playing, he was inside the family grocery devouring as much junk food as he could shovel into his mouth with both hands.

"We had the store, and us kids helped Mom in there," he said. "I used to take pop and sweets out of there. I've always been big on sweets. Maybe that's why I was so fat when I was a little boy. My particular favorites were Almond Joys and Hostess cupcakes."

Despite growing out as well as up, Archie was proficient in every athletic endeavor he tried. He was an accomplished wrestler, enjoyed baseball and basketball, and could beat every other boy in the neighborhood who dared challenge him to a footrace. But Archie's football career was nearly derailed before it ever got started.

When he was nine, he joined his first organized team, but didn't play much because the other boys ranged in age from twelve to fif-

Archie as popular nesting dolls.

teen. He was also short and stocky, and therefore was relegated to backup duty plugging the middle of the defensive line.

"I was a fat, dumpy little kid, and the kids called me 'Tank.' I wasn't very good," Archie said. "I played middle guard, but I just wasn't ready to play with those guys. But they'd let me get in for the last few minutes. I played for that team for two years, and then we moved out to the north end of Columbus and I

played for another team, called Caldwell Temple. I was still playing guard, but one day, none of the fullbacks showed up for practice and the coaches tried me. I guess I was about twelve by then. Well, I never went back to the line again."

Griffin was a natural at the running back spot, using a unique combination of brute strength with the ability to switch directions in the blink of an eye. When he got to junior high, though, his problem with baby fat continued to dog him and, because of a school-mandated weight limit, he was faced with trimming about ten pounds from his frame.

That was when Archie proved his resourcefulness. His summertime workout regimen included wrapping himself in plastic dry-cleaning bags, then turning the family bathroom into a sauna by turning on all the hot water and putting towels under the door so the steam couldn't escape. As he

Archie's mutton chops were as smooth as his running style.

performed jumping jacks, sit-ups, and pushups amid the fog, he would sweat so much the plastic melted to his skin.

When his mother or another family member chased him from the bathroom, he improvised again. There was a junk car behind the house, and Archie would get in the back, push the front seats down, and do pushups and sit-ups in the musty old jalopy. He later fashioned a set of barbells by filling a pair of wooden crates with dirt and attaching them to either end of an old mop handle.

That kind of homemade ingenuity helped transform Griffin from a pudgy, straight-ahead power back into a leaner, quicker runner who could beat opposing defenses with his speed and finesse as well as his strength.

The football world first took notice when Archie was smashing records at Columbus Eastmoor High School and leading the Warriors to the City League championship. In addition to his other exploits, Griffin also exhibited toughness. He rushed for 267 yards in the City League title game against Linden McKinley despite playing with a broken bone in his foot.

From there, it was only a few miles to Ohio Stadium where he achieved almost instant rock star status. In only his second game as a Buckeye, Archie set a new single-game school rushing record with 239 yards during a 29–14 victory against North Carolina. It was the beginning of a career that produced a then-NCAA record 5,589 rushing yards, four consecutive Big Ten championships, a trio of first-team All-America honors, and a feat unparalleled in college football history—back-to-back Heisman Trophy seasons.

Through it all, he remained humble and stayed true to the faith his parents had instilled in him. Woody Hayes used to tell about how he'd nearly stumble over a kneeling Griffin each time the team came roaring out of the locker room "because Arch'd be down on his knees praying."

Griffin went on to become a first-round selection of the Cincinnati Bengals in the 1976 NFL draft, and although injuries curtailed his pro career, he managed to play seven seasons and appeared in the Bengals' 26–21 loss to the San Francisco 49ers in Super Bowl XVI.

He retired from the NFL following the 1982 season, attempted a brief comeback in the upstart USFL three years later, then returned to Columbus to work in the athletic department at Ohio State, rising to the position of associate athletic director. Since 2004, Archie has served as president and CEO of the Ohio State Alumni Association, becoming one of the university's most recognized and beloved goodwill ambassadors.

He remains a living, breathing folk hero to Buckeye fans, an almost larger-than-life legend who serves as a conduit to the glory days of Ohio State football when Hayes roamed the sideline and getting to play in the Rose Bowl was every young football player's dream. Despite his mythic stature, however, Archie remains as unassuming and humble as the days when he used to sneak candy bars out of his parents' store.

"Sincerity is the key to the whole thing with Archie," longtime OSU football beat writer Kaye Kessler once said. "We've been exposed to a lot of great football talent in Columbus, but of all the qualities that go into greatness, Archie has more of them than anyone else. I've never seen him change—not for one minute. He was the same fine young man the day he left school as he was when he arrived.

"They say success spoils just about everybody, but Archie Griffin has true humility. He's the same with everybody he meets. He's just a nice human being. I've never heard anyone say a bad word about him."

Perhaps his old coach said it best.

"Archie Griffin is a better person than he is a football player," Hayes said, "and he's the best football player I've ever seen."

CORNELIUS GREENE

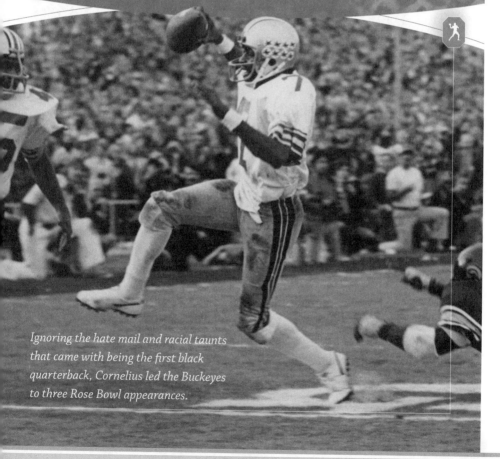

OSU QUARTERBACK 1973–1975

NICKNAME: Corny, Flam

HOMETOWN: Washington, D.C.

HEIGHT: 6 ft 0 in   **WEIGHT:** 172 lb

7

Ignoring the hate mail and racial taunts that came with being the first black quarterback, Cornelius led the Buckeyes to three Rose Bowl appearances.

Cornelius Greene has a 50,000-watt smile that could light up Broadway and a nickname to match. But behind the confident bravado of a player called "Flam" because of his flamboyant style on and off the field, there was a scrawny little homesick kid told by his coach that he was too small to play major-college football.

"When I was being recruited, lots of schools were offering cars and cash, and most of the coaches promised me I'd start right away," Greene said. "But when I got to Columbus and first met Woody Hayes, he told me I was so small that I might get my neck broken if I tried to play at Ohio State. He told me straight out that I'd only play if I was good enough, and if I wasn't, I wouldn't. It was a little disturbing hearing that from him when I was hearing just the total opposite from other coaches."

One more thing: Ohio State had never before in its history had a black starting quarterback.

"Corny knew what the odds were and the obstacles he was facing," two-time Heisman Trophy winner Archie Griffin said. "But he had a lot of confidence in himself, and he chose to take the hard road when a lot of people were telling him he was crazy. He left his hometown, left his friends, went to an entirely new place with completely new surroundings and worked his tail off. I don't know that I could have done something like that at that time in my life, and I have always admired him for that."

Cornelius Greene was born on January 21, 1954, into one of the many poverty-stricken ghettos scattered throughout Washington, D.C. He was a naturally gifted athlete and always on the move, eager to get out of the projects as quickly as possible. He ran with a small group of close-knit neighborhood friends who called him Butch and needled him endlessly about his extremely slight build, often telling him he was so skinny his pants had only one belt loop. The youngster would always flash a bright smile and chuckle along with the joke, but his sunny disposition was just a mask, a defense mechanism for the despair he faced at home.

His father was blind, and his four sisters and three brothers tried to help their mother as best they could. Young Cornelius was shuttled off to be raised by his aunt and uncle, and he spent many of his summers staying with other family members in Flint, Michigan. The youngster dreamed of the day when he could strike out on his own, and it didn't take long for him to figure the best way out of his situation was to get an education. And the only way to do that was through athletics. Luckily for him, he had been bestowed with natural instincts and lightning speed, and despite his small frame, the youngster quickly earned notoriety as one of the most electrifying athletes in the D.C. area.

At Paul Laurence Dunbar High School, a predominantly black school named for one of the first nationally accepted African-American writers, Cornelius excelled in everything he tried. He averaged 25 points per game in basketball, using his catlike quickness in the open court to slash to the basket. His keen hand-to-eye coordinaton made him a .500 hitter on the baseball team, while a strong, whip-like arm led to a 30–2 career record as a pitcher. But it was football where his skills were really on display as a free-lancing, scrambling quarterback whose now-you-see-him-now-you-don't ability made Dunbar one of the top high school programs in the area.

More than eighty colleges and universities offered enticements of one sort of another. He was even offered a small bonus by the Baltimore Orioles to join their minor-league organization as a shortstop. "They offered $25,000, which at that time was more money than I ever knew existed," Cornelius said. "But I was looking for something more. I wanted an education."

Michigan State University really seemed a perfect fit. The beautiful, sprawling campus in East Lansing was less than an hour west of Flint where he had spent several summers, and the Spartans had been recruiting Cornelius for years, using former player Jimmy Raye—that school's first black starting quarterback—to convince the youngster to come to Michigan State. But on his official recruiting visit to East Lansing, Cornelius was abandoned at a party by his host player, leaving the youngster to find his own way back to his hotel. The Spartans were quickly eliminated.

A few weeks later, Cornelius found himself at another party, this time at Ohio State with a completely different vibe. "I hit it off with some other black players who took me under their wing," he said. "We hung out, went to some parties, hung around with some white guys, and it gave me a good feeling. I was in an environment with less than five percent blacks, but I felt comfortable. It felt like a fraternity."

When he returned home to D.C. and told everyone he was going to sign with Ohio State, his decision was met with derision and scorn. Friends, rival recruiters, and even family members expressed their doubt, reminding Cornelius what he already knew.

"They said Ohio State had never had a black quarterback or a black middle linebacker because those positions were supposed to be for the smartest players," he said. "But to me, that was just an old stereotype. Plus, I was cocky enough that I wanted to do whatever other people told me I couldn't. I wanted to show them that I could."

When he arrived in Columbus, however, he thought he had made the biggest mistake of his life. His roommate was supposed to be fellow freshman Woodrow Roach, another black player the Buckeyes had recruited out of the D.C. area. But after his first day of summer practice, he returned to his dorm room at Stradley Hall to find Brian Baschnagel, a white kid from the Pittsburgh suburbs, unpacking his bags. Hayes was already testing his freshman quarterback's mettle. If Corny was going to be the first black starter at his position in program history, he had better learn how to relate to his white teammates.

Somehow, the black kid from the projects and the white city kid hit it off, discovering they had more in common than they thought. "I was just worried about making the team and maintaining a starting position, and to me, Corny was in the same boat as I was," said Baschnagel, whose mop top of black hair and quintessentially-1970s mustache was a sharp contrast to his roommate's towering Afro hairstyle. "There were a lot of athletes out there, black and white, who were fighting for security on the team, trying to get some playing time on the field. The reality, at least for me personally, was that I was oblivious to the color."

Cornelius agreed, adding, "I'd never been around white people, but Brian and I ended up as best friends. We did everything as brothers, and he taught me a lot. We covered for each other and shared our backgrounds, and the whole experience made me a better person."

It was a good thing Corny was making new friends among his teammates, because he wasn't endearing himself to the Ohio State coaching staff. He was late for his first team meeting and got an earful from Hayes. He was sixth on the depth chart at quarterback as he struggled to grasp an offensive scheme much different from the one he ran in high school, and whenever he did get the rare chance to show what he could do, it usually ended in disaster.

"The starter, Greg Hare, was having a bad day, so Woody called me up," Corny remembered. "But I didn't know the plays and didn't have the sense to tell him. He called the play in the huddle, and I turned the wrong way and ran into the fullback and fumbled. Woody goes off on me, screaming, 'Get him out of here!' So I went right back down. I had spent all of about two minutes on the varsity, and I was devastated. For the rest of the summer, I was getting ulcers and couldn't sleep. I finally went to our team doctor, who told me not to worry. He said I was about the fifth quarterback Woody had given an ulcer to."

Hayes continued to ride his young quarterback mercilessly, but he obviously saw tremendous potential. An excellent spring camp in 1973 followed by more improvement in the fall pushed Cornelius to No. 2 on the depth chart behind Hare. Then, when the senior co-captain pulled a hamstring muscle just before the 1973 season opener against Minnesota, the scrawny sophomore from the D.C. ghetto was about to make history as the first black player to start at quarterback for the Ohio State Buckeyes.

"It was surprising, it was fearful—there was a lot going through my mind," Corny said. "But I knew I was prepared. I guess the butterflies of starting your first game, it seemed like I had those same butterflies almost before every game, so I didn't see too much difference. I knew the significance of it, of what I was doing. But there was so much to learn and so much to do that I tried to block that side of it out."

After leading the Buckeyes to a 56–7 rout of the Golden Gophers, Corny had removed all doubt about his ability to lead a major-college offense. He went on to become one of the most prolific dual-threat quarterbacks in school history and one of the most successful, leading Ohio State to three Big Ten championships and three consecutive Rose Bowl appearances. He was named to the all-conference first team in 1974 and '75, and earned team Most Valuable Player honors as a senior despite playing on the same team as Griffin, who won his second Heisman Trophy that year. It was Griffin who cast the deciding ballot for Corny, paving the way for the senior quarterback to be named the Big Ten's Most Valuable Player.

He was also quite possibly the flashiest Buckeye ever, nicknaming himself "Mr. Flamboyant," which was quickly shortened to "Flam." He tooled around Columbus in a flashy Grand Prix with "FLAM 7" on his custom license plates, and began showing up for team functions dressed in bold-colored, three-piece suits and platform shoes. It wasn't long before his sartorial splendor rubbed off on his teammates.

"When I first met Archie, he wore black shoes with everything," Corny said. "I always used to say I was flashy and he was classy. But I got him shaped up. It wasn't long before he got red shoes, green shoes, all kinds of color shoes. We had a ball."

In return, Archie turned his friend onto religion.

"When I first got to Ohio State and I wasn't starting right away, I was very disappointed, very low," Corny said. "I'd sit there watching *Kojak* on TV and Archie, he'd be reading the Bible. It got to working on me, you know, and pretty soon he made me receive Jesus Christ into my life.

"I found that being a quarterback under Woody Hayes, you needed all the faith you could get."

EARLE
BRUCE

OSU COACH 1979–1987

HOMETOWN: Cumberland, Maryland

RECORD: 81-26-1

BIG TEN CHAMPIONSHIPS: 1979, 1981, 1984, 1986

The only foot race Bruce ever claimed to lose was one run against his mother.

*I*t was an atypical Monday morning inside the brand-new Woody Hayes Athletic Center, the gleaming practice facility that bore the name of Ohio State's most storied football coach. For the first time in sixteen years, the Buckeyes had lost their third consecutive Big Ten game, and grim-faced players and assistant coaches were attempting to focus on the formidable task at hand: how to salvage a mediocre season by beating archrival Michigan.

Urban Meyer was a 23-year-old receivers coach on that mid-November morning in 1987, mustachioed and full of the same kind of fire-and-brimstone bravado of his boss Earle Bruce. Rock-solid confident he and his fellow assistants would be able to formulate a winning game plan to beat Michigan and salvage the season, Meyer clutched a cup of hot coffee and headed down the hallway for a meeting with his position players. As he stuck his head in Bruce's office, he noticed his fellow coaches were already inside, huddled around a conference table. Leaning against a far wall was director of athletics Rick Bay, who motioned for Meyer to come inside.

"I knew this wasn't going to be any ordinary meeting," Meyer said. "Rick Bay was leaning against the wall, and he looked at me and said, 'Are you the last one?' I looked around the room, nodded and said, 'Yes, sir.' He told me to close the door and sit down."

Bay told the young men assembled that Bruce would no longer be coach after the Michigan game and that he had resigned as athletic director in protest.

"Just like that," Meyer said. "It hit me like a ton of bricks."

Bruce, the proud Ohio State alum who had spent six seasons as an assistant under Hayes and then succeeded the legendary coach in 1979 was understandably bitter about being dismissed after nine seasons as head coach, especially after winning four Big Ten championships and more than 75 percent of his games. But while others chafed at his treatment, Bruce did what he was taught at a young age—keep your head down, never complain, and remain focused on the task at hand.

"I was kind of in awe that week as I watched how a man gets back up after he's been knocked down," Meyer said. "We were all kind of shell-shocked, but not Earle. He wouldn't let us get distracted. We had a job to do and he was going to make sure we did it."

It couldn't have been any other way. Bruce was born March high school football and track star in the blue collar town of Cumberland, Maryland. He was state champion in the 220-yard dash and rarely ever lost a footrace—except once to an unlikely opponent.

"One time, my high school football team was playing a game at Johnstown, Pennsylvania," Earle remembered. "I took the kickoff

"Undefeated, or dead."

—*Earle Bruce*, describing how Buckeye fans liked their OSU coaches

8, 1931, the first of four sons to Earle D. Bruce Sr. and his wife, Mildred. Bruce's father was a no-nonsense man of strong will and an even stronger constitution, having toiled in the steel mills along the tri-state area where the borders of Pennsylvania, Maryland, and West Virginia converge.

Young Earle inherited his father's grit and determination, as well as a passion for sports. He could barely stretch himself to 5-foot-9 and tipped the scales at a mere 155 pounds, but because of his blinding speed he became a and ran it ninety-five yards for a touchdown, and my mother ran all ninety-five yards with me down our sideline. Sometimes, she embarrassed me a little bit. I'd try to get her to settle down, but she wouldn't. It wasn't her nature."

Self-proclaimed as a rough and scrappy kid, Earle was as strong-willed as his father. After University of Maryland head coach Jim Tatum conducted a recruiting interview with a cigarette dangling from his lips, Earle immediately crossed the Terrapins off his list. "Here's this coach, trying to recruit

Earle learned the good, the bad, and the ugly ways to coach from his head coach, Woody Hayes.

me, and he's smoking," Bruce said. "I knew at that moment that even if they really wanted me, I wasn't going to Maryland."

Ohio State and head coach Wesley Fesler made a much more favorable impression. Two things impressed the youngster about Fesler—the coach called him by his childhood nickname "Lefty" and later sent him a telegram on his birthday. That was all Bruce need-ed to make up his mind. He spent the 1950 season on the freshman team, trying to learn Fesler's sin-gle-wing offense, but shortly after the Buckeyes lost a 9–3 decision to Michigan at the end of that sea-son, Fesler resigned and Hayes was named as his replacement.

The following year, Bruce ex-pected to be moved from halfback to a receiver position to take ad-vantage of his speed, but he slipped on wet grass during a preseason practice drill and twisted his knee. At first, team trainers believed the injury was a simple muscle pull, but several days later the pain had yet to subside and Bruce sought a second opinion. He had suffered cartilage damage to the joint and the meniscus tendon had been torn away from the bone. Today, he would have undergone reconstructive surgery and returned the following season. But in 1951, he had sustained a career-ending injury.

Figuring he was no longer of any use to the Buckeyes, Earle packed his bags and returned home to Cumberland. By the time he got there, however, Hayes had already called and left a message with Bruce's mother—get back to Columbus as soon as you can, finish your education, and help coach the team.

In those days, injured players typically lost their scholarships, but Hayes didn't follow that philosophy, believing schools and coaches should honor their commitments regardless of the situation. Bruce re-joined the team as a student assistant with no formal title, and he continued his educa-

tion, considering law school and a career with the Federal Bureau of Investigation. But he found he enjoyed his role on the coaching staff, however minor it was.

It was the beginning of an extremely successful coaching career that included back-to-back undefeated seasons at Massillon High School, six seasons as a full-time assistant on Hayes's staff at Ohio State, and successful runs as head coach at the University of Tampa and Iowa State. When he returned to Ohio State in 1979 as Hayes's successor, his first team came within an eyelash of the national championship, its only loss a 17–16 heartbreaker to the University of Southern California in the Rose Bowl. The Buckeyes won at least nine games each season during Bruce's first eight years as head coach and captured victories in five different bowl games.

But as successful as Bruce was, his gruff exterior and old-school mentality rubbed some influential friends of the program—as well as university president Dr. Edward H. Jennings—the wrong way. Tension reached such a pitch that Bruce briefly toyed with the idea of leaving Ohio State following the 1986 season when Arizona tried to lure him away with a lucrative contract. In the end, the coach's loyalty to his alma mater won out, and he began making preparations for his ninth season in Columbus.

"What a colossal mistake," Bruce said later. "I had declined an offer-of-a-lifetime from Arizona, and I would be fired with the year."

When the 1987 season began, the Buckeyes were the No. 5 team in the country, but their late-season losing streak ended all hopes of another championship. And then the axe fell.

"I remember it like it was yesterday," said Derek Isaman, who knows a thing or two about getting up after being knocked down. Recruited by Bruce to play linebacker at Ohio State, Isaman was also a boxer who won two national amateur titles, and once traded punches with Mike Tyson during a Golden Gloves match.

"During the pre-practice meeting that Monday, Coach Bruce stood before us and announced, 'I have been let go by the university.'

As tears ran down his face, he told us it was not going to affect our determination, desire, and willingness to play error-free football. 'This is the most important game in your entire life,' he said. 'That School Up North is good, but they're not great.' His face was getting red and the tears were streaming down his face. 'Strap on your helmets, boys, because there is no game like this one, and we'll be flying around the field and cracking skulls. This will be the hardest-hitting game of your lives. We are going up to Michigan and we are going to kick their ass!' Hell, we were ready to play Michigan right then and there."

Just before the traditional coin toss, Ohio State players had a surprise for their coach. Each removed his helmet to reveal a white headband emblazoned with the word "EARLE," a sign of both solidarity and protest.

"I got the idea from watching NFL games at the time," OSU offensive lineman Jeff Uhlenhake said. "Chicago Bears quarterback Jim McMahon used to wear a headband with (then commissioner) Pete Rozelle's name on it whenever the league did something McMahon didn't like. He got in trouble for it, but he made a statement. That's what we wanted to do. We wanted to say something about the way we felt the whole thing was handled."

Bruce, who was pacing back and forth nearby, did a double take. "I'd gone out near the middle of the field for the captains' toss and I looked back at the rest of the team," he said. "For some reason, they had all come out to the middle of the field with their helmets on. I had never seen them line up like that and I wondered what the devil they were doing. All of sudden, I turned around and their helmets were off and I saw something around their heads. I thought, 'My God! We don't do that here! We don't have headbands on. We don't do that!'

"As I looked back again, I saw what the headbands had written on them, and I thought, 'Oh, my God! I can't say anything now.' So I acted like I didn't see it. But I'll tell you something right now and I couldn't say then. Those headbands were pretty nice."

In the end, emotion carried the day. Michigan jumped out to an early 13–0 lead, but the Buckeyes came storming back to claim a 23–20 victory and then hoisted their fallen head coach on their shoulders in triumph. Then—and only then—did Bruce allow himself a public display of emotion, thrusting his fist into the air several times in defiant jubilation.

Bruce left Ohio State and assumed other coaching jobs, but his heart really never left Columbus. The now-octogenarian Bruce remains his fiery, opinionated self as a radio analyst during football season and a goodwill ambassador for the Buckeyes year-round.

But while the body is a little slower and the voice a little shakier, the memory of Earle Bruce for most Ohio State fans is the one of the determined little man in a fedora and charcoal suit—knowing he had only one more game to coach—defiantly stalking the sideline at Michigan and willing his team to win.

As the old saying goes, "Winners don't whine; they roar." Earle Bruce is roaring still.

ARTHUR (ART) SCHLICHTER

OSU QUARTERBACK 1978—1981

NICKNAME: King Arthur

HOMETOWN: Bloomingburg, Ohio

HEIGHT: 6 ft 3 in   **WEIGHT:** 208 lb

NFL DRAFT: 1982, Baltimore Colts

Art Schlichter (right) and his wide receiver Doug "White Lightning" Donley.

*H*e has been largely reduced to a grotesque caricature, condemned and ridiculed because of a gambling addiction that cost him his professional career, most of his friends, and untold millions of dollars. The list of felonies, frauds, and forgeries committed to fuel his addiction is longer than that of most career criminals, and he has paid a heavy price for his scams and swindles with lengthy prison terms.

Yet the story of Art Schlichter cannot be told—the entire story, at least—without mentioning the God-given talent and improvisational artistry he had for the quarterback position during his four years at Ohio State. More than three decades before Johnny Football, there was King Arthur, a transformative quarterback who played the position with guts and guile. He possessed a cannon of an arm that could find blanketed receivers with pinpoint accuracy, and he had the elusiveness of an escape artist, able to evade oncoming pass-rushers in the blink of an eye. In other words, equal parts Howitzer and Houdini.

"Art was the best high school quarterback I've ever seen, and I've seen a lot of them," said George Chaump, a longtime high school head coach in Pennsylvania as well as Schlichter's quarterback coach at Ohio State. "Everybody would just shake their heads when they saw what that kid could do. Running, throwing, there wasn't anything he couldn't do. There was no question in my mind that he was going to be a star."

But did Schlichter fall victim to his own seemingly endless potential? Was he pushed too far too fast by an overbearing father and an aging head coach desperate to keep up with a game that was threatening to pass him by?

Arthur Ernest Schlichter was born April 25, 1960, the youngest of three children to a farming family just outside Washington Court House, Ohio. His mother Mila was beautiful inside and out, a soft-spoken, nurturing woman who was perfectly content to remain in the background. Meanwhile, his father Max was an ego-driven blowhard who pushed young Art mercilessly, dreaming for his son the athletic stardom he was never able to achieve.

Meanwhile, Woody Hayes had recruited countless athletic quarterbacks during his long tenure with the Buckeyes, but those players were usually more adept at running the ball. After all, the coach was famous for his saying, "Three things can happen when you throw the ball and two of them are bad." As a result, some of the best quarterbacks in the Hayes era before 1978 were little more than option-style players whose chief duty was to hand off to a stable of running backs. Even three-year starters such as Rex Kern and Cornelius Greene became known more for their slashing running styles than the strength of their arms.

But when Hayes scouted Schlichter at Miami Trace High School, tucked between two Fayette County cornfields about forty miles southwest of Columbus, the old coach had to be thinking of his own future. Schlichter set records by the truckload in high school as his team piled up victory after victory. And he was a natural-born athlete, running track and leading the Panthers to the state championship game in basketball.

Football was his true calling, though, and some of his early exploits were legendary. He won the state Punt, Pass and Kick competition, and could throw a football eighty yards in the air—fifty from the seat of his pants. Nearly every major college coach from coast to coast mapped their way to the Schlichter farm, including Bo Schembechler of Michigan and Joe Paterno of Penn State. But he had grown up in the shadow of Ohio Stadium and eventually followed his heart to Ohio State.

Schlichter admitted he had a lot of trepidation as he embarked upon his first fall training camp at Ohio State. "Don't get me wrong—I wanted to be there. It was a dream come true to be able to play for Woody Hayes," he said. "But the one thing I remember is driving away from home on the day fall camp started. I cried my eyes out. I remember thinking, 'Wow, my life's getting ready to change. I've got to be a man now.' I was going from being a big fish in a little pond, and there are qualities of that kind of life that are nice."

Things didn't get much better when he got to Columbus. He had his wisdom teeth pulled during the first week of practice, and said, "I was sick as a dog on picture day." By the second week of camp, he had recovered and was working exclusively with the first-team offense, something that didn't exactly sit well with some of his teammates, especially the ones who were close friends with the incumbent starting quarterback, senior co-captain Rod Gerald.

"Some of the older guys let it be known that they weren't too crazy about me coming in and taking Rod's job," Art said. "They weren't very excited about that, and looking back I don't blame them. Older guys don't want to see a younger guy playing because it's their time. They want to be the focus. It was a bold move on Woody's part to try and change things, but it was coming at the expense of a senior and a pretty popular one."

However, while several of the upperclassmen spurned the rookie quarterback, Schlichter found an unlikely ally in Gerald. Well-suited to run the kind of option attack the Buckeyes had been using for more than a decade, Gerald started as a sophomore in 1976 and led Ohio State to a 9-2-1 record, a Big Ten co-championship, and an Orange Bowl victory over Colorado. The following year, the Buckeyes captured another conference co-title, their only two regular-season losses coming by a combined nine points, and Gerald was the first team All-Big Ten quarterback.

"No one would have blamed him for being upset, but that wasn't Rod," Art said. "He treated me better than anyone else on the team did, and I have the utmost respect for him for that. He was a team guy. Rod was all about the team. He saw that I had a lot of potential and that they were going to play me. If he ever had any animosity toward me, he never showed it. When some of the other guys were shunning me, he treated me with a lot of respect. He helped me when he could and I wanted to see him succeed. He helped me get better."

Schlichter slowly won over his older teammates, and trotted out onto the Ohio Stadium field for the 1978 season opener against Penn State. Unfortunately, the battle-tested Nittany Lions were more than ready for the freshman phenom. They pressured and pummeled Schlichter mercilessly, coming away with a 19–0 victory that really wasn't as close as the final score might indicate. Art managed to complete only twelve of twenty-six passes for 182 yards to go along with five interceptions, a single-game school record that still stands. Making matters worse, the Buckeyes also fumbled the ball away three times—one by Schlichter—giving Penn State eight turnovers for the game.

"We just weren't ready to be a passing team," Art said. "It was nobody's fault and it was everybody's fault. We didn't protect very well, and I was probably guilty of holding the ball too long. And we were playing against some great players. We had guys who were great linemen, but they were used to just coming off the ball and making holes for the running game. They weren't ready to pass protect yet. Nothing against them—we just weren't ready to be a passing team."

Schlichter never fully recovered from the beating he sustained dur-

> "Art could read you like you had a teleprompter sticking out of your skull advertising your thoughts. He read your face, your body language, the double helix of your DNA."
> —*Sarah Hawley,* Art Schlichter's book publicist

ing his debut, and neither did the Buckeyes. Their string of six consecutive Big Ten championships came to an end as did the coaching career of Hayes, fired the day after he slugged an opposing player toward the end of the team's 17–15 Gator Bowl loss to Clemson.

Schlichter managed to rebound from that tough first year, leading the Buckeyes to within a whisker of the 1979 national championship the following season, and he finished his collegiate career as the top passer in Ohio State history with 7,547 yards (still a school record) and fifty touchdowns. He was All-Conference as a sophomore and a senior as well as Big Ten Player of the Year in 1981. He also finished third in the Heisman Trophy voting as a sophomore and fourth as a senior.

In the spring of 1982, he became a first-round NFL draft selection of the Baltimore Colts, but soon afterward, Schlichter's gambling addiction came to light and then NFL commissioner Pete Rozelle suspended him from the league—twice. He played briefly in the Canadian Football League and Arena Football League before being reinstated by the NFL. Art caught on with the Buffalo Bills but was waived when the Bills signed future Hall of Famer Jim Kelly shortly after the United States Football League folded. Schlichter never played professional football again.

As his gambling addiction took over his life, the memory of Schlichter's swashbuckling days as a quarterback faded while friends and fans tried to make sense of why someone so gifted could throw it all away. Psychologists and pundits alike have weighed in on possible causes, but Art's old position coach has always believed he has a clue as to the answer.

"I've thought about it a lot over the years," Chaump said. "I don't think I've ever seen anyone so psychologically defeated as I saw Art after that first game against Penn State. After that, I think we threw the ball maybe five or six times a game, and that's not what Art came to Ohio State to do.

"To say the least, it was very frustrating for him, and I have always wondered if what happened to Art that day had anything to do with the difficulties he has had in life. That's always bothered me, and it continues to bother me to this day."

Art's Achilles Heel was gambling, a pastime that's led to a lengthy prison sentence.

JOHN
FRANK

OSU TIGHT END 1980–1983

HOMETOWN: Mount Lebanon, Pennsylvania

HEIGHT: 6 ft 3 in   **WEIGHT:** 226 lb

NFL DRAFT: 1984, San Fransisco 49ers

89

John Frank became the all-time leading receiver among tight ends in OSU history.

John Frank seemed the very embodiment of Clark Kent. He was 6-foot-3 and 225 pounds, although with his soft-spoken, studious manner, it seemed that he wouldn't hurt a fly, a bespectacled two-time Academic All-American more intent upon becoming a doctor than playing football. But when he changed into the Scarlet and Gray of an Ohio State football player, he was transformed into intensity personified, a player with a warrior-like mentality willing to sacrifice himself for the good of the team.

"I wish I could have given his intensity to every athlete I coached," said Earle Bruce, who was head coach for the Buckeyes during Frank's entire college career from 1980–1983. "He was really something after he caught the ball. He just didn't know how to give up. If he hit you and got his feet moving, he'd take you off the planet."

John E. Frank was born April 17, 1962, in suburban Pittsburgh, the second oldest of Alan and Barbara Frank's four children and the couple's only son. Like most youngsters growing up in and around the Steel City in the late 1960s and early 1970s, John was a born-and-bred Steelers fan and played football every day around his Mount Lebanon neighborhood.

At the age of ten, John wanted to try out for a team in the local Pop Warner youth league. At first, his parents balked. Alan was a tough inner-city Jewish kid who had been an outstanding basketball and baseball player as a youngster, even earning a contract offer from the Pittsburgh Pirates. But his parents had forbidden him from playing organized football, telling him to concentrate on more mundane pursuits, such as studying hard and getting a good job. Alan heeded their advice, working as a mechanical engineer while attending night classes at Duquesne Law School, eventually becoming a well-known and successful attorney.

Once John exhibited an interest in playing football, however, Alan embarked upon a frenetic campaign to turn his pudgy, pre-pubescent boy into a gridiron star. John was put on a strength and conditioning program to shed his baby fat. He went through countless pass-catching drills—catching on the run, catching dry footballs, catching wet footballs, catching overinflated balls, catching underinflated balls, catching while looking into the sun, catching in the lengthening shadows of dusk. Alan hired a college track coach from nearby Carnegie-Mellon to improve John's running ability, and college and professional offensive line coaches tutored the youngster in blocking techniques.

For several summers, while his friends were playing other sports or hanging out at the local swimming pool, John was eating, sleeping, and living football. By the time John reached high school age, his parents had separated, but his father continued to insist his son continue his training.

Although Alan was no longer living with the family, "He would show up every morning to make sure I ate a big breakfast, so I'd grow up strong," John said. His father would come by the house on weekday evenings to help John with his studies, and then on weekends go over film of his son's football performance the night before. Always afraid to say anything in fear of letting his father down, John went along with anything his father wanted him to do. That included interests away from football: motorcycles, skiing, and working on cars. Father and son even seemed to share the same taste in music.

"His advice always led to success," John said. "Everything he said was so right. I couldn't argue. I didn't want to disappoint him. I always felt we were working toward a common goal. It was a perfect relationship."

The hard work paid off in a host of scholarship offers, both for academics and athletics, and John's hometown university seemed to be the favorite to land his services.

"Everyone, including myself, thought he was going to the University of Pittsburgh," Bruce said. "I recruited that area of western Pennsylvania along with assistant coach Steve Szabo, and Steve was tenacious in pursuing John. But I finally told Steve, 'Get off him. You're wasting your time. He's going to Pitt.' That was one time I was glad one of my assistants didn't listen to me."

Ohio State had everything John was looking for in a university—a major football program, an outstanding medical school, and a campus close enough that his parents could come to his games but far enough away that he could finally strike out on his own. He became a success both on the field and in the classroom, immersing himself into football as much as his pre-med workload. He carried a 3.90 grade-point average and was a first-team Academic All-American as a junior and senior after being a second-team pick as a sophomore. One of his research papers was even published in a medical journal between his junior and senior years.

But he excelled even more on the football field. Over the course of his OSU career, John became the all-time leading receiver among tight ends in school history and turned in some of the most memorable individual performances of his era.

During the second game of the 1983 season, a contest against second-ranked Oklahoma, John established career highs with seven catches for 108 yards and two touchdowns during the Buckeyes' 24–14 upset victory in Norman. The performance was even more remarkable given the circumstances.

Playing conditions for the September 17 contest were brutal. Each team woke up that mid-September Saturday morning to unseasonable heat and humidity as temperatures rose into the low nineties by kickoff. It was reportedly 135 degrees on the stadium's artificial surface midway through the contest and medical staffs on both sidelines were scurrying for ways to keep the players hydrated.

It was especially difficult for John and became even more so as the game wore on. The Ohio State tight end was observing the Jewish holiday of Yom Kippur and had abstained from eating or drinking for two days. He seemed almost in a daze as the team made the trip from its hotel to the stadium, prompting several teammates to ask if he felt well enough to play. John simply glared at them. He seemed to know that he was going to play a big role in the outcome that afternoon and already had his game face on.

"That tight end," Oklahoma head coach Barry Switzer told reporters after the game. "He's just slow enough that he's open all the time."

After the game, an exhausted and dehydrated Frank lay on a training table, taking fluids intravenously in both arms. He had to be helped to team bus and then onto the charter flight back to Columbus but through it all wore the smile of a champion.

Asked years later about fasting before the game and playing at less than 100 percent efficiency body-wise, Frank replied, "I didn't care. None of us cared. We literally exploded off that bus and I don't think Oklahoma knows to this day what hit them."

It was the kind of performance that endeared Frank to his teammates, who voted him Ohio State's Most Valuable Player during his senior season. "John was an outstanding student and he brought that same work ethic to the way he studied film," OSU All-American lineman Jim Lachey said. "He always knew the game plan like the back of his hand, and once the whistle blew, he was ready for action. That

was his mentality. He was a warrior. He was always front and center. He had a lot of athletic ability, but he also got things done with intensity and sheer willpower."

Frank went on to a successful National Football League career with the San Francisco 49ers, winning two Super Bowl championships in only five seasons. But his world had begun to unravel. For the first time in his life, he was having difficulty in the classroom as he struggled with offseason studies back at Ohio State while a string of injuries caused him to second-guess his football career.

Nothing had prepared John for what happened in early 1986, however, when his father was indicted on charges of income tax evasion, forgery, and theft stemming from bank loans of $500,000 secured by John, purportedly to help his father start a vending-machine leasing company. Alan briefly fled the country but later returned and was eventually acquitted of the forgery and theft charges. But he was convicted of tax evasion and unlawful flight with John forced to testify for the prosecution at the tax-evasion trial. In August of 1988, Alan Frank was sentenced to six years in federal prison.

John was devastated, but through therapy and introspection, the inner strength on which he had relied so often as a football player served him well. "For many years, I desensitized myself," he said. "I kept pushing my feelings back and back, repressing any sort of human emotion, especially when I saw an injury. You get into a frame of mind; it's the whole macho thing. Football players carry this further than the average male. Who draws the distinction between the person you are on the field and the one you are off it? And does anybody really care who you are when the game's over?"

Frank returned to Ohio State and finished his medical degree work in 1992 and then spent six years in residency at Loyola University in Chicago. After a year and a half spent traveling through Europe—with some volunteer and professorial work mixed in—he returned to Loyola for additional training in the field of cosmetic and facial plastic surgery. Current-

ly, he is a board certified otolaryngologist in New York City with his own clinic that specializes in surgical hair transplantation.

Married with two young children, John also continues to stoke his competitive fires as a member of the Israeli bobsled team he helped co-found in 2002. The squad has performed well in competitions worldwide and just missed qualifying for the XX Winter Olympiad in Torino, Italy.

"I guess I would describe myself as a Type-A personality. I guess I have a little Woody Hayes in me," John said. "I've done everything with a lot of intensity, and that was particularly true in football. I gave it all I had every play because I never wanted to let the team down."

And he never did.

KEITH BYARS

NICKNAME: Bramble

HOMETOWN: Dayton, Ohio

HEIGHT: 6 ft 2 in   **WEIGHT:** 245 lb

ALL–AMERICAN: 1984

NFL DRAFT: 1986, Philadelphia Eagles

41

Keith was a state champion in both high school track and basketball.

Ohio State football fans can mark their eras with simple pieces of clothing. For a certain generation, a black baseball cap and a pair of horn-rimmed glasses signifies Big Ten titles, Heisman Trophy wins, and a healthy dislike for "That School Up North." For others, a white dress shirt worn under a scarlet sweater vest conjures memories of a most improbable march to the national championship.

And then there is a size-15 shoe with a scarlet Nike swoosh tumbling end over end near midfield at Ohio Stadium during a 1984 game against Illinois. It was perhaps the most famous footwear since a prince combed the countryside looking for the owner of a glass slipper.

"There aren't many days that go by when I'm not reminded about that shoe," said Keith Byars, who kicked it off in mid-stride during a touchdown gallop that fueled a comeback victory for the Buckeyes that mid-October afternoon in the Horseshoe. "There must have been more than a hundred thousand people in the stadium that day because that's how many I've met who swear they were there."

It was the signature run of an outstanding collegiate career at Ohio State for Byars, the youngest of three sons born to Reginald and Margaret Byars. Keith Alan Byars arrived October 14, 1963, with a passion for food and a body with the unique capacity for taking that fuel and transforming it into a blend of power and speed. By the time he arrived at Roth High School in Dayton, Keith had already become a massive young man, standing 6-feet-2 inches tall and weighing 220 pounds. He never saw the inside of a weight room until late in his teens, and no one in his family was particularly large, but Keith was a mountain of a young man, rock solid from his 19-inch neck to his 18-inch calves.

"I was just born big, I guess," he said. Big enough that one coach observed, "He must put tree trunks in his pant legs," while another said after his team was assaulted by the Byars juggernaut, "They've got a lot of weapons in their arsenal. As a matter of fact, they've got a whole arsenal in one uniform."

Keith wasn't only big; he was fast. Sneaky fast with a short, almost stutter-step gait that lulled opposing players into thinking they could easily catch him until he got farther and farther from view after shifting into high gear. He inherited his speed from his father, a foreclosure officer for the county treasurer's office during the day, an associate minister at the Apostolic Tabernacle Church on weekends, and an urban legend on the softball diamond who could circle the bases in the blink of an eye.

Following a high school career that included two state championships in basketball and a state track title as a member of the Roth 4x100 relay team, Keith was ready to take the next step toward college stardom. "I want to say it was an easy decision to come to Ohio State because when I was a young boy, I watched all of the games on TV and I knew I wanted to play for Woody Hayes," he said. "But once I grew up, and all the schools in the country started to recruit me, it was easy for me to get confused."

Like any red-blooded son of Ohio, Keith grew up hating Michigan with a passion, but repeated overtures from head coach Bo Schembechler led to an official visit to Ann Arbor—a visit that didn't go as either Byars or Schembechler envisioned.

"I got up there and they gave me so much food," Keith said. "They gave me food I'd never even heard of. Oysters, Porterhouse steak...I didn't know what that was. I'd been to Ponderosa and seen T-bones, but a Porterhouse? They said it was the biggest steak, so I took it. And shrimp cocktail. I said, 'It's not even cooked. Shouldn't it be boiled or something?' But I shoveled it all in. Then, as Bo is taking me back to the hotel, I said, 'Coach, you've got to speed it up.' But he's explaining this and explaining that, and I said, 'No, Coach, you've *got* to speed it up.'

"Well, he'd just pulled into the parking lot—in his brand new car—and there came all that food. I finally looked up at him and said, 'You still want me to come here?'"

Schembechler had lost that new-car smell and a top running back prospect all in the same night.

When he joined the Buckeyes as a freshman for the 1982 season, Byars moved into a crowded backfield that featured veterans Tim Spencer and Jimmy Gayle at tailback, and Keith carried only four times for 17 yards. But with Spencer and Gayle gone the following season due to graduation, Keith had a breakout year that included 1,199 yards and twenty touchdowns, a campaign punctuated by a 99-yard kickoff return for a touchdown during a 28–23 win over Pittsburgh in the Fiesta Bowl.

And still the best was yet to come. Keith set himself up as a

The Fighting Illini jumped out to a seemingly insurmountable 24–0 lead early in the second quarter before Ohio State finally began to show signs of life. Byars ran for a 16-yard touchdown and quarterback Mike Tomczak threw a touchdown pass to freshman receiver Cris Carter to get the Buckeyes back in the game, then Byars blasted into the end zone from four yards away to make it 24–21 just before halftime. As television cameras showed the OSU bench fol-

> "I remember a play where Byars picked a wild pass out of the hands of an opposing cornerback that was already running for a pick-six. I've never seen anything like it. The cornerback was literally in the middle of embracing the ball and Byars just went 'Wooop, I'll take that...'"
> —*Leo Pizzini*, analyst for Philadelphia

Heisman Trophy candidate early during the 1984 season, averaging more than 160 yards per game during his first five games. Then, on October 13, the Buckeyes hosted defending Big Ten champion Illinois at Ohio Stadium.

lowing the score, Byars suddenly turned around, faced the camera, and with a huge smile declared, "We're coming back!"

The Buckeyes eventually took the lead and were clinging to a 28–27 advantage midway through the third quarter when thunder stuck. Byars burst through the line of scrimmage on a draw play and quickly cut toward the right sideline. He picked up downfield blocks from Carter and fellow receiver Jamie Holland, then began to pull away from two final would-be tackles nipping at his heels. All the Illinois defenders could catch was Byars's left shoe, which had come off about midfield. The OSU tailback never broke stride, finishing the 67-yard romp as the crowd inside the Horseshoe came unglued.

"My mom always told me to make sure you don't have any holes in your socks, and I'm glad I listened to her," Keith said with a smile. "That play was just a simple draw play. I remember cutting to the right and turning upfield, and as soon as I was getting ready to run up toward the end zone, I felt my shoe coming loose. So I just kicked it off and turned it into high gear. I just remember thinking, 'Get to the end zone before anyone steps on your foot,' and I ran faster than I ever ran in my life. I felt like I was running on a cloud. I still don't know how that shoe came off because the shoestring was still tied tightly after they handed it back to me."

Tomczak just sat back and marveled at how his teammate had singlehandedly altered the course of the game. "I was the one who ran over and picked up the shoe," the OSU quarterback said. "It was like being a member of Keith's pit crew."

The shoeless jaunt was the fourth touchdown run during the afternoon for Byars, who wound up establishing new school records with 274 yards and five touchdowns in the eventual 45–38 victory. It was the seminal game during a season in which Byars finished with 1,764 yards and twenty-two touchdowns. Still, it wasn't good enough to wrest the Heisman Trophy away from Boston College quarterback Doug Flutie, who cemented his candidacy by heaving a last-second touchdown pass during a thrilling 47–45 victory against the defending national champion Miami Hurricanes, a game televised to a nationwide audience the day after Thanksgiving.

Despite Flutie's runaway win, there was no question in the mind

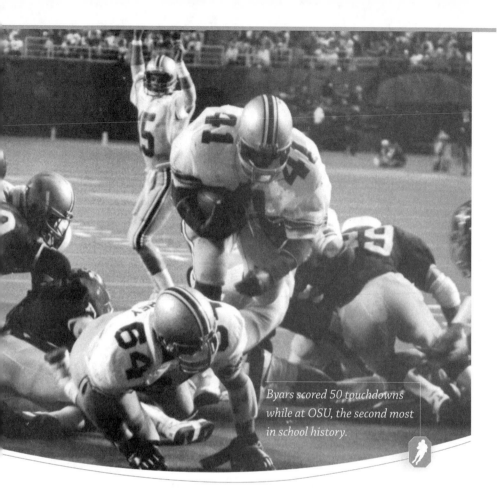

Byars scored 50 touchdowns while at OSU, the second most in school history.

of Keith's coach as to who should have won the Heisman. "I will always believe the TV people wanted Flutie to win it because they replayed that Hail Mary pass over and over again until the Heisman ceremony," Earle Bruce said. "They never replayed Keith's shoeless run against Illinois."

For Byars's part, he was disappointed but good-natured about it. "Everybody knows who won it," he said. "It's just that my trophy is sitting in Doug Flutie's living room. When we both played in the NFL, I used to ask him, 'Hey, Flutie, how's my trophy doing?' I should have won it, but things don't always work out the way you want them to."

Those words were never more prophetic. Byars entered his senior season as the prohibitive favorite to win the 1986 Heisman, but during a preseason practice session he suffered a broken bone in his right foot. He missed the first five games of the 1985 season and then reinjured the foot in his second game back. Byars attempted another comeback in the team's Citrus Bowl win over Brigham Young University, but the injury flared up again on the Buckeyes' second offensive series of the game.

Despite losing almost his entire senior season, Byars finished his Ohio State career with 4,369 total yards, 3,200 rushing yards and fifty touchdowns. Those numbers were good enough for National Football League scouts, and the Philadelphia Eagles made him the tenth overall selection in the 1986 draft. He went on to play fullback and tight end for four different teams over the span of thirteen seasons, earning selection to the Pro Bowl in 1993 when he was with the Miami Dolphins and playing in Super Bowl XXXI with the New England Patriots. He became one of the game's most versatile players during his career, finishing with 3,109 yards and twenty-three touchdowns on the ground as well as 610 recep-

tions for 5,661 yards and thirty-one TDs. He also completed six passes during his career with all six going for touchdowns.

Since his playing days ended, Byars has dabbled in a number of activities, including a brief stint as a high school coach in Florida and serving as a football analyst on radio and television. Still, he knows he will always be remembered for the afternoon during which he threw a shoe like a racehorse galloping toward the finish line.

"Only to the day I die will I hear about that, and that's okay with me," Keith said. "If you're going to be remembered, it's nice to know that it's something that brings a smile to people's faces. That makes you feel pretty good."

CHRIS
SPIELMAN

OSU LINEBACKER 1984–1987

NICKNAME: Spiels

HOMETOWN: Canton, Ohio

HEIGHT: 6 ft 0 in **WEIGHT:** 247 lb

ALL–AMERICAN: 1986, 1987

NFL DRAFT: 1988, Detroit Lions

Chris went to the Pro Bowl four times and was an All-Pro three times.

If only one word could be used to describe Chris Spielman, the word would be intensity.

Charles Christopher Spielman exploded onto the scene October 11, 1965, appropriately enough in the shadow of the Pro Football Hall of Fame in Canton, Ohio, and he has been a sort of perpetual motion machine ever since. Whether it has been starring on the football field at the high school, college, and professional levels or embracing the fight against breast cancer, the disease that ultimately claimed his wife, Spielman has always jumped headlong into any endeavor.

Fellow Ohio State linebacker Derek Isaman summed up Spielman succinctly when he said, "Chris was one tough son of a bitch. He slept and ate OSU football, and nobody matched his determination, hard work and effort."

That mentality began as a youngster when Chris got his first football helmet for Christmas at the age of five. "My grandma came over to the house and said, 'Hey, Chris, you wanna play some football?' I tackled her right there in the living room. I mean, I took her out," Spielman said. "She bounced right up, though. You could tell she was a Spielman."

Chris and his older brother Rick often staged impromptu football battles in the family home, shaking it from foundation to rafters. By the time Chris was 12, the parents of the other boys in their peewee football league tried to have him banned from the league. He was breaking too many helmets not to mention arms, legs, and collarbones. He was obsessively competitive no matter what the activity.

"Electric football? I'm sure I wasn't the only kid who would get frustrated," Spielman said. "But I'm positive that not everybody would smash the game or just throw the players away because they were uncoachable. I was a coach's son, and from an early age, I loved the game and studied the game so that I could be the best I could be."

It was study time well-spent as Chris starred in high school at the same Massillon High School that produced such legendary players as Harry Stuhldreher, who became one of the famed "Four Horsemen" at Notre Dame, as well as Ohio State coaches Paul Brown and Earle

Bruce and longtime Baldwin-Wallace coach Lee Tressel. Spielman keyed countless victories for the Tigers during his high school career and won state player of the year honors during his senior season in 1983. He was also named winner of the Dial Award, symbolic of the national high school scholar-athlete of that year, and became one of the select few athletes honored with his likeness on the front of a Wheaties cereal box.

When it came time for him to select a college, however, Chris was torn between archrivals Ohio State and Michigan. He agonized over choosing to play his college football for Michigan head coach Bo Schembechler, with whom he had formed a close bond, or Bruce, who shared a Massillon Tigers background. In the end, Chris locked himself in his bedroom to make the decision. After agonizing for several hours, he emerged and told his father, Sonny, he had finally made up his mind.

"Michigan!" the youngster exclaimed. "I'm going to Michigan!"

Sonny Spielman looked the youngster squarely in the eye and replied, "It's great that you've made a decision, Son. Now get back in that room and make the right one."

That was the genesis of a storied four-year career for the undersized linebacker who bristled anytime someone suggested he was an overachiever. "A lot of stuff doesn't bother me," Chris said, "but that's one thing that does. Overachiever? I've heard that a million times. Maybe I do bring it on myself, but if I hadn't done the extras, maybe I wouldn't be where I am."

Spielman brought his special brand of intensity with him to Ohio State and immediately won a starting job at inside linebacker, a rarity for a true freshman. But he had aggravated an ankle sprain just before the 1984 season opener against Oregon State, and defensive coordinator Bob Tucker determined the youngster wasn't physically ready to play come game day. It was going to be the first organized football game in Spielman's life that he would not start, and he was beside himself. He paced back and forth along the sideline throughout the first half, staying within earshot of

Bruce. "I was like a caged animal," Chris said. "I was pawing, I was growling. I just remember saying, 'Put me in. You've gotta put me in. This is why you recruited me! I've gotta be in there!'"

At halftime, Bruce sought out Tucker in the locker room. "Why isn't Spielman playing?" the head coach asked. "He's just a freshman.

on twenty or twenty-five tackles a game. He was always at the ball."

Spielman topped off his freshman season with nine tackles in the team's 21–6 victory over Michigan, a win that gave Ohio State the Big Ten championship and sent them to the Rose Bowl, where the team lost a narrow 20–17 decision to the University of Southern California.

"Spielman takes the stairs sideways because it improves his lateral mobility. He routinely performs pass-rushing techniques on garbage cans. He turns the heat on high in his truck on a hot summer day as a personal test. Sometimes he prepares for a game by inhaling smelling salts."
—*Associated Press,* 1996

He isn't ready," Tucker replied. Bruce narrowed his eyes and snorted, "He's ready."

"And then all he did was go out and make the first ten tackles (of the second half)," Bruce said. "He played a heckuva game and we won. The thing I remember about Chris in that game—in every game, every play—he gave great effort. His game was about making tackles. It wasn't unusual for him to be in

The promise of the following season was dashed before it began when running back Keith Byars, who had finished second in the 1984 Heisman Trophy balloting, broke a bone in his right foot during preseason practice and was lost for nearly the entire season. The Buckeyes managed to press on without their offensive star but were having uncharacteristic problems on defense when top-ranked Iowa brought its high-octane offense to Columbus for a November 2 date with the Buckeyes. Bruce insisted that his talented team had yet to play its best game, but his assertions were beginning to fall upon deaf ears.

On the morning before the game, *Columbus Citizen-Journal* columnist Burt Graeff wrote what most OSU fans had been thinking, opining that the Buckeyes would be fortunate to hold Iowa's Heisman Trophy candidate Chuck Long to under 1,000 yards. As Spielman would later put it, "The motivational factor was that we were the underdogs in Ohio Stadium. If somebody wants to fight me in my own back yard, he had better bring an army with him and kill me if he wants to win."

Spielman was a one-man wrecking crew against the Hawkeyes, recording nineteen tackles and two interceptions as the Buckeyes celebrated a 22–13 upset victory. It was the kind of no-frills, workmanlike performance in which Spielman excelled during his college career. He was a self-described hermit who had simple goals, yet was the kind of inspirational leader who spurred others to excellence.

"My goals were going to school, playing football, and maybe going to the NFL later," Chris said. "Let me put it this way: They didn't let me host many recruits because they didn't want them hosted by a hermit." That wasn't always the case, however. John Kacherski, a linebacker prospect from Long Island, New York, was much in demand during the 1987 recruiting season, and he was torn between several schools until he visited Columbus.

"The player who cemented my decision to choose Ohio State was Chris Spielman," Kacherski said. "Unlike other recruiting visits, where recruits were wined and dined and shown campus nightlife, Chris took me back to his apartment to eat pizza and watch game film. Right then and there, I began to understand that football at Ohio State was more than just a game—it was a way of life."

What little spare time Chris did find away from football, he spent with his high school sweetheart, Stefanie Belcher. They first met at a school hangout in Massillon when he was seventeen and she was two years younger. Stefanie was dancing to a slow song with the quarterback from another school when Chris simply cut in. Asked years later how he managed to separate his future wife from the grasp of the other young man, Chris would only smile and mumble something about knowing how to handle opposing quarterbacks.

Spielman went on to finish his OSU career with back-to-back All-America honors, and in 1987 earned the Lombardi Award as college football's best lineman or linebacker. His senior season also included a victory over Michigan in Bruce's emotional final game as head coach as well as a team-leading 205 tackles, the second-highest single-season total in program history.

After college, Spielman was a first-round selection in the 1988 NFL draft, joining the Detroit Lions. He anchored the Lions' defense for eight years, earning four Pro Bowl honors, and leading the team in tackles every season he played in Detroit. In 1996, he moved on to the Buffalo Bills and established a team record with 206 tackles that season. He missed the last half of the 1997 season because of a neck injury that required delicate spinal surgery, then sat out the entire 1998 campaign to support his wife during her initial bout with breast cancer. Spielman tried a comeback with the Cleveland Browns in 1999, but announced his retirement with no regrets after sustaining another neck injury in the preseason.

Since that time, he spends his autumns as a color analyst for college football telecasts on ESPN and the rest of his time involved in charity work, most notably the Stefanie Spielman Fund for Breast Cancer Research, which has raised more than $11 million since 1999 for the fight against breast cancer. Stefanie passed away in 2009 following a brave eleven-year battle against the illness, a fight Chris says changed his life both literally and figuratively.

"I learned that I can't control everything—that I can't out-prepare, outwork, out-lift, or outrun cancer," he said. "That's hard for a competitive guy, who basically thought that success was based solely on effort and toughness and strength and endurance. It's not. There are some things you cannot control, so you

Chris loved his wife Stefanie way more than he loved football. And he loved football with his entire being.

have to humble yourself and realize there is meaning and purpose that you are not going to get to dictate. Now, it's your job to recognize and seize on that opportunity, which essentially I did—and we did—but it is humbling to learn that.

"I've had two great loves in my life. One was my love for my wife Stefanie. The other was my passion for my football career. But my love for Stef vastly trumped the other."

The way Chris supported Stefanie throughout her long battle, and the way he has persevered as the father of the couple's four children, has earned Spielman an even larger appreciation among fans who already remember him as a rough-and-tumble player ever-willing to sacrifice his body and spirit for the greater good.

Is there any better way for a man to be remembered?

CRIS
CARTER

OSU WIDE RECEIVER 1984–1986

NICKNAME: CC

HOMETOWN: Troy, Ohio

HEIGHT: 6 ft 3 in   WEIGHT: 208 lb

ALL–AMERICAN: 1986

NFL DRAFT: 1987, Philadelphia Eagles

Even though he didn't play as a senior, Carter held the OSU school record for receptions then, with 168.

A teammate once referred to Cris Carter as the most talented player he had ever played with or against. Another called Carter the biggest asshole he had ever encountered inside a locker room. Many of the same teammates that marveled at his skills one minute wanted to rip his throat out the next. Ask any number of people to describe Carter and chances are you'll get answers that span the spectrum from cocky and selfish to the most gifted receiver ever to catch a football.

The perceived dichotomy of Carter's personality first became evident during his mercurial career at Ohio State. He exploded onto the stage as a freshman with a record-setting performance in the Rose Bowl, only to be kicked off the team just before his senior season, a suspension that played no small role in getting head coach Earle Bruce fired after nine seasons.

There were bouts with alcohol and substance abuse, as well as lingering periods of self-doubt for Carter, who always wondered whether he could live up to the substantial legacy of his older brother,

Butch, a star basketball player at Indiana University who went on to a lengthy playing and coaching career in the National Basketball Association. When the going got rough, however, Cris would retreat inside himself to battle his own demons, unapologetic for any toes he had stepped on, friendships he had torched, or careers he had ruined... that is, until recently.

During his August 4, 2013, acceptance speech for induction into the Pro Football Hall of Fame, a misty-eyed Carter looked out over the crowd at Fawcett Stadium and declared, "To all the Buckeye fans, from the bottom of my heart, I sincerely apologize for signing with a sports agent and losing my eligibility my senior year. That's the only regret I have in my athletic career, that I couldn't play for the Buckeyes as a senior. Buckeye fans, Cris Carter says, 'I'm sorry.'"

It was perhaps the symbolic removal of a chip on his shoulder carried by young Graduel Christopher Darin Carter since being born November 25, 1965, in Troy, Ohio, the same sleepy Dayton suburb that had produced Ohio State fullback Bob

Only three NFL wide receivers have more TDs than Carter; Jerry Rice (208), Randy Moss (157) and Terrell Owens (156).

Ferguson. But while Ferguson went from a stable family environment to become a record-setting running back at the local high school, Troy held no promise for Carter's mother, Joyce, a single mother with seven children. Joyce had dropped out of high school to begin raising a family, and when a job opportunity presented itself, she moved her family to Middletown, a sprawling community tucked away in the rolling hills of the southwestern part of the state.

Cris was just seven when the family moved into a tiny four-bedroom unit at People's Place Apartments, a housing complex near Douglas Park at the intersection of Lafayette Avenue and Minnesota Street. "It was the projects," Cris said. "I came from the bricks, man. I came from the projects and a lot of people don't make it out of there. But I had some great role models. My mom and my brothers—great role models. I know where I came from, and I never take that for granted."

Each of his three older brothers—Clarence, George, and John—had played college basketball, but the most famous was Clarence, who went by the nickname of Butch. "He was my hero," Cris said. "He was the best basketball player in the state of Ohio. He was also my father figure. He was my role model. He did everything the way you were supposed to do it—the way he conducted himself, dressed in the appropriate manner, did well in school, worked extra jobs, helped our mom. Butch Carter was and still is my hero."

Inspired by the success of his brothers, Cris became a basketball prodigy in his own right, earning All-Ohio honors at Middletown High School. But he also exhibited so much raw talent on the football field that his coach made a startling comment one afternoon after practice. Bill Conley, who played football for Woody Hayes at Ohio State, took over the Middle-town program as head coach during Carter's junior season and told the youngster he was pursuing the wrong career.

"I was one of the best basketball players in the state of Ohio, I had a brother in the NBA, and I was only playing football to stay in shape," Cris said. "But Coach Conley looked me straight in the eye and said, 'Son, you have a better chance to be Lynn Swann than you do Isiah Thomas.' I thought he was crazy."

Conley, who later coached Carter while both were at Ohio State, said it was no-brainer. "Cris was a very good athlete, especially when it comes to the technical part of the game—ran great routes, had leaping ability, had the ability to catch the football. You could see right away that he just had tremendous skills," Conley said. "He was also an extreme competitor. The closer a game was, when it came time to make a crucial play, he got it done. He loved to compete and thrived on that competition. The third thing was his extreme confidence in himself. You'd better not tell him he couldn't do something because he would always meet the challenge."

Slowly, Cris began to entertain the idea of playing both basketball and football at the college level, and he decided he would pursue both at a school about as far away from Middletown as he could get—the University of Southern California. Those plans were derailed, however, by a Midwestern snowstorm. USC assistant coach Norv Turner was on his way to Ohio to discuss details of signing Carter when his plane was grounded in Kansas City. Rather than wait out the storm and travel to Middletown the following day, Turner decided to board a different plane and headed home to Los Angeles.

"When I found out about that, I canceled my visit to USC and decided not to go to school there," Cris said. "I didn't know where I was going to go; I just knew I wasn't going there."

Ohio State seemed a natural fit, but the two major figures in his life were pulling him in opposite directions. Butch was telling his baby brother that life as an OSU receiver would be frustrating since the Buckeyes seldom threw the ball, but Cris's mother told him she had always hoped one of her sons would someday wear the Scarlet and Gray.

"My mom wanted me to go to Ohio State because her dad had grown up being an Ohio State fan," Cris said. "Plus, she loved Woody Hayes because she thought that what he did for young people was tremendous. She also liked Ohio State's staff. She liked how accountable they were and what they promised her about off-the-field things. So one day we were talking and she said, 'I've always dreamed of one of my kids playing for Ohio State.' Right then, I decided that was what I was going to do. I was going to listen to my mom."

Cris became part of one of Ohio State's finest recruiting classes in years, arriving on campus at the same time with such future stars as William White, Alex Higdon, Jeff Uhlenhake, Tom Tupa, and Chris Spielman. But during his first few practice sessions, Cris began to hear his older brother's voice ringing in his ears. Bruce ran a tight training camp with the first and second team getting most of the snaps, and all freshmen relegated to the scout team. After the first week, Carter had seen enough, telling Bruce that he was leaving. "I told him, 'This is not what you told me while you were recruiting me. You promised me a chance to make

Throughout a superlative three-year college career, Carter rewrote Ohio State's record books, repeatedly bringing crowds to their feet with remarkable, gravity-defying catches. Strong and graceful, he

One recruiter offered Cris's mom a horse if Cris signed with his school. Cris's mom said, "I live in the projects. Where would I keep a horse?"

the varsity.' The next day, they announced they were moving Spielman and me up to third-string—although there really wasn't any such thing as third-string."

That signaled the beginning of what would become an All-America football career for Carter with the Buckeyes. The team won the Big Ten championship during his freshman season and earned a trip to the Rose Bowl where Cris won offensive player of the game honors after totaling nine receptions for a game-record 172 yards. As he clutched the MVP trophy in Pasadena, Cris remembered thinking, "That was the first day I became convinced I would never play basketball again. I would just stick to football."

had no equal. He became a student of his position, understanding that opponents would have to respect his speed and leaping ability, and using that knowledge to analyze and then manipulate the movements of any defensive back who dared challenge him.

He also had an uncanny knack for making the impossible catch as he did during a crucial part of a 10–7 victory against Brigham Young University in the 1985 Citrus Bowl.

"I was actually trying to throw that ball away," Ohio State quarterback Jim Karsatos said. "When I saw it later on film, I couldn't believe it. He went up and caught the ball with one hand, tucked it in, then it looked like he just levitated back inbounds.

I thought I threw that thing so hard and so high that no one would have a chance at it. That was Cris, though. Just unbelievable."

Primed for a spectacular senior season in 1987, Carter was suspended after it was discovered he had already signed with a sports agent. It was the first of several extremely selfish acts that dogged him well into his professional career. A wellness management program offered by the Minnesota Vikings helped to lead Carter away from substance abuse, and he became one of the National Football League's most productive receivers. When he retired following the 2002 season, he was second only to Hall of Fame receiver Jerry Rice in career receptions and touchdowns, and he remains in the all-time top five in both categories despite having left the game more than a decade ago.

Spielman, who admittedly wanted to tear his teammate apart when he was suspended in 1987, has marveled at how Carter blossomed, both as a football player and as a man.

"Getting humbled, guys go one of two ways," Spielman said.

"They say, 'Maybe it's me as opposed to everything around me that made me make poor choices.' To his credit, Cris said, 'It's me.' One of the gifts he had was he recognized how talented he was. He didn't want to throw that away. If he weren't a great competitor, he would have said the heck with it. For him to beat the odds, I always say how proud I am of him. I can't think of many guys who have made a comeback like he has."

All the way to the Hall of Fame.

JOHN
COOPER

OSU COACH 1988–2000

HOMETOWN: Knoxville, Tennessee

RECORD: 111-43-4

BIG TEN CHAMPIONSHIPS: 1993, 1996, 1998

John Cooper was inducted into the College Football Hall of Fame as a coach in 2008.

John Cooper arrived in Columbus in 1988 armed with an impressive résumé, a cocksure attitude, and a seemingly endless supply of homespun homilies that he delivered rapid-fire with a rich Southern drawl. Thirteen seasons, 111 victories, three Big Ten championships, and a number of excruciatingly tough losses to Michigan later, the coach met the same fate as nearly every one of his predecessors—he was fired.

In between, though, Cooper did something for which he will likely never be credited because of his 2-10-1 record against Michigan: He transformed the Ohio State football program from its stodgy we-do-it-this-way-because-Woody-did-it-this-way approach to a more streamlined program better equipped to recruit as well as perform on a significantly higher level.

How far had OSU's star fallen when Cooper arrived in 1988? The answer is debatable because predecessor Earle Bruce had produced four Big Ten championships while averaging exactly nine wins per season during his nine-year tenure. But for all intents and purposes,

the Scarlet and Gray brand was dying on the vine. Ohio State had finished among the top five teams in the final Associated Press poll only once during the a 12-season span from 1976 to 1987.

Cooper's personality was most definitely a one-eighty turn from Hayes or Bruce, and his shoot-from-the-lip style was a beat reporter's dream. But the new coach soon discovered that his easygoing nature and brutal honesty would be used against him, especially as loss after agonizing loss in the final two games of the season began to pile up year after year. The coach's legacy at Ohio State could not be chronicled without mentioning his record against the Wolverines as well as a 3-8 mark in bowl games. However, a record of 106-25-3—a stellar .802 winning percentage—in all other games cannot be ignored, nor can the fact the coach overhauled the entire OSU program from top to bottom.

Cooper ditched what had been for generations a mostly plodding offense, replacing it with a high-octane attack designed to stretch opposing defenses to their breaking point. He expanded the Buckeyes' recruiting footprint, making vital inroads into such fertile high school states as Florida and Texas. And he oversaw a makeover of the weight and conditioning program, making it the envy of college football.

"I think sometimes Coach Cooper doesn't get the kind of respect he deserves," longtime OSU football historian Jack Park said. "If you go back to a huge loss at Penn State late during the 1994 season, the week after that the team came back home as underdogs to Wisconsin and beat them. In my opinion, that was the beginning of one of the best eras in the history of the program."

Park's opinion is borne out by facts. Beginning with that 24–3 victory over Wisconsin in 1994, the Buckeyes won forty-six of their next fifty-four games, a stretch that included coming within an eyelash of winning two national championships during a three-year period.

"I know some people would disagree with this, but I would rank John among my top five Ohio State coaches of all-time," Park said. "Of course, you have Woody and Earle, and I would include Jim Tressel and

Paul Brown. But if you take the totality of what John accomplished at Ohio State—upgrading the facilities, expanding the recruiting base, things of that nature—I don't see how you couldn't put him in the top five all-time."

Others disagree, of course, citing the repeated Michigan failures. Three-time All-America linebacker Chris Spielman, whose four-year career ended the year before Cooper arrived in Columbus, likens the coach to a salesman who annually puts up good numbers but can seldom make the close on his largest account.

"Coach Cooper is a Hall of Fame coach, and his stats say that," Spielman said. "But when you're talking about Ohio State, I don't care what his record is. What's his record against Michigan?"

Born July 2, 1937, in Knoxville, Tennessee, Cooper spent his childhood in nearby Powell, a speck on the map so off the beaten path the coach often joked about going toward town just to hunt. One of six children, the son of a hard-working carpenter admittedly had little ambition as a youngster.

"Where I came from, back there in the hills of eastern Tennessee, very, very few people went to college," Cooper said. "As a matter of fact, I don't know of anyone in my senior class that went to college. You basically went to school, got out, got a job, and that's what you did for the rest of your life. I didn't have a clue what I was going to do, but I was pretty sure college wasn't going to be part of my future."

Cooper played all three sports Powell High School offered—basketball, baseball, and football—and proved his eagerness time and again, eventually working his way up from

Despite scholarship offers from several small schools, Cooper decided to pursue his dream of playing at the University of Tennessee. "I was small—only about 160-165 pounds—but I was pretty sure of myself, so I was ready to walk on at Tennessee and earn myself a scholarship. Then I showed up to register there, and those lines were a mile long...I got to thinking that I didn't have any money and I was dating (future wife) Helen, so I turned around and left and got myself a job."

Cooper spent the next few months working odd jobs until de-

> "About the time you're feeling pretty good about yourself, be sure and check your hole card."
>
> —John Cooper

team manager of the football squad to two-way starter at quarterback and safety. Following his senior season on the gridiron, he further distinguished himself by earning Most Valuable Player honors in a statewide all-star game. Still, colleges didn't seem to notice much.

ciding that fall to enlist in the U.S. Army. During his fifteen-month hitch, he re-evaluated his football career and spent countless hours crafting letters and sending them to prospective colleges and universities, trying to secure a scholarship offer. His queries met with only limited response until he received a positive reply from Iowa State.

"My first year, there were more than a hundred players on that football team," Cooper remembered. "But that didn't last long. You talk about boot camp. Basic training in the Army was nothing compared to this. They'd slap you upside the head, kick you in the rear, threaten to take away your scholarship—lots of things they wouldn't dare try today. There were players dropping out left and right because you went full-go in full gear every day of practice. But they couldn't run me off. I was a poor old country boy, and if I had quit, I would have had to go back home and get a job."

From those hundred players in camp during the fall of 1958, head coach Clay Stapleton and his staff had run off all but about thirty players who returned the following season. But the ones who stayed became one of the most storied teams in ISU program history. Nicknamed the "Dirty Thirty," the Cyclones finished 7–3 in 1959, compiling Iowa State's best record in nearly two decades.

Cooper was a three-year starter for the Cyclones and capped his college career in 1961 by being voted captain as well as MVP by his teammates. After that season, he and his wife longed to return to their eastern Tennessee roots where John had lined up a high school coaching position. But Stapleton had other ideas.

"I was in his office one day after the season was over," Cooper said, "and he leaned back, put his feet up on the desk, and said, 'John, I think you'd make a hell of a coach. As a matter of fact, I'll tell you what I want you to do. I want you to stay here at Iowa State and coach my freshmen team next year.'"

That began a coaching career spanning four decades and included piloting the programs at the University of Tulsa, Arizona State, and Ohio State. He won five consecutive Missouri Valley Conference championships at Tulsa and captured a Rose Bowl title with Arizona State (beating Michigan, no less) before arriving in Columbus in early 1988.

Ohio State fans had grown tired of nine years of what they consid-

Cooper and quarterback Joe Germaine hoist the winner's trophy after OSU's 1997 Rose Bowl victory.

ered underachievement with Bruce at the helm, and they initially welcomed Cooper with open arms. His first spring game attracted a record 54,302 fans to Ohio Stadium, and the coach began to get more and more comfortable in his new surroundings—perhaps a bit too comfortable. The new coach signed a promotional contract with a local grocery chain, and his face became omnipresent in Columbus during the summer of 1988, thanks to a barrage of television commercials. Unfortunately, that led to one of his first gaffes when in one of the spots he referred to Ohio Stadium as "Buckeye Stadium."

Candid almost to a fault, Cooper's sometimes brutal honesty led him to opine the talent cupboard was bare when he arrived, and his roster was filled with "too many slow, white guys." In mid-August, the new coach appeared bare-chested with a towel hanging from his neck as part of a four-page *Sports Illustrated* article titled "In Woody's Shadow." It would not be the last time Cooper would take his shirt off in public that summer. He was joined by members of his family in a hot tub for a television commercial.

Thanks to a firestorm of indignation from Ohio State fans used to the staid nature of Woody Hayes and Earle Bruce, the spot aired only a handful of times. But the damage had been done. Critics were already out in force as they railed against what some perceived as a man exercising poor judgment and others called a self-promoting huckster.

The criticism seemed to disappear following a near-perfect victory against Syracuse in the 1988 season opener. But a week later, the honeymoon was officially over. As the grim-faced coach emerged from the visiting locker room following a 42–10 loss to the University of Pittsburgh, fans pelted him with a steady stream of sharp criticism that echoed back and forth off the exposed steel girders of old Pitt Stadium.

For the remainder of Cooper's thirteen-year run as head coach of the Buckeyes, that kind of heated criticism really never went away, mostly because of his team's shortcomings against Michigan. Still, he enjoyed many successes, including a come-from-behind victory against Arizona State in the 1997 Rose Bowl that made him the only man in history to coach both a Pacific-10 and Big Ten conference team to a Rose Bowl victory.

Cooper remains an enigma to many Ohio State fans. Some can appreciate his many contributions to the program, although many others will never understand how he lasted so long. Nevertheless, his victory total with the Scarlet and Gray stands behind only that of Hayes, and Cooper will always represent the bridge between a program that had grown stagnant and a new period of prosperity, a record-setting era that he helped build.

RAYMONT HARRIS

OSU RUNNING BACK 1990–1993

NICKNAME: Ultraback and Quiet Storm

HOMETOWN: Lorain, Ohio

HEIGHT: 6 ft 0 in   **WEIGHT:** 230 lb

NFL DRAFT: 1994, Chicago Bears

On Raymont's Twitter profile he describes himself as, "Man, father, husband, true hip hop purist and scrabble addict."

*I*t was the day before Halloween of 1993 and Raymont Harris was awake early. Penn State was in town, and the Big Ten's new kid on the block was boasting about throwing its weight around. The Nittany Lions hadn't visited Ohio Stadium since manhandling the Buckeyes and rookie quarterback Art Schlichter during a 19–0 victory in 1978, and Joe Paterno's team saw no reason why it wouldn't repeat that earlier performance.

"That was Penn State's first year in the league, and they were supposed to come in and dominate," Harris said. "I remember getting up the morning of the game and looking outside. I couldn't believe it. October? And it's snowing? But that just put a smile on my face because I knew under those conditions we would run the ball more. I liked that. I liked that a lot."

As the late afternoon sun began to set behind Ohio Stadium's majestic colonnades, and the wet snow turned the venue's frosty green playing surface into a slippery brown quagmire, Penn State's potent passing attack became a liability while star running back Ki-Jana Carter's cutback ability—his bread and butter—was neutralized.

Meanwhile, the Buckeyes handed the ball to Harris, whose punishing, no-frills approach was perfect for the conditions. By the time the game had ended, the senior tailback had established new career-highs with 151 yards on thirty-two carries, and Ohio State had literally and figuratively pounded out a 24–6 victory.

"We just did what we do best," OSU left guard Jason Winrow said. "Run the ball inside the tackle box. We knew we had them right where we wanted them. Just give the ball to Raymont and let him pound on them."

The game not only proved to be a breakout moment in the college career of Harris. It represented a signature achievement for the determined young man known as "Quiet Storm," a youngster whose life was filled with obstacles and heartache from the beginning.

Raymont LaShawn Harris was born December 23, 1970, in Lorain, Ohio, a proud, blue-collar Lake Erie town located just outside Cleveland, best known for its U.S. Steel mill and Ford Motor Company assembly plant. But while the blast furnaces and assembly lines provided good-paying jobs for many of Lorain's residents, they couldn't support the entire city's population, and Raymont was born into difficult surroundings made even worse when his mother died of complications while giving birth.

"I come from a poverty-stricken environment," he said. "I come from a single-parent family household. My mother passed away giving birth to me. Statistically, I really wasn't supposed to make it."

But make it he did. Growing into his 6-foot, 200-pound frame, Raymont became one of the lakefront area's top running backs at Admiral King High School. He won All-Erie Shore Conference honors as a junior and was poised for a superlative senior season when a broken collarbone limited him to only four games in 1988. Before he was injured, however, he delivered a performance against crosstown rival Lorain High that is still being talked about. He rushed for 332 yards and five touchdowns in the victory, establishing new single-game Lo-

rain County records for yards rushing, total yards from scrimmage, carries, and touchdowns.

"That's probably one of my fondest memories from high school," Harris said. "There were severe bragging rights on the line because they had beaten us the last few years, and I was just getting back to 100 percent. I wanted to perform well so badly in that game because of who it was against."

Admiral King assistant coach Harvey Herrmann, one of a handful of mentors Harris credits for getting him and keeping him on the straight and narrow, recalled that his star tailback had missed the first three games that season with a bad knee. "He played in the fourth game at about 90 percent, then was at full strength against Lorain. It was an outstanding game. The more yards Raymont gained, the better the line blocked. It was almost like he ran that whole game downhill. He just kept picking up speed and momentum as the game wore on."

But just as he was celebrating his greatest triumph, Harris suffered a broken clavicle the following week against Elyria and his high school career was over. Despite the injury and a relatively short high school résumé, Raymont was still courted by a host of major college programs. He originally committed to Michigan head coach Bo Schembechler upon his official visit to Ann Arbor, but immediately began having second thoughts. When he arrived at Ohio State a few weeks later, he met running back Scottie Graham, who was to be his host for the weekend. Graham, now director of player engagement for the NFL Players Association, showed Raymont around the campus and introduced him to other players, all the while calmly laying out the plan head coach John Cooper had for his fledgling program. Before Raymont left Columbus, he had changed his mind.

"As strange as it sounds, I grew up being a fan of both Ohio State and Michigan," Raymont said. "So when Bo Schembechler, one of the greatest coaches in college football, asks you to become part of his team, how do you turn that down? But then you get away from that initial euphoria and you begin to put it all together. The guys at Ohio State were different. Michigan was putting great teams on the field, while Ohio State was struggling to get started under John Cooper and the players seemed hungrier. They were ambitious, and that fit my personality more."

Immediately, friends and family told Raymont he had made a mistake. "They were telling me that Ohio State was too big, that I ought to go to a smaller school," he said. "But I never felt like I couldn't do well at Ohio State. I never felt like there was *anything* I couldn't do. I always had the ultimate belief that when it came to getting something done, I could do it."

Getting to Ohio State was one thing. Seeing meaningful playing time was another. After redshirting in 1989, Harris played only sparingly the next two seasons as the Buckeyes used an established stable of running backs that included Graham, Carlos Snow, and Robert Smith.

"It was really tough because deep down I knew I was just as good or better than Carlos Snow and just as good as Robert Smith at that time," Raymont said. "We were all effective in different ways. But sitting there on the sidelines, watching this other guy do the things he does well, and you know in some ways you can do them better, that was tough as an 18-, 19-, 20-year-old man. You learn a lot about yourself when you're in that spot. Places like Ohio State chew kids up and spit them out, and that's hard to deal with."

At the same time, Harris wasn't doing himself any favors among his teammates. He had only a few close friends on the team, and kept his mouth shut while seething inside.

"His first couple of years, I didn't think he could play," said All-Big Ten receiver Joey Galloway, who later became one of Harris's closest friends. "I didn't know. I mean, how could I? He just didn't seem like he was that likeable of a guy."

The memory brings a smile to Raymont's face. "I was used to letting my actions speak for me," he said. "And he's right. I didn't talk much. That's where I got my nickname—Quiet Storm. But those first couple of years, not having the kind of success I wanted to have, it was really, really tough. And being young and immature, I'm sure I didn't do myself any favors."

Finally, the competitive fire threatened to burn too hot. In his spare time, Raymont put together his own highlight tape, planning to send it to other schools that might give him more of a chance to play. He kept his plans to himself until one day confiding in strength and conditioning coach Dave Kennedy.

Raymont remembered what happened next. "He looked straight at me and said, 'Are you crazy? You're going to let these other guys beat you out?' Then after a couple of minutes, he said, 'Well, OK. Go ahead. Transfer.' And when he said that to me, it all just clicked. I don't think it was a coincidence that I truly got on the field and starting playing well right after that."

During his senior season in 1993, Harris became the featured back in Ohio State's offense and piled up 1,344 yards while rushing for twelve touchdowns. His yardage total represented the highest for the Buckeyes in nearly a decade and was achieved through sheer determination and hard work.

"I'm not sure I have ever seen a more serious student of the game," said Bill Conley, a former

Ohio State player and assistant coach who is currently head coach at Ohio Dominican University. "Raymont knew what he wanted, knew where he wanted to go, and knew how to get there. He certainly wasn't the biggest running back we ever had at Ohio State, but he was among the toughest. He is truly a self-made man."

And like all rags-to-riches stories, Raymont couldn't have scripted a better ending, rushing for 235 yards and three touchdowns as the Buckeyes took a 28–21 victory against Brigham Young University in the Holiday Bowl. The yardage total established a new school postseason record at Ohio State, and Harris told reporters after the game that his blocking was so good he often had trouble deciding which massive hole he wanted to run through.

One of his linemen indicated otherwise, however. "It's a pleasure to block for a guy like Raymont," two-time All-American right tackle Korey Stringer said. "He makes you look better than you are."

Harris went on to play six seasons in the National Football League, including four with the Chicago Bears, but his take-no-prisoners style of running soon exacted a heavy toll on his body, and he was forced to retire after playing only four games in 2000. He bounced around after football, trying a variety of different things from radio analysis to banking until returning to his alma mater where he served as assistant director of development for the Fisher School of Business before becoming director of development for the Ohio State athletic department.

"I never even knew what development was when I was a player," Raymont said. "If you would have asked me then I would probably have said it was something that had to do with construction. But it's part of my personal journey— a long and winding road that has brought me to where I want to be."

That seems only natural since Ohio State is the place the Quiet Storm truly came of age.

EDDIE
GEORGE

OSU RUNNING BACK 1992–1995

NICKNAME: Sir Edward

HOMETOWN: Philadelphia, Pennsylvania

HEIGHT: 6 ft 3 in   **WEIGHT:** 240 lb

ALL–AMERICAN: 1995

NFL DRAFT: 1996, Houston Oilers

27

Eddie's number, 27, was retired on November 10, 2001.

If perseverance ever goes searching for a poster child, it needs to look no further than Eddie George. From a spindly child whose mother wouldn't allow him to play organized football to Heisman Trophy winner and four-time Pro Bowler, George picked himself up after being knocked down so many times he finally lost count. It never crossed his mind not to keep getting up, though. He was too busy chasing big dreams.

"Adversity is a wonderful seed to plant," Eddie said. "You can nurture it, you can cherish it, you can learn from it and you can just keep feeding it water until it finally grows and blossoms."

Edward Nathan George Jr. began sharing his life with the seeds of adversity shortly after he was born, September 24, 1973, in suburban Philadelphia. His father, Edward Sr., wasn't around much during the youngster's childhood, officially separating from his mother, Donna, when Eddie was only seven. The couple later divorced, leaving Donna as a single mother to care for Eddie and his older sister Leslie.

Eddie didn't know it at the time, but his mother was passing her strong will and determination down to her son. Donna George was a loving mother, but she also had no hesitation to mete out whatever discipline was necessary for the situation. She insisted her children set goals for themselves, not only for the present but for the future. That insistence led to her son establishing a lofty ambition for himself.

"Eddie was about eight years old, and I asked what his goals were, what he wanted to get out of life, what he wanted do, and one of them was to win the Heisman Trophy," Donna said. "He didn't know hardly anything about the Heisman Trophy except that he wanted to win one."

Donna let her son continue to fantasize about college football greatness, making sure a helmet or jersey found its way under the Christmas tree each year. Whenever it came time to smile for holiday photos, Eddie put on his new helmet, tucked a football under his arm, and struck the famous Heisman stiff-arm pose. But his mother made sure he always kept football in proper perspective, refusing to allow Eddie to play the sport in an organized setting until he was eleven, even though he had been begging to play on a team since he was five.

As Eddie began to grow from a gangly all-arms-and-legs youngster, his athletic talents came to the fore. When he was just a sophomore at Abington High School, he won the state track championship in both the low and high hurdles, but he wasn't satisfied. He was desperate for stardom on the football team, continuing to chase his Heisman dream to the point he had even written an acceptance speech. Football was suddenly all that mattered in his life, and with that as his sole focus, he began to run with the wrong crowd, his grades began to slip, and a well-nurtured character started to show cracks.

That didn't last long, though. Sensing that she was beginning to lose her son to the same dark elements that had pushed too many young men toward a path of self-destruction, Donna took Eddie out of public school and enrolled him at Fork Union Military Academy, a discipline-first institution tucked away in the Virginia foothills. He was understandably upset with his mother's decision, although it really didn't matter what he thought of the situation.

"It's not like I had a choice," Eddie said with a smile. "Once I got used to the place, things were all right, but at the time I wasn't happy at all. I was used to hanging with my boys, staying out all night and getting into stuff. Nothing major, but you know how young kids are when they don't have anything else to do. Then I got to Fork Union and my life changed overnight."

Getting used to the military academy and its stringent rules, with nearly every minute of every day regimented between schoolwork, athletics, and military drills, took some getting used to. "Man, I cried myself to sleep every night the first week I was there," Eddie said. Slowly, the strictness of his new surroundings paid off, and he began to appreciate the dedication, discipline, and attention to detail it took to excel as a Fork Union cadet.

"There's no question that I am where I am today because my

mother sent me there," Eddie said. "No question whatsoever. If she hadn't had the foresight to send me to Fork Union, there's no telling where I might be today."

In addition to rebuilding his character and reinforcing the life lessons his mother had instilled, Fork Union allowed Eddie to begin to realize his dream of stardom on the football field. In two seasons with the Blue Devils, he rushed for 2,572 yards and thirty-two touchdowns, drawing the attention of several major college programs, including Virginia and Penn State. But Eddie found himself drawn to Ohio State, partly because he liked the school colors and partly because his formative years had been spent watching OSU tailback Keith Byars terrorize opposing defenses.

But if Eddie wanted to become a Buckeye, he had to first convince his mother. The University of Virginia was only about thirty miles northeast of Fork Union, while Penn

State not only was Eddie's home-state school, its football program offered the stability of longtime head coach Joe Paterno. That was not the case with John Cooper at Ohio State, whose four-year tenure in Columbus had been beset by public relations missteps off the field and a lack of consistent winning on the field. Cooper was rumored to be out as OSU coach following the 1991 season, fueling even more skepticism from Eddie's mother. But Cooper

Eddie striking an almost Heisman-like pose on the field.

received a contract extension to remain with the Buckeyes, and Eddie resumed trying to convince his mother that Ohio State was the best place for him.

In the end, it was Cooper who finally sold Mrs. George, but only after what the head coach described as an intense in-home visit. "I usually went into the house and told the parents what going to Ohio State was going to mean to their son and they would ask a couple of questions and nod their heads the rest of the time," Cooper said. "This time, Eddie's mother did most of the talking and I did most of the nodding."

Finally, Eddie was going to realize his dream of becoming a Buckeye, a dream that nearly turned into a nightmare. After slowly working himself into the tailback mix as a freshman during the first four games in 1992, he fumbled twice near the goal line against Illinois in early October. One of the fumbles was returned 96 yards for a Fighting Illini touchdown that ultimately accounted for the losing margin in an 18–16 final. The fumbles proved disastrous for George,

who found himself on the bench for much of the rest of the '92 season and for a good part of his sophomore campaign as well.

He briefly considered a transfer, although he knew his mother would never stand for her son quitting something he had started. So he dedicated himself to an offseason training regimen that reshaped his body and his spirit. As a result, Eddie became the go-to running back for the Buckeyes in 1994, and he carried 276 times for a team-best 1,442 yards and twelve touchdowns.

That set the stage for a superlative senior season during which he shattered a host of Ohio State records, including the single-game rushing mark with 314 yards during a 41–3 win against the same Illinois team where he had fumbled twice three years earlier. It was another example of Eddie taking adversity and using as fuel to achieve his goals.

"Reflecting back, the game against Illinois during my freshman year was pivotal," he said. "I was known for the longest time as the guy who fumbled twice inside the five-yard line. People said I couldn't make it at Ohio State, that I should transfer out. But I believed in myself and continued to work hard."

"Adversity teaches a man to know himself, and Eddie had a lot of adversity with that first Illinois game," said OSU administrator Bill Myles, a former assistant coach under Woody Hayes. "Then he came back three years later and had the greatest game of his career against Illinois. That's the measure of a man."

George capped his senior season with Big Ten Most Valuable Player and All-America honors, and then captured the sixty-first annual Heisman Memorial Trophy, flashing a huge grin and celebrating the moment in New York City as his proud mother looked on. He went on to a nine-year NFL career, eight of them with the Houston Oilers who later became the Tennessee Titans. Throughout his time in Houston and Tennessee, Eddie rushed for more than 10,000 yards, scored seventy-six touchdowns and made four Pro Bowls.

Perhaps his finest achievement as a pro, was the fact he never failed to answer the bell during his first eight seasons, persevering through injuries to play in 128 consecutive games—the very embodiment of perseverance.

"His work ethic was the best," Cooper said. "I can't imagine another football player in history having a better work ethic. He is a great athlete with tremendous focus, and that is why he did so well at Ohio State and as a professional. He always was physically and mentally tough, and he always knew exactly what he wanted and exactly what it took to get it."

Deserving of every accolade that ever came his way, Eddie George is the textbook example of how far you can go through good, old-fashioned hard work and enough self-confidence to pursue your dreams no matter how many hurdles adversity throws your way.

KOREY
STRINGER

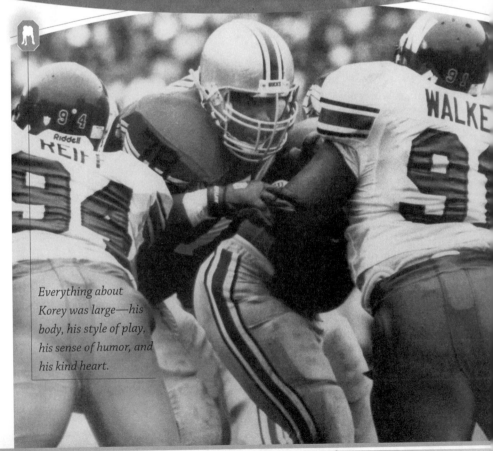

OSU OFFENSIVE TACKLE 1992–1994

NICKNAME: Big K

HOMETOWN: Warren, Ohio

HEIGHT: 6 ft 4 in   **WEIGHT:** 346 lb

ALL–AMERICAN: 1994

NFL DRAFT: 1995, Minnesota Vikings

78

Everything about Korey was large—his body, his style of play, his sense of humor, and his kind heart.

Ask anyone who knew him and they would all say the same thing. Korey Stringer was an oversized man with an oversized heart.

There was the time he was driving home after playing in a game for the Minnesota Vikings when he stopped along the road to help a young man change a flat tire. He donated pencils and notebooks as well as his most precious commodity—time—to elementary schools in the Twin Cities area. On Beggar's Night each year, he would sit on his porch with a huge bowl of candy and encourage each child to take as much as they wished. When he made one of his final visits to his Northeast Ohio hometown, he endorsed his $15,000 Pro Bowl check and gave it to a local peewee football organization.

And when the 6-foot-4-inch, 335-pound teddy bear of a man died suddenly in 2001 from heat stroke, the outpouring of love and affection was overwhelming. "There was not a more well-liked player on our football team," said Pro Football Hall of Fame receiver Cris Carter, who was Stringer's teammate with the Vikings from 1995–2000.

"There was not a player that anyone enjoyed spending more time with than Korey. I pray that one day, when they put me in a casket, that I would be like Korey—not famous, but unforgettable."

Those Minnesota teams of the mid-1990s featured a wide array of divergent personalities with feathers often ruffling freely in the locker room. Stringer, however, was the mother hen, able to defuse any potential conflagration before it got a chance to start. Following one particular loss to bitter division rival Chicago, several Vikings grumbled and groused as they headed for the showers. As reporters approached mercurial star Randy Moss, the All-Pro receiver angrily pushed them aside and shouted, "Get out of my space! Why don't you go over there and watch Big K get dressed?"

Stringer looked over his shoulder, smiled, and dropped his towel. "Have to put a dollar in the G-string if you want to watch," he said. "Not gonna perform for free." Everyone in the locker room—including Moss—roared in laughter.

"He was a great lineman, but he was even more than that. Korey was one of the best players I ever coached," said John Cooper, who had the good fortune to have Stringer at right tackle and Orlando Pace at left tackle on his 1994 Ohio State team. "Technique, footwork, the way he used his hands—he was one of the best. And he was one of the most likeable guys in the locker room. If anybody ever said a bad word about Korey Stringer, I certainly never heard it."

High praise indeed, especially on a college football team where tensions run high among young men struggling to form their own identities. Once told he needed to develop more of a mean streak, Stringer decided to get a tattoo with the initials FTW, supposedly an acronym for "Fuck the World." But Korey regretted the ink almost as soon as he got it, and began claiming the initials stood for "Find the Way." That seemed more fitting for a young man who preferred the word "Peace" as a parting sentiment rather than "Goodbye."

"Gone too soon. Much too soon," said former Ohio State teammate Steve Tovar. "Korey was such a fun guy, and we took it for granted. It was just him. Every time I saw him, he had a smile on his face or was trying to make people laugh. That's the way I remember him."

Korey Damont Stringer was born May 8, 1974, in Warren, Ohio, a manufacturing town that always seemed to dwell in the shadow of Youngstown, its bustling neighbor to the southeast. But while Youngstown represented the hub of Ohio steel country, Warren manufactured everything from automobiles to light bulbs. In fact, in 1890, it became the first town in the United States to install electric street lamps. Warren's chief export, however, has always been football players, including such Ohio State stars as Paul Warfield, Randy Gradishar, and Van Ness DeCree, and Korey seemed destined to follow in those footsteps.

As the first-born son of James Stringer Jr. and Cathy Reed Stringer, young Korey displayed a prodigious appetite, quickly earning the reputation for eating anything that wouldn't eat him first. His penchant for food and plenty of it came from his father, but Korey's personality came from his mother, a hard-working, fun-loving woman who worked for more than thirty years at Delphi Packard Electric, the same company that had installed Warren's electric street lights in the late nineteenth century. When she wasn't working—or cooking for her young son—Cathy spent hours reading, singing, and laughing, and it was from her Korey inherited his ready smile and dry sense of humor.

As Korey continued to grow, he was naturally attracted to football and became a consensus first-team All-American lineman at Warren G. Harding High School. By the time he was a senior, Korey was already known as "Big K" and not just for his size. As one of the country's leading offensive line prospects, he had a scholarship offer list that stretched from one end of a football field to the other and back again.

University of Michigan head coach Gary Moeller, an Ohio State team captain in 1962 for Woody Hayes, thought he had a chance to sign Stringer. After all, Harding had produced almost as many Wolverines as it had Buckeyes, and Michigan was having its way in the series with its archrival. In the end, however, Moeller never really had a chance. Ohio State was Cathy Stringer's favorite team, so there wasn't much doubt where her son would be playing his college football. "It was kind of a no-brainer," Korey said at the time.

When he arrived in Columbus, the Ohio State program was still trying to gain traction with Cooper as head coach. In his first four seasons, the coach could muster no higher than a third-place finish in the Big Ten standings. The recruiting class of 1992 began to turn things around, however. Stringer, along with such other future stars as Eddie George and Luke Fickell, produced a conference championship and two runner-up finishes over the next three seasons.

The Buckeyes also became one of the most potent offenses in college football, thanks in part to Stringer, who was named to the All-America first team as both a junior and a senior.

"He just dominated. Most of the time, the guy who lined up opposite Big K never had a chance," said ESPN college football analyst Kirk

Herbstreit, who was Ohio State's starting quarterback during Stringer's freshman year in 1992. "Guys came into the huddle and you could often read in their eyes what they were about. Korey always had that run-the-ball-behind-me look. If we needed a yard, we ran behind him because we knew we'd get that yard. He was just a natural beast."

Eddie George had an even more unusual perspective. He had the good fortune to run behind Stringer early during his college career before winning the 1995 Heisman Trophy with Pace clearing the way for him. And while he was effusive in his praise for Pace during his Heisman acceptance speech, the former OSU running back indicated that Stringer might have been even better.

"Korey was probably the greatest tackle in Ohio State history as far as athletic ability and attitude," George said. "He was a big teddy bear off the field and a great guy to be around in the locker room, but when the bell rang, look out. He brought a toughness to the line that was just special."

Following his junior season with the Buckeyes, Stringer left school early to make himself eligible for the National Football League draft and was selected by the Vikings with the twenty-fourth pick of the first round. He won the starting right tackle position as a rookie in 1995 and never relinquished it, starting ninety-one of the ninety-three games in which he played during his six pro seasons.

As the 2001 season was about to get under way, Stringer was entering the prime of his career. He had made his first Pro Bowl the year before, and the Vikings were Super Bowl contenders after winning the NFC Central Division title. During a late July practice session, however, when the heat index reached 110 degrees, Korey collapsed. He was rushed to Immanuel St. Joseph's-Mayo Health System hospital, but never regained consciousness. Stringer was gone, the victim of heat stroke. He was only 27.

"What can you say?" asked Raymont Harris, another Ohio State tailback who enjoyed success running through massive holes created by Stringer. "You lose someone like that, it's a devastating loss. Unbelievably devastating."

In the days that followed the tragedy, countless stories were told by friends and family regarding Stringer's kindness and good nature, stories that transformed the man called "Big K" into "Special K." Perhaps the best was shared by Steven Arnold, an assistant coach at Harding High School when Korey played there.

"A lot of guys who make it to the big time forget where they came from, but not Korey," Arnold said. "He was always back here, always involved with the people in this town. In fact, he had been here about a month before he passed. A friend and I were sitting in my living room, talking about what we could do to get one of our local peewee football teams some equipment when Korey stopped by. We talked for a while, and he said, 'Wait a minute. Don't go anywhere. I'll be right back.'

"Korey went out to his truck, came back about a minute later, and he's got this check in his hand. It was the check he got for playing in the Pro Bowl—his first-ever Pro Bowl—and he signed it over to us. I couldn't believe it. It was a lot of money. A short time later, he called me from camp to make sure I was getting the best equipment for the kids, too. But that was Korey."

In the wake of Stringer's death, the NFL adopted more stringent guidelines with regard to its players when practicing in extreme heat, while Korey's widow, Kelci, became as advocate for athletes, especially in terms of heat-related illnesses. She helped found the Korey Stringer Institute at the University of Connecticut in 2010 to provide information, resources, assistance, and advocacy for promotion of prevention of sudden death in sports via health and safety initiatives.

With the founding of the institute and increased awareness in heat-related illnesses that have undoubtedly helped to save countless lives, Korey Stringer's death has at least left a lasting legacy. But placed against his effervescent personality and the good works he might have done with the remainder of his life, what a bittersweet legacy it is.

ORLANDO PACE

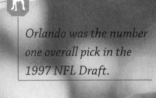

OSU OFFENSIVE TACKLE 1994–1996

NICKNAME: Big O

HOMETOWN: Sandusky, Ohio

HEIGHT: 6 ft 7 in   **WEIGHT:** 325 lb

ALL–AMERICAN: 1995, 1996

NFL DRAFT: 1997, St. Louis Rams

75

Orlando was the number one overall pick in the 1997 NFL Draft.

*B*ig body, big smile, big laugh, big appetite, big ambition—there was never anything small about Orlando Pace. Every Ohio State football fan worth his Scarlet or Gray could tell you Pace was born to play football, but it might surprise them to know Orlando thought he was born to play the sport at the University of Michigan.

Orlando Lamar Pace entered the world on November 4, 1975, in Sandusky, Ohio, the town made famous as an Underground Railroad stop in Harriet Beecher Stowe's anti-slavery novel *Uncle Tom's Cabin*. By the early 1900s, the town on the Sandusky Bay just south of Lake Erie was home to a burgeoning paper mill, as well as Cedar Point, the second oldest operating amusement park in the United States.

The city is also nearly equidistant between Ohio Stadium—some 108 miles to its south—and Michigan Stadium—located about 113 miles to its northwest—and on any given autumn Saturday, a drive along Washington Street or a walk around the Jackson Street Pier provides a bountiful vista of fall foliage against a backdrop of colorful flags,

some scarlet, others blue, fluttering from porches and storefronts.

"You had a lot of Michigan fans there, but everybody in my family liked Ohio State...except me," Orlando said. "For some reason, I was different. I thought Michigan had cool uniforms, cool helmets. Growing up, I always thought I would go to Michigan."

His mother, Joyce, who as a single parent raised Orlando and his older sister Katrina, didn't think much of that idea, but she was at least subtle about it. She worked for several years at the factory famous for churning out those ubiquitous yellow No. 2 pencils, but the plant also manufactured colored pencils and crayons, and whenever Joyce brought home samples for her son, the box always seemed to be missing any color resembling maize or blue. That was as close to deception as Orlando's mother would ever get, though, as she worked hard to provide her son with a stable foundation while making sure his feet were firmly planted in reality.

"I've always been pretty grounded," Pace said. "Especially with money. If you speak to my friends, they would call me tight. But I'm a saver by nature. I never got caught up in spending money, getting a lot of flashy cars, stuff like that. I have my mom to thank for that."

As little Orlando grew—a misnomer because nothing about the youngster from his shoe size to his appetite was ever described as small—he quickly became enamored with sports, especially football and basketball. Already 6-foot-5 and nearly 300 pounds, he was a second-team All-Ohio center on the Sandusky High School basketball team, and he admittedly enjoyed the spotlight that came with being a star basketball player.

"I got into basketball because I never got any stats as an offensive lineman," he said. "But when I realized I wouldn't be the next Michael Jordan, football worked out well for me. My cousin was probably eight or nine years older than me, and when he went to Bowling Green to play football, he got me thinking about going to college. Then when I first walked onto my freshman football team, a coach told me, 'In four years, you can go to any school you want to go to.' It was just a statement he made, but it really stuck with me."

Orlando wasn't just big; he seemed born to play football. "Some guys who are great players on the offensive line, their technique has to be perfect on every play," said Jim Lachey, an All-America guard at Ohio State and three-time All-Pro lineman in the NFL who now serves as color analyst on Buckeye radio broadcasts. "But Orlando could take a bad step and his feet were good enough that he could recover and still get the job done. He had everything you needed in an offensive tackle."

College coaches, eager to witness the talented offensive lineman for themselves, flocked to Sandusky to recruit Pace, but he had long ago made up his mind to attend Michigan. His mother suggested he was doing himself a disservice if he didn't check out at least one other school, and if, after that visit, Orlando still wanted to play for the Wolverines, he would have his mother's blessing. "Then I took a visit to Ohio State and that changed everything," Orlando said.

"I was going to Michigan all the while up until that visit."

Helping seal the deal was the closing sales pitch from Cooper, who showed Pace his team's depth chart for the 1994 season with a hole at offensive tackle opposite All-American Korey Stringer. "That was an eye-opener because I thought of myself more of a defensive guy," Orlando said. "I was a defensive guy, Michigan was recruiting me as a defensive guy, and I thought I'd be a defensive tackle in college. The op-

State in the mid-1990s, "but I stood there that first day, and all I could think was, 'Wow!' I mean, 'Wow!!' He was incredible."

Pace's freshman season was an up-and-down one as the Buckeyes lost a 63–14 decision to top-ranked Penn State in late October before rallying to win the final three games of the regular season including an emotion-filled 22–6 victory over Michigan. It was OSU's first win over its archrival since 1987 and Cooper's first victory at Ohio

"The case for Orlando Pace is slightly loopy, and yet perfectly logical. Pushing a tackle for the Heisman Trophy is an exercise in football folly. Yet Pace probably deserves nothing less."

—*Tim Sullivan*, Cincinnati Enquirer

portunity to play right away on offense at Ohio State, that was probably the deciding factor."

It took only about a week in fall camp before the freshman behemoth rose to the top of the depth chart at left tackle. "We knew he was good," said Lee Owens, who coached the offensive line at Ohio

State over the Wolverines after seven tries.

The Buckeyes were an offensive juggernaut the following season with Pace leading the way for tailback Eddie George, who rushed for a school-record 1,927 yards on his way to the 1995 Heisman Trophy. George later remarked, "If it hadn't been for Orlando Pace, you probably would never have heard of Eddie George. All I had to do was run behind the big guy." It was a statement that was rooted as much in truth as humility, as Pace earned first-team All-America honors and became the first sophomore to win the Lombardi Award as the nation's best interior lineman.

During Pace's junior year, the Buckeyes had to replace George and several other offensive stars, but they kept right on percolating, outscoring their opposition by a 455–131 margin and topping off the season with a thrilling 20–17 Rose Bowl victory over second-ranked Arizona State, a game Pace described as "the most fun college game I played in."

By that time, Orlando had become one of the superstars of college football, making the "pancake block"—knocking opponents flat on their backs—part of the sporting lexicon. He wasn't just a force in the trenches, either. He could often be seen leading speedier running backs down the field, swatting away helpless defensive backs like mosquitoes. "My first year, to be honest, I was kind of shaky," Orlando said. "Not shaky in the sense that I wasn't getting the job done, but just that I wasn't as dominant as I wanted to be. That's the one thing I set out to do as a junior—dominate my man every play, every game. I was pretty successful at doing that."

After that 1996 season, Pace earned another All-America team honor, won the Lombardi Award again, becoming its first two-time recipient, and added the Outland Trophy, symbolic of college football's best lineman. He was also a finalist for the Maxwell Award, given to the top college player regardless of position, and became the first offensive lineman since 1949 named Big Ten Most Valuable Player. Then, when the 1996 Heisman Trophy votes were tabulated, Pace finished fourth, the highest finish for an offensive lineman in nearly a quarter-century.

Pace would have been extremely tough to beat for the '97 Heisman and could have easily won the Lombardi and Outland awards again, but he elected to forego his senior season of eligibility and became the overall No. 1 pick of the 1997

NFL draft. He was the first lineman to be selected with the league's top pick in nearly thirty years, and the St. Louis Rams were never sorry. During most his twelve seasons in St. Louis, he anchored the left side of the Rams' offensive line, making the Pro Bowl seven times and helping his team win Super Bowl XXXIV.

Injuries forced his retirement prior to the 2010 season, but Orlando made an easy transition to his life after football. Along with wife Carla and their four young children, Orlando makes his home just outside St. Louis, where his diverse interests include part-ownership in a radio station and remaining active in community affairs as well as serving as spokesman for several charitable organizations. Orlando also returns several times each year to his northern Ohio hometown, where he owns a popular sports bar as well as a number of houses that he rents to low-income families.

Still, Sandusky will always remember its favorite son, the mountain of a man nearly as big as the Cedar Park roller coasters, because he was simply one of the best players who ever graced a football field.

"People ask me all the time," College Football Hall of Fame coach John Cooper said, "who was the best athlete I ever coached, and that's hard especially when you consider the players we had just from our time at Ohio State. My gosh, we had guys like Joey Galloway, David Boston, Robert Smith, Eddie George...I don't know how you can put one of those guys in front of the others.

"But the best I ever coached? The absolute best football player I ever coached in my life was Orlando Pace. Big, strong, mobile, hostile, blocked like he was in a bad mood—he was just born to play the game of football. I don't know how you would ever find a better player than Orlando Pace."

JOSEPH
GERMAINE

NICKNAME: Joe

HOMETOWN: Mesa, Arizona

HEIGHT: 6 ft 2 in   WEIGHT: 225 lb

NFL DRAFT: 1999

St. Louis Rams

7

Joe was the Rose Bowl Player of the Game in 1997.

*J*oe Germaine buckled the chin-strap on his helmet and clapped his hands together. This was crunch time and he knew it. He surveyed the field, looking left, right, and then over the middle. Crouching slightly, he took a deep breath and then barked, "Red 32! Red 32! Hut! Hut!" The football felt like an extension of his right arm as he drew back a couple of steps before feeling pressure coming up the middle. Like any experienced quarterback, Joe deftly moved out of harm's way, sprinting to his right. Suddenly, his right arm went up and his elbow cocked into place. Out of his hand tumbled a spiral so tight, a thin vapor trail seemed to follow the football to its intended target.

Seconds later, the game-winning touchdown secured as the final seconds ticked away, the young quarterback jumped up and down triumphantly, his arms stretched to the heavens as he shouted, "We win! We win! I'm going to Disneyland!" As the on-field celebration continued, and Joe contemplated another Rose Bowl victory for his team, the jubilation was suddenly interrupted by a solitary voice beckoning from a distance. "Joe!" the voice said. "It's time to come inside and get cleaned up! It's time for dinner!"

Ten-year-old Joe Germaine yelled back, "In a minute, Mom!" Then he smiled and nodded as he surveyed his own personal field of dreams—a walled backyard in his Mesa, Arizona, hometown, a rectangular brown patch of desert about twenty-five yards long and ten yards wide filled with cinder-block pilasters playing the role of wide receivers and budding cacti serving as members of the opposing team.

By his own unofficial count, Joe won thousands of Rose Bowls in that backyard over the years, rallying his Arizona State University football team from behind with a last-second touchdown pass. The late rally, the game-winning touchdown pass—lofty childhood dreams that would eventually come true for Germaine in the eighty-third Rose Bowl Game. Except Joe's real-life dream had a bit of a twist to it. Rather than leading the Sun Devils to victory, the Prodigal Son returned to plunge a dagger into the heart of his hometown team.

Joe had come off the Ohio State bench after Arizona State had taken a 17–14 lead with only 1:40 to play and led the Buckeyes sixty-five yards for the game-winning touchdown, connecting with freshman wide receiver David Boston on a five-yard touchdown pass with only nineteen seconds remaining. The 20–17 victory on New Year's Day 1997 was bittersweet for Germaine, who was named the game's Most Outstanding Offensive Player. It robbed Arizona State—the team Joe had led to all of those Rose Bowl victories in his backyard, and the team for which his father was a season ticketholder—of their first national championship.

Joseph Benton Germaine was born November 16, 1975, into a sprawling Mormon family that included four siblings and untold numbers of aunts, uncles, and cousins. Little Joe was born in Denver, the youngest of five children who were seven to fifteen years older, and he tried his best to grow up quickly. His father, Big Joe, a gregarious cowboy hat-wearing man worthy of his ex-

pansive nickname, earned his living as a fence and gate contractor. Joe's mother, Phillis, kept the family on track and helped her husband instill a sense of respect, loyalty, and love in each of their children, especially their youngest.

"I really believe that family should be the cornerstone of each person's life," Joe said. "You should care and concentrate the most about your family because they are your family. That is how important it is to me."

Sometimes, however, living up to the family credo becomes difficult. Joe's first encounter with organized football came when at the age of eight when his mother signed him up in the Pop Warner youth football league. Being a huge Walter Payton fan, Joe naturally assumed he would be his team's starting running back, but the coach had other ideas. When informed he would be a quarterback, Joe was furious and wanted to quit the team. But when he pled his case to his mother, she gave him a stern look. "We don't quit in this family," she said. "If you sign up for something, you see it through."

Joe was the Big Ten Offensive Player of the Year in 1998.

Joe went back, apologized to the coach, and gutted it out. "I was furious," he said. "I don't know if I cried, but I probably did. Eight years old, you can be pretty emotional. But it turned out to be a valuable life lesson." A few seasons later, he quarterbacked his team to a state championship.

"One thing my parents taught me was toughness," he said. "That is something I have taken from them the most because it has been one of the keys to the successes I've had. It helps you tremendously in football because when you are mentally tough, you are able to handle anything that is thrown your way."

By the time he reached high school, Joe was an outstanding football and basketball player, as well as an honors student. But it was as a quarterback at Mountain View High School that he received the most attention, throwing for more than 2,000 yards in each of his junior and senior seasons and leading the Toros to back-to-back state championship game appearances.

Yet despite such a successful high school career, it seemed no major college was interested in the smallish kid with the baby face and rifle arm. Neither Arizona State nor Arizona wanted him, with his only scholarship offer coming from Brigham Young University, and that only as a token gesture because of his Mormon faith. Then, when the Cougars suddenly signed an All-America quarterback prospect from California, even they decided there was no room on the roster for Germaine.

Reluctant to give up his dream of becoming the quarterback at a major college program, Joe enrolled at Scottsdale Community College and flourished, showcasing his strong arm and pinpoint accuracy while running a high-octane offense and displaying the kind of leadership skills every coach wants his quarterback to possess. Ohio State assistant coach Larry Coker, who was defensive backs coach on John Cooper's staff in 1993 and '94, had scouted Germaine in high school and lobbied for the Buckeyes to extend a scholarship offer. Cooper wasn't exactly sold on a 6-foot, 180-pound quarterback prospect, but he decided to take a chance.

Ohio State fans weren't so sure, demanding to know who this no-name prospect was and why the Buckeyes would gamble a precious scholarship on a junior college transfer. Germaine would have to prove himself all over again as the program searched for an heir apparent to starter Bobby Hoying, one of the most prolific passers in school history. When that criticism made it back to Arizona, Joe's junior college coach sounded off.

"They don't have a clue," Fighting Artichokes head coach Lane Jacobson said on National Signing Day in 1995. "He'll be special. Bobby Hoying is a heck of a player, but before Joe is done there, people are going to forget about Bobby Hoying but they're going to remember Joe Germaine for a long time."

Those were strong words to live up to, especially when Germaine joined the Buckeyes later that fall and took his place as the fifth-team quarterback. The following two seasons, Germaine and fellow quarterback Stanley Jackson battled one another for the number one position, but it was a rivalry that never seemed to produce a clear winner. Jackson was the starter most of the time, but it was Germaine who came up with the better stats.

"The coaches told us in camp that whoever separated himself from the other was going to play," Joe said. "I guess they didn't think anybody stood out, so they decided to play both of us. I was never sure what the fans thought back then, if they ever favored one over the other, but I did receive a lot of support. The Ohio State fans were just great to me. All the same, I wonder what I would have done if I would have played more. For example, against Wisconsin in '96, we were behind in the third quarter and I came in and threw a touchdown pass. 'Now, we're rolling,' I thought, but I got taken out and never played the rest of the game."

While he struggled to adjust to the two-quarterback system with the Buckeyes, Joe was also having a difficult time being away from home for the first time. Mesa is a city with a large Mormon population, while Columbus is more of a Midwestern melting pot, and he admitted, "At first, it was very difficult because of my church not being as strong in Columbus and not having as many members. However, my family did a good job instilling our principles and beliefs at a very early age. And it helped also that the people in Columbus were great."

His Mormon teachings as well as his mother's admonishment to finish whatever he started also helped. "When I was a little kid, I was a roughneck," he said. "I got into a lot of fights. But as you get older, you learn self-control. Sure, I'll get angry if during a game a play doesn't go well, but not to the point where I would openly vent my frustrations on my teammates. Everybody wants to do well. But at the same time, people shouldn't think of my personality and think I'm not competitive or someone they can take advantage of. I am one of the most competitive people there is."

Germaine played well enough as a backup during his sophomore season in 1996 that Cooper rewarded him with his first college start against Michigan. Unfortunately, the Buckeyes suffered a 13–9 loss to the Wolverines, and when the team began Rose Bowl preparations in December, Cooper announced he would go back to Jackson as his starter in Pasadena. But with only 1:40 showing on the clock, the Buckeyes were trailing by three points and in need of a miracle. When Cooper asked offensive coordinator Mike Jacobs which quarterback he preferred for what would be the team's last gasp, the question was met with deadly silence. After a few awkward seconds, quarterbacks coach Walt Harris piped up. "We've got to go with Germaine," he said. Cooper just looked at Joe and pointed toward the field.

"We had practiced the two-minute drill every Friday that year, and when I got into the huddle there wasn't a lot of talking," Joe said. "We just weren't going to let the game end like that. We hit a couple of crucial third-and-longs, and then came the big play. We were on the five-yard line and sent Dimitrious Stanley to the slot on the right and David Boston out wide to the right. The primary receiver was supposed to be Dimitrious, who would run a corner route. David would run inside on a hitch and then back toward the pylon. As I dropped back, I could tell they had Dimitrious defended. They had cut him off. So, I looked down at Boston and he was wide open."

The victory propelled Ohio State to the number two position in the final national polls, and gave the Buckeyes one of their most memorable Rose Bowl victories in history. It also helped fulfill a certain junior college coach's prophesy: It's safe to say Buckeye Nation will always remember Joe Germaine.

MICHAEL DOSS

NICKNAME: Mike

HOMETOWN: Canton, Ohio

HEIGHT: 5 ft 10 in   WEIGHT: 190 lb

ALL–AMERICAN: 2000, 2001, 2002

NFL DRAFT: 2003, Indianapolis Colts

2

In 2002, Mike was awarded the Jack Tatum Trophy which is given yearly to the top collegiate defensive back.

Mike Doss sat huddled in the visiting locker room showers beneath Ross-Ade Stadium, fully clothed and crying like a baby. The Ohio State sophomore safety was inconsolable after being victimized by Purdue quarterback Drew Brees, who threw a 64-yard touchdown pass to receiver Seth Morales with 1:55 remaining to complete a late comeback and give the Boilermakers a 31–27 victory on a sunny late October afternoon in 2000.

The victory allowed Purdue to continue its quest for a first Rose Bowl appearance in thirty-four years, while the loss began a downward spiral for Ohio State that eventually led to the dismissal of longtime head coach John Cooper.

"I felt so down," Doss said of the loss during which he had two interceptions before allowing Morales to get behind him for the game-winning score. "I ran in the shower in a corner and cried like a little baby. I was wondering if the seniors would be looking down on me, but they all said, 'You played hard. You had a great game. They just made a play. Nobody is going to look at you any differently.'

"But I looked at myself differently. That was a game where I had my opportunity. That was a time in my career where I felt it was me and a situation, and the situation beat me. You prepare all your life for those situations—to be on a big stage and to showcase your talents. That was the first time, and really the only time in my career, where I could say the situation got the better of me."

Two years later, Doss paid a return visit to Ross-Ade Stadium and left the playing field once again with tears in his eyes—only this time, they were tears of joy. Quarterback Craig Krenzel delivered the late-round knockout blow, connecting with receiver Michael Jenkins on a 37-yard touchdown pass with only 1:36 remaining to give Ohio State a 10–6 victory and preserve the Buckeyes' march to the 2002 national championship.

"What a difference those two years made," Doss said. "When Mike made that catch, I just started crying. I guess I'm just an emotional guy, but it kind of hit me. To go from where we were after that game in 2000 to where we were headed two years later...the emotion just overtook me for a second or two. It's something I'll never forget as long as I live."

Doss went on to help lead Ohio State to the national championship in 2002, including nine tackles, breaking up two passes, and grabbing one interception during the team's 31–24 title game victory in double overtime against the University of Miami Hurricanes. Following the season, he became only the seventh player in program history to be named to the All-America first team for a third consecutive year, after which the Indianapolis Colts made him a second-round selection in the 2003 National Football League draft.

It was pretty heady stuff for Michael Allen Doss, who was born in Canton, Ohio, on March 24, 1982, into a family that was on the verge of disintegration. His parents, Eugene and Diane Doss, divorced when Mike was at an early age, and Eugene moved to New York City to pursue work as a professional photographer. Mike and his younger sister moved with their mother to Cleveland, but Diane struggled trying to keep her young family together in the inner city. As a result, Mike went to live with his grandmother, Clara. But when she died of cancer in 1985, the three-year-old began a personal odyssey that saw him move from relative to relative every few months.

When he was seven, Mike decided he'd had enough. He left elementary school one day and walked ten miles to Canton, showing up at his uncle's house unannounced. The youngster tearfully begged his uncle to take him in, but 28-year-old Larry Doss was unsure.

"When he came out of Cleveland, he had an attitude problem," Larry said. "He was very aggressive. Even though he was only seven, being part of the projects, he was kind of tough. But I agreed to take custody of him as long as he would live by my rules."

Mike agreed, but later admitted it wasn't easy. A combative nature and hair-trigger temper often flared, resulting in a number of fights and scrapes. Things got progressively better as he aged, however, and when his uncle suggested Mike channel his aggression through athletics, the proverbial light bulb switched on. Despite being smaller than most other boys his age, the eight-year-old became an instant star in a local league normally reserved for ten-year-olds.

"That began my love affair with football," Mike said. "Although Michael Jordan was my idol—his famous dunk from the free-throw line, that poster was on my bedroom wall—I always wanted to play football. And I especially liked defense because it was where you take out your frustrations against the other team. I played some on offense, but I really thrived on being a hitter, something that would fire up the crowd. I was confident enough to believe I could play man-to-man with any receiver out there, but I was an aggressive type of strong safety. If you have a chance to make a nice tackle, you do it."

While Doss was becoming a budding football star, his trophy case began to overflow. Every team he ever played for won a championship, including Canton McKinley, which won the state championship as well as the national high school title during Mike's junior year.

"He was a winner. You could tell that the first time you laid eyes on him," said OSU defensive tackle Kenny Peterson, a teammate from peewee league through high school and college. "Doss overcame a lot of adversity. Everything he got, he worked hard for and deserved. He had some family problems, but he never let that affect his game. At McKinley, he was a great player. Doss was always the guy who wanted to stand out, and most of the time, he did just that."

Despite standing just six feet tall and tipping the scales at a modest 190 pounds, Doss was one of the most sought-after prospects as college recruiters drooled over his strength, speed, and football knowhow. However, Mike had known from an early age where he was planning to go to college. Since the fifth grade, he had been a participant in Ohio State's Young Scholars program, an organization designed to instill a zest for learning into promising youngsters, many of them from disadvantaged backgrounds. So when it came time to choose a college, Mike repaid the promise Ohio State had seen in him and committed to the Buckeyes shortly after his junior season at McKinley.

Despite being short of stature, Mike was never bashful about establishing lofty goals, declaring that he wanted to make the All-America team as a freshman. That boast became impossible when he began his rookie year riding the bench behind starting safeties Gary Berry and Donnie Nickey. Mike did manage to play well enough in 1999 that he drew starting assignments in the final two games of the season before earning his way into the regular lineup as a sophomore in 2000.

Despite the up-and-down season for the Buckeyes that year, Doss led the team in tackles and scored a pair of defensive touchdowns. The following year, with Jim Tressel taking over for Cooper as head coach, Ohio State had another disappointing record, but Doss again led the Buckeyes in tackles and earned his second All-America honor. He was poised to leave school early and make himself eligible for the NFL draft following his junior season but wrestled with making a final decision.

"In my mind, I really wanted to leave," he said. "My mother was still living in Cleveland, and I wanted to do something to change her life. I remember calling her the day I was going to make the decision, and the day I actually made the decision was on her birthday (January 9). I called her and said, 'Mom, I'm about to go pro. I'm about to change your life.' And this lady tells me, 'I think you should stay in school.'

"All I could think was, 'Does my mom even watch football? Does she know I'm a two-time All-American?' I told her, 'Mom, I want to go pro and make things better for you.' And she said, 'Son, I've made it this long. I can make it one more year.' And I thought, OK. I'll go back to school because that's what my mom wants me to do."

Doss returned for a superlative senior season that included winning a national championship ring as well as his third All-America honor. When the team arrived back in Columbus following its double-overtime victory in the national title game, Mike immediately hopped into his car and headed north.

"I remember going to West Seventh in Cleveland where my mom lived at the bottom of the hill in the projects, walking in the door and just telling her, 'Get your driver's license.' She looked at me with this puzzled look on her face, but I just said, 'Get all your identification. We're leaving this place right now and moving to Columbus to start a new, fresh life.' That, to me, was the most important thing I've ever done. To be able to take care of my mother, who took care of me, was huge. That was my whole motivation.

"That was a driving force growing up to be a success...whether it was playing sports, getting my degree, or being a trash man. It was about being able to do something to change my mother's life, and those of my sisters and little brother."

Mike's mother, who spent most of her life fighting an uphill battle against poverty, got to live the good life for only six years. She was diagnosed with breast cancer in 2008 and died that December at the age of 45. Mike was understandably devastated, but he remained thankful of the time he shared near the end of his mother's life after being apart for so many years.

"It was a blessing for me to have her for twenty-seven years and provide for her the last six," he said. "That was an honor for me. I always wanted to make her feel like she didn't have to worry about things. I held up my part, and she held up hers."

Anyone who has ever played with or against Mike Doss will tell you there was no more fierce competitor. Away from the football field, however, he belied the desperate situation of his early childhood. The angry, bitter youngster grew up to be a caring and loving person who never took no for an answer—a person who felt that any obstacle in his way, he could overcome.

And did.

CRAIG
KRENZEL

OSU QUARTERBACK 2000–2003

NICKNAME: Circle K

HOMETOWN: Utica, Michigan

HEIGHT: 6 ft 4 in   **WEIGHT:** 228 lb

NFL DRAFT: 2004, Chicago Bears

16

Craig scored a 38 on the Wonderlic Test that is given to all football players at the NFL Combine. The highest score you can receive is a 50.

*E*choes from the cheers of more than 100,000 fans had long since died away when Craig Krenzel walked onto the Ohio Stadium field for the last time as a Buckeye. The senior quarterback had just helped his team to a thrilling three-point overtime victory against Purdue, and his attention had already shifted to the next opponent. As Krenzel exited the warmth of the home locker room, he looked up into the cold November sky and noticed the lights were still on inside the venerable old Horseshoe. Instead of heading for his car and any number of postgame parties, he motioned to a handful of fellow seniors and together they made one final walk down the concrete ramp toward the south end zone.

After plotting and executing so many narrow escapes in two years as Ohio State's starting quarterback, after notching two victories against his school's archenemy, after leading the Buckeyes to their first national championship in more than three decades, the quiet solitude of an empty stadium following his final home game served as a fitting postscript on Krenzel's storybook career.

"That is my favorite memory from my college career," he said. "After that final home game, I went back into the stadium. The lights were on and I just sat there for a while with a couple of my teammates, silently in admiration of the best stadium in the country. It was also nice to sit there that night knowing that even though I would never play another game in Ohio Stadium, we never lost a game there while I was a starter."

That a proud son of Michigan found his calling at archrival Ohio State was remarkable enough without the stardom that came with being a championship quarterback.

Craig L. Krenzel was born July 1, 1981, in the southeastern Michigan town of Utica, the youngest of three children whose parents each had a head for numbers. Al Krenzel was a U.S. Army veteran who served a sixteen-month tour of duty in Vietnam before embarking upon a career as an accountant, while his wife, Debbie, worked as a school bookkeeper.

"We always told the kids, 'Do anything you want, but put your heart and soul into it. Don't just show up,'" Al said. Evidently, his kids were listening. Brian, the eldest, played safety for four years at Duke before becoming an orthopedic surgeon specializing in hip and knee replacements, while middle child Krysten became an elementary school teacher.

Meanwhile, Craig wanted nothing more than to follow his older brother into football and medicine, but he was just a skinny freshman at Henry Ford II High School with no real sense for the game of football, much less the intricacies of playing the quarterback position. Still, when Ford High coach Terry Copacia saw the youngster throwing a ball around during a gym session one afternoon, something clicked. Copacia saw something in Craig's throwing motion and immediately immersed his new pupil in quarterback fundamentals. "Pretty much everything I understood about being a quarterback," Craig said, "it came from Coach Copacia."

By the end of his sophomore season, he was getting most of the varsity snaps, unusual for a team that was more accustomed to upperclassmen at the controls. But Craig seemingly never faced a challenge he couldn't overcome. That went for the classroom as well where he carried a 3.80 grade-point average, scored 30 on the ACT and aligned himself with advanced classes so that he could pursue a degree in medicine when he got to college.

After throwing for more than 3,000 yards and thirty touchdowns during his final two seasons at Ford, Craig became a hot commodity on the recruiting trail. He had grown up just about an hour from the University of Michigan campus, but that didn't automatically make him a fan of the Maize and Blue.

"My brother and I were actually Notre Dame fans in the '80s when they had Tim Brown, Tony Rice, and the Rocket (Raghib Ismail)," he said. "Then when I was in high school, I was a big Tennessee fan when Peyton Manning was there. I loved the way he played the game."

Further complicating Michigan's pursuit of Krenzel was the fact they had signed another in-state Michigan schoolboy phenom named Drew Henson the year before. Henson had attended Brighton High School, one of Ford's archrivals, so that immediately scratched the Wolverines in Craig's estimation. Michigan State expressed keen interest while spirited pitches came from such other programs such as Boston College, Stanford, and Duke. But an unusual offer from an unlikely source intrigued the young quarterback prospect.

"Coach Copacia put together a little highlight tape and sent it from home," Craig said. "Mom and Dad could make all the games but couldn't show up on my doorstep unannounced. Plus, it just felt right."

That feeling didn't last. He saw no action his first season and only token snaps as a redshirt freshman in 2000. Cooper was fired after that season, but Krenzel's prospects for playing time didn't get any better when new head coach Jim Tressel

"Craig's so calm, I think he's a little weird."
—Chris Gamble, OSU defensive back

around, and on the basis of that four-minute tape, Ohio State offered me a scholarship the January before my senior year," Craig said. "They had never even seen me play a down of football in my life, but they offered anyway. All they had to go on was that little highlight reel."

Four months after the initial offer, Craig found himself on the Ohio State campus for the first time where head coach John Cooper and recruiting coordinator Bill Conley reaffirmed their interest.

"It was a good school, a good medical school, a good football program, and just the right distance took over. Things got so frustrating in 2001 that Craig asked his new coach if he could miss a mid-October game to attend his sister's wedding. Krysten had scheduled her wedding two years in advance so that her brother could be there, but the events of September 11, 2001, forced the cancellation of the Buckeyes' scheduled game the following weekend against San Diego State. The contest was moved to October 20, the day of the wedding.

Getting no first-team snaps in practice the Monday before the game, Craig wrestled with his options and then decided to ask for

Craig was a two-time Fiesta Bowl MVP in 2003 and 2004.

the time off. "He went into it with so much class," Tressel remembered. "He was considerate of his teammates and the coaching staff, and when he asked me if he could go home, I said 'Yes.' Let's face it, the fall of 2001 after 9/11 was not a time for conventional thinking."

A little more than a month later, however, a twist of fate had Krenzel starting at quarterback for the Buckeyes during their traditional season finale against Michigan. Regular starter Steve Bellisari had been suspended for the final home game of the season following a drunken driving arrest, and Scott McMullen was ineffective as the starter in an eventual 34–22 loss to Illinois. Krenzel had come off the bench to throw for 163 yards and a touchdown against the Fighting Illini, a performance good enough that Tressel entrusted him with the starting assignment a week later against Michigan, a trust that was repaid with a 26–20 victory, Ohio State's first win in Ann Arbor in fourteen years.

"People always hope for an opportunity," Craig said, "but you have to be ready because—at least in my case—there might not have been another one. So, I was mentally ready."

Krenzel's performance against Michigan carried over into the 2002 season, and he was at the controls for one of the most magical seasons in recent Ohio State history. Seven of the Buckeyes' fourteen victories that year were won by a touchdown or less, including a dramatic, come-from-behind 10–6 win at Purdue when Krenzel completed a fourth-down touchdown pass to wide receiver Michael Jenkins with only 1:37 remaining in the game.

"No one thought we would end up doing what we did on that play," said Krenzel, who explained that his down-the-middle heave to Jenkins was his fourth and final option in the do-or-die situation. "I'm pretty sure Coach Tress was leading the bandwagon of four-letter words when that ball was flying through the air."

Tressel, who had called a similar pass that had just worked for a solid gain to reliably sure-handed tight end Ben Hartsock, admitted to thinking his quarterback had taken leave of his senses when he saw Krenzel step up in the pocket and make his desperation heave.

Craig was a wizard on and off the field, graduating from OSU with a GPA of 3.75 and obtaining a degree in molecular genetics.

"I thought Ben would be open, but I was wrong," Tressel said. "I thought maybe the backs would get open for a check-down, but I was wrong. Then (wide receiver) Chris Gamble ran the wrong route. Craig was looking for him and Chris was over on the Purdue bench. So, Craig had one choice. And while he was telling you what I was thinking, I'm sure he was thinking four-letter words right before that, saying, 'I can't believe they called this play.' But as you know, the number one attribute of great quarterbacks is that they make great decisions, and no one made better decisions during my thirty-eight years of coaching quarterbacks than Craig Krenzel."

An overtime win at Illinois and an emotional victory at home against Michigan closed the 2002 regular season, and then Krenzel led the heavy underdog Buckeyes to an improbable victory against the University of Miami, a 31–24 thrill ride over the defending national champions that took two overtimes to decide. The win was a total team effort, but it was Krenzel who earned Offensive Player of the Game honors, mainly for repeatedly throwing his 6-4, 225-pound body into harm's way against one of the toughest defensive units in college football and finishing with a career-high 81 yards and two touchdowns.

Although Ohio State could not duplicate its national title run in 2003, Krenzel finished his college career with another solid season and then embarked upon a brief professional football career. He always told himself he would return to medical school once his playing days were over, "but after having the fortune—or misfortune—of seeing Brian going through what he did, I thought there are a lot of other ways in this world to make a living."

Now as a partner in a lucrative insurance business with time left over to dabble in other interests, Krenzel remains a celebrity in and around Columbus—not because he was the flashiest quarterback in Ohio State history or the one with the strongest arm. Craig Krenzel remains forever etched in the hearts of Buckeye fans everywhere because he consistently displayed the one attribute that separates all great players from the merely good ones.

He was a winner.

JIM
TRESSEL

OSU COACH 2001–2010

HOMETOWN: Mentor, Ohio

RECORD: 106-22

BIG TEN CHAMPIONSHIPS: 2002, 2005-09

NATIONAL CHAMPIONSHIPS: 2002

Tressel's nickname, derived from his sideline attire, is "The Vest."

*T*he decade-long tenure of Jim Tressel as head football coach at The Ohio State University was once described as a jarring contrast of Ozzie and Harriet virtue and Ozzy Osbourne excess.

As victory piled on top of victory and an unparalleled period of success against archrival Michigan convinced many in Buckeye Nation that Tressel could turn water into wine, others pointed to an aloof, almost-robotic creature who micromanaged his program to the nth degree. Some believed the coach was the very embodiment of humility and integrity, while some disputed his perceived authenticity, citing scandals that hounded him at Youngstown State and eventually cost him his job at Ohio State.

If Woody Hayes and Bo Schembechler squared off in what is affectionately remembered as "The Ten-Year War," historians might one day refer to the Tressel era in Columbus as "The Ten-Year Paradox."

"However you want to look at Jim Tressel—as all that is right with college football or all that is wrong—you can probably find evidence to support your case," said Bruce Hooley, a radio talk-show host who covered Ohio State football for nearly twenty years for *The (Cleveland) Plain Dealer*.

There is little doubt to Tressel's success as a head coach. He won more than seventy percent of his games during a fifteen-year stay at Youngstown State that produced four Division I-AA national championships, and then posted a 106–22 record at Ohio State, winning seven Big Ten titles in ten years, as well as the 2002 national championship. His career winning percentage is the best among those who coached at OSU for more than two seasons, his impeccable 9-1 record against Michigan represented the most successful period for the Buckeyes in the series that began in 1897, and his teams finished in the top five of the national rankings seven times.

Yet amid all of those successes, there were messy off-the-field embarrassments. Several players experienced legal problems, academic deficiencies, or a combination of both. Maurice Clarett, the freshman running back who helped lead the Buckeyes to the 2002 national title, had a contentious one-year stay that was marred by allegations of improprieties by coach, player, and university. A year before he won the 2006 Heisman Trophy, quarterback Troy Smith received a two-game NCAA suspension for taking money from a booster. And there was the final straw, the infamous "Tattoogate" scandal that resulted in Tressel's ouster.

Role model or hypocrite? Who can say, especially weighed against other discretions by other coaches at other programs in the often murky world of major college football, where it becomes more and more difficult each day to ascertain the line between right and wrong.

"Tressel was a man of both opportunism and altruism who helped many more people than he hurt," longtime *Plain Dealer* columnist Bill Livingston wrote in 2012. "He was also an icon of propriety who had a past of improprieties, for which he had escaped punishment. To fans, Tressel had a quality of nobility, even at the end. He was the coach who took the fall for his players, the selfless figure (albeit one leaving with a lavish

settlement) who fell on his sword for Ohio State. The coverup of the tattoos, though, branded Tressel as a liar. It is a mortal sin in the creed of the NCAA (and) Tressel's penalty was to lose his dream job."

James Patrick Tressel was born December 5, 1952, in Mentor, Ohio, where his father was head coach of the high school football team. Lee Tressel was a square-jawed man who favored crew cuts, bowties, and no nonsense, and his acumen as a coach helped lead Mentor High School to win thirty-four games in a row during one stretch. When Jim was six, his father moved the family to Berea and Baldwin-Wallace College, where Lee compiled a 155-52-6 record over the next twenty-three seasons that included the 1978 Division III national championship.

There wasn't much doubt that Jim would eventually enter the family business. "The great impact my father had on his players was readily apparent to me," he said. "It wasn't just in watching him with the team he was coaching each year. It was also the number of players who came back year after year seeking counsel on some life issue or wanting just to sit in our living room and way I felt about Ohio State and Woody Hayes and Rex Kern."

"My dad taught me a long time ago, you'll have a thousand chances to keep your mouth shut. Use every one of them."
—Jim Tressel

talk. They valued my father's opinion. Many looked up to him as the father they never had. There was something that really made me feel good about his contribution, and I could see how rewarding a career in coaching might be."

Before coaching, however, Jim wanted to try his hand at playing football, eager to emulate the playing style of his hero, Ohio State quarterback Rex Kern.

"When I was small, Ohio State was all I cared about," Tressel said. "Then when I got into high school, I became a big Rex Kern fan. I had to know what Rex Kern was doing all the time. I remember Rex was on the cover of the *Plain Dealer* holding his Rose Bowl MVP trophy and his Bible. I said maybe I ought to be reading the Bible because if Rex Kern is reading the Bible, that's what I ought to do. That's just the

That affinity continued to manifest itself as Tressel grew older. After graduating cum laude from Baldwin-Wallace with a degree in education, he embarked upon a coaching career that took him first to the University of Akron as a graduate assistant and later to Miami University and Syracuse. As he was making the transition from Miami to Syracuse, his father was diagnosed with lung cancer, a disease to which he succumbed in April 1981 at the age of 56.

During the final week of the elder Tressel's life, he had a visitor. "Coach Hayes drove to Cleveland and sat with him on his deathbed," Jim said. "That was the kind of guy Woody Hayes was."

It was also the random act of kindness that brought the young assistant coach to the realization that he needed to get back closer to

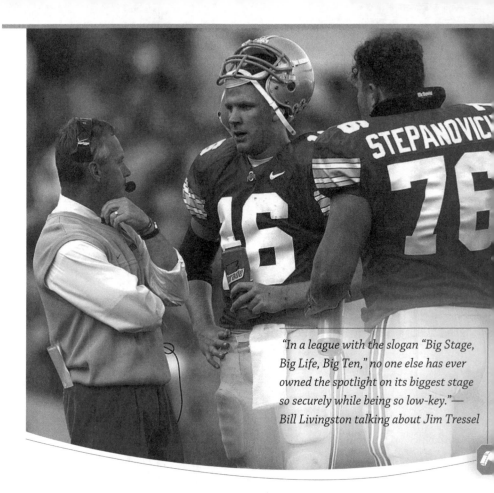

"In a league with the slogan "Big Stage, Big Life, Big Ten," no one else has ever owned the spotlight on its biggest stage so securely while being so low-key."— Bill Livingston talking about Jim Tressel

home, and after two seasons at Syracuse, he began a three-year stint as quarterbacks and receivers coach on Earle Bruce's staff at Ohio State. Although Jim left following the 1985 season to pilot his own program at Youngstown State, there was always the inkling that if the Buckeyes ever came calling again, he would be eager to take over the top job.

To illustrate the sway Ohio State continued to have over Tressel, he once shifted a Saturday afternoon game at Youngstown State to Friday night when it was originally scheduled for the same day as the OSU-Michigan game.

Then, of course, when he was hired to become the twenty-second head coach in Ohio State history, he immediately endeared himself to Buckeye fans. Just hours after his first news conference in Columbus, Tressel told a crowd of more than eighteen thousand at Value City Arena, "I promise you'll be proud of our young people in the classroom, in the community, and most especially in 310 days in Ann Arbor, Michigan, on the football field."

The arena exploded in a roar of applause, and 310 days later the unranked Buckeyes made good on that promise, upsetting the number eleven Wolverines by a 26–20 score.

Tressel's speech gave two bits of insight into his personality. First, he showed he was unafraid under fire—remember that predecessor John Cooper had won only twice in thirteen tries against Michigan and never in Ann Arbor—and second, he understood what that game meant to the program's legion of fans.

"He emphasized that game; he embraced it," former Ohio State offensive lineman Doug Datish said. "He never tried to ignore it or run away from it. He knew the importance of it and emphasized it. He called it *The* Game because it is *The* Game. If you've never played in that game, it's very hard to describe. It's not like any other game you've ever played in, and he un-

derstood that. Maybe that's why he had such success over them. I'll tell you this: As bad as our fans want to win that game, multiply that by a hundred and that's how bad he wanted to win."

The victory over Michigan that first year propelled the Buckeyes into the 2002 season, a heady rush of games decided by a touchdown or less that kept fans with one hand attached to their seats and the other reaching for antacid tablets. There was a heart-pounding defensive stand to preserve a mid-September win against the University of Cincinnati, harrowing back-to-back escapes against Wisconsin and Penn State, the infamous "Holy Buckeye" pass to beat Purdue and an overtime victory at Illinois—all simply tantalizing appetizers before a 14–9 win over Michigan to send Ohio State to the national championship game in Tempe, Arizona.

Waiting for the Buckeyes in the Desert Southwest were the University of Miami Hurricanes, defending national champions and owners of a winning streak of thirty-four games. Ohio State was a double-digit underdog, but somehow Tressel and his coaching staff devised a master game plan, allowing the Buckeyes to engineer a 31-24 win in double overtime and marking one of the most entertaining battles in the Bowl Championship Series era.

Following the game, Tressel dropped his guard and allowed some emotion to show when he accepted the crystal football trophy and told the crowd, "We've always had The Best Damn Band In The Land! Now we have The Best Damn Team In The Land!"

In the years that followed, Tressel guided Ohio State to two more national title game appearances and tied a Big Ten record with six consecutive conference championships. All of those accomplishments quickly faded into a scandal-filled haze, however, when several of Tressel's players were suspended for trading or selling memorabilia at a Columbus tattoo parlor. What began as a small brush fire quickly escalated into a five-alarm blaze when the NCAA became involved. Tressel was eventually discovered to have known about the incident and failed to share it with Ohio State director of athletics Gene Smith or the university's compliance department.

After initially vowing to stand behind their embattled coach, Smith and OSU president Dr. E. Gordon Gee suspended Tressel for the first five games of the 2011 season. Then, when the university caught wind of a scathing expose scheduled for publication in *Sports Illustrated*, it forced Tressel's resignation. No matter that the *SI* piece contained little more than a rehash of already-known information, and the firestorm so much feared by university officials quickly faded. Tressel was out and with him went one of the most successful periods in the history of Ohio State football.

The Buckeyes soldiered on as a fractured entity under interim head coach Luke Fickell in 2011, losing seven games in a season for the first time in more than a century. But the team rebounded quickly under Urban Meyer, posting back-to-back undefeated regular-season records in 2012 and 2013. It was an unprecedented feat due in no small measure to the solid modern-day foundation of success built by Jim Tressel.

TROY
SMITH

OSU QUARTERBACK 2003-06

HOMETOWN: Columbus, Ohio

HEIGHT: 6 ft 0 in   **WEIGHT:** 225 lb

ALL–AMERICAN: 2006

NFL DRAFT: 2007, Baltimore Ravens

In winning the 2006 Heisman, Smith took 86.7% of the first place votes, a record that has not been broken.

Troy Smith spent his first Ohio State-Michigan game in uniform as a redshirting freshman, freezing on the home sideline as the Buckeyes executed another of their many narrow escapes during a march to the 2002 national championship. When the clock in cavernous Ohio Stadium reached all zeroes that day, Smith and his teammates were swept away in a tsunami of Scarlet and Gray well-wishers that had flooded the field to celebrate the 14–9 victory.

Smith was a mere bystander that frigid late November afternoon, no more involved in the action than any member of the record Horseshoe crowd of 105,539 squeezed into the stands. Still, just to be wearing an Ohio State football uniform on that day represented a significant achievement for an inner-city Cleveland kid who struggled as much for acceptance as he did for his own identity.

It was only the beginning of what turned out to be a superlative career, however. Four years later, Smith stood on college football's mountaintop, having overcome every crag and more than a few pitfalls to become the seventy-second recipient of the Heisman Memorial Trophy.

"I don't think a lot of people realize just how tough it was for Troy as he was growing up," said Ted Ginn Sr., longtime coach at Glenville High School in Cleveland and one of several father figures in the life of a youngster who had no relationship with his real father. "He saw things, experienced things that kids shouldn't ever have to be exposed to. He was kind of left for a time to grow up on his own and that's tough for any kid."

Troy James Smith was born July 20, 1984, in Columbus to a teen-aged mother and a man who had little interest in being a father. Troy's mother, Tracy, had already known her share of heartache from a young age. She met Kenneth Delaney and became pregnant at sixteen with Troy's older sister, Brittany, but was quickly informed she was no longer welcome in her mother's house. A few years later, when Tracy became pregnant again, this time with a little boy, Delaney had decided he wanted nothing more to do with his young family. Tracy had little choice but to pack up her two young children and move to Cleveland and its rugged East Side neighborhoods filled with drug-dealing, drive-by shootings, and desperation. It was there young Troy saw his first fistfight and his first police chase. It was the first place he saw someone fire a gun. He also saw anger and bitterness take human form when he witnessed a spectator at a pickup basketball game take an empty beer bottle and smash it into a player's face.

"My struggles and what I had to go through was no different than any other kid in my situation," Troy said. "I don't want to make it seem like my life was the worst of anybody else growing up off of 112th and St. Clair. The things I saw growing up were not always good, but they also helped make me what I am today."

> ## "I will have to say this time and again in every interview that I do. I don't see color. I look at myself as a quarterback, not a black quarterback."
> —*Troy Smith*

From the ages of nine to fourteen, as their mother struggled to get on her feet, Troy and Brittany were placed in the Ohio foster-care system, shuffled back and forth among at least eight homes throughout the state, including a stay in Springfield where Troy learned one of his first lessons in toughness. After being kicked in the stomach during a pickup basketball game at school, the principal immediately instructed Troy to go back into the game. It was also in Springfield where the youngster's quick temper first showed itself.

"I got into my first fight with a kid who hit me in the head with a snowball," he said. "I wasn't living with mother at the time, but I kept hearing her voice in the back of my head. She always said, 'Once you start something, finish it. Don't ever quit.' I take that to the extreme in just about everything."

That first fight was far from the last. As he and his sister moved from town to town, trouble seemed to follow. Back in Cleveland, he was kicked off the Lakewood St. Edward High School basketball team during his junior year for viciously elbowing an opponent. It didn't matter that the opponent had used a racial slur against him. He was no longer welcome at the private Catholic school in the western Cleveland suburb. But the incident had a silver lining. Troy left St. Ed's and transferred to inner-city Glenville High School where Ginn was building a perennial high school powerhouse. Under Ginn's guidance, Troy flourished both as a football player and as a young man.

"Troy is probably the best offensive player I ever coached," Ginn said, who also coached his own son Ted Jr., a record-setting receiver and kick returner both at Ohio State and in the National Football League. "People ask me who the smartest player I ever had, and it would have to be Troy. He was so smart on the field, almost like another coach. He had the strongest arm of any quarterback I've ever seen, but it was his mind that set him apart."

Unfortunately, most college recruiters couldn't get a handle on exactly where Smith fit into their plans. At only six feet and 173 pounds, he didn't fit the prototypical mold of a drop-back quarterback. Meanwhile, his 4.74 speed in the forty-yard dash was regarded as borderline slow, and he didn't seem to possess the strength needed to withstand the pounding a big-time college quarterback could expect. So despite a host of accolades accompanied by Ginn's personal recommendation, Troy became one of the final players signed in 2002 by Ohio State head coach Jim Tressel.

It wasn't as if Smith had no other offers. At one point, he seemed headed to West Virginia, where head coach Rich Rodriguez had promised Troy he would start at quarterback as a freshman. But Rodriguez has neglected to mention he already had a quarterback on his roster, Rasheed Marshall, who had been promised the starting job in 2002. When Troy didn't get a good

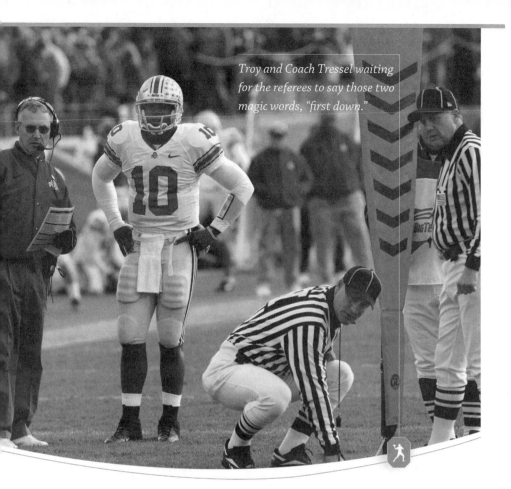

Troy and Coach Tressel waiting for the referees to say those two magic words, "first down."

vibe during a late November visit to Morgantown, he decided Ohio State was the place for him.

Still, when he arrived on campus, he got that familiar feeling of being unwanted. Despite all he had accomplished as a high school quarterback, it seemed the Buckeyes already had plenty of players at that position, including juniors Craig Krenzel and Scott McMullen as well as Smith's classmate Justin Zwick,

who had broken nearly every state high school record on the books while playing at storied Massillon Washington High School. During his freshman year, Troy was a player without a position and a young man without direction.

"Joe Daniels loved the way he threw the ball and I loved the way Troy competed at receiver, cornerback, and quarterback," Tressel said. "I'd only been at Ohio State one year and we finished with a 7–5 record, so I didn't pretend to know everything. But I knew I wanted Troy on my team. I loved his demeanor, and I loved that he was dying to go to Ohio State. To me, that meant a lot."

Still, Troy wasn't totally convinced he wanted to buy what the Ohio State coaches were selling.

"Coach Daniels would say, 'Come in here and watch this film with us,' but I was always making silly excuses because I thought every other thing was more important," Troy said. "I was in the dorms, parties were every weekend. Plus, I'm redshirting, so I'm thinking, 'What

assignments was to run the scout team, whose job is to prepare the first-team defense for its upcoming opponent. But he wouldn't always run the play the way it was called, something that quickly earned the ire of defensive coordinator Mark Dantonio.

"If no one was open, I wouldn't throw the ball and that used to really piss off Coach Dantonio," he said. "But I never threw interceptions. Ever. I hated interceptions, so I hated throwing to covered receivers. Coach Dantonio would yell, 'Troy! Throw the ball!' and I would answer back, 'Y'all are gonna have to kick me out of practice

"When you're the quarterback at Ohio State, it's pretty much like you're the governor of the state. Everybody's watching, and everybody has something to say."
—Troy Smith

do I need to watch film for? They're not going to use me.' That was my downfall, though."

Whenever Smith did get a chance to showcase his talents on the field, his stubbornness threatened his progress. One of his first

because I'm not to throwing to somebody who's not open."

Smith finally got his chance in the second half of a 33–7 loss at Iowa in week six of the 2004 season when Zwick was injured, and he rallied the Buckeyes to victories in four of the final five regular-season games, including a 37–21 upset over seventh-ranked Michigan during which Troy rushed for 145 yards and a touchdown and threw for 241 yards and two scores. It was the first of three straight victories over the Wolverines as a starting quarterback for Ohio State, the third of which clinched the 2006 Heisman Trophy.

When Smith's name was announced at the New York City awards ceremony, his sister jumped to her feet in an explosion of happiness while his mother stood silently behind her son, misty-eyed while she tried to comprehend the moment.

"Sometimes," she said, "I can't believe it's my little baby doing all this stuff. He could have turned the wrong way, but he chose to turn the right way. I couldn't be more proud if I tried."

Troy currently plays football for the Montreal Alouettes.

Troy Smith had made it from the mean streets of East Cleveland to the bright lights of Broadway, and when he hoisted that twenty-five pound trophy and looked at his mother, he flashed a smile to match.

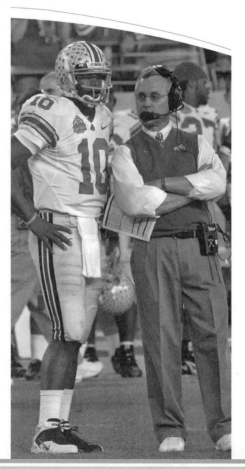

JAMES
LAURINAITIS

OSU LINEBACKER 2005-08

NICKNAME: Animal and Shrek

HOMETOWN: Minneapolis, Minnesota

HEIGHT: 6 ft 2 in   WEIGHT: 248 lb

ALL–AMERICAN: 2006, 2007, 2008

NFL DRAFT: 2009, St. Louis Rams

33

James Laurinaitis before a game during the national anthem.

*M*ost wide-eyed freshmen would have been scared to death, but James Laurinaitis didn't have time to be frightened. Ohio State linebacker Bobby Carpenter had just hobbled to the sideline after breaking a bone in his lower leg on the first defensive play against Michigan, and Laurinaitis was faced with trying to fill in for his team's best pass rusher and one of its most vocal leaders as the ninth-ranked Buckeyes looked to finish their 2005 season with a victory over the archrival Wolverines.

"James got thrown to the wolves, so to speak," said former OSU head coach Jim Tressel, fully aware of his pun. "To his credit, he didn't panic. He knew what he was supposed to do, and went out and did it."

The freshman linebacker didn't exactly distinguish himself that day, being credited with only one assisted tackle. But as his head coach remembered, Laurinaitis did what he was supposed to do, helping the Buckeyes limit a vaunted Michigan rushing attack to only thirty-two yards during a 25–21 win.

"Running in there, I realized I was in the huddle with A.J. Hawk and Anthony Schlegel and all those other studs," James said. "I knew I didn't need to do anything special because I had a bunch of special players around me."

That no-drama personality was instilled almost from birth by parents who were not only athletically gifted but emotionally grounded. James Richard Laurinaitis was born December 3, 1986, in Minneapolis to Joe and Julie Laurinaitis, not exactly your run-of-the-mill Midwestern couple. Julie was an accomplished high school athlete who later excelled in the world of bodybuilding. And then there was Joe, one-half of the Road Warriors tag-team partnership that dominated professional wrestling for more than thirty years.

Joe was a star linebacker at Golden Valley Lutheran College in the early 1980s, a junior college in suburban Minneapolis, and had landed a tryout with the New Jersey Generals of the old United States Football League. Just before leaving for tryout camp, however, Joe was asked if he wanted to make some easy money as a professional wrestler. He joined forces with high school friend and fellow bouncer Mike Hegstrand, and the rest is squared-circle history.

Together, Joe and Mike became Animal and Hawk, better known as the Road Warriors or the Legion of Doom, and headlined wrestling cards all over the world. Best-known for sporting Mohawk haircuts, spiked shoulder pads, and face paint, the duo immediately struck fear into the hearts of opponents while entering the ring accompanied by the driving guitar riffs and slightly demented voice of Black Sabbath lead singer Ozzy Osbourne belting out *Iron Man*.

"I guess it took me until late elementary school or early middle school to realize that Dad's job was different," James said. "To me, Dad was just Dad and that's the way he was. I always called it a unique childhood, though, watching Dad on TV and seeing him do what he did. But I remember eating Oreos with guys named Earthquake and Typhoon, so that was what was normal to me."

It was an unusual childhood environment, but still one that served James well, especially when he was faced with difficult situations like the one in Ann Arbor that late November day. After all, facing a bunch of Wolverines was nothing compared to the afternoon when a teen-aged James stared down six-time World Wrestling Federation heavyweight champion "Stone Cold" Steve Austin.

"I brought James and his hockey team down to the Civic Center one afternoon to watch some of the wrestling matches," Joe said. "This is long before the show started, and the kids are down in the ring, wrestling around, and as I was sitting in the back, I looked around and who's there sipping a cup of coffee? Stone Cold. He said, 'Hey, Joe. Is that your boy? Flick that switch right there.'"

Suddenly, a spotlight hit the ring and arena loudspeakers belched the sound of breaking glass, signaling the beginning of Austin's theme song. That's where James's boyhood friend Dominique Barber picks up the story.

"We were all in the ring, and all of a sudden Stone Cold's music comes on," Barber said. "We all scattered out of there as fast as we could. All of us except James."

As the 6-foot-2, 250-pound Austin came barreling into the ring, James went right into a well-known routine. "He threw Dom out of the ring, and then he throws me against the ropes," James said with a huge smile. "And then he gave me the Stone Cold Stunner."

The stunner was Austin's patented finishing move in which he throws his opponent against the ropes, and then catches him by the neck on the rebound, twisting himself around before dropping to his knees while the opponent's head is jammed into Austin's shoulder.

"I think all of my friends thought I was dead," James said with a laugh.

The youngster wasn't afraid of the intimidating world champion wrestler because his father had schooled him in the finer points of how professional wrestling worked.

"James wasn't afraid of Stone Cold because he knew exactly what to do," Joe said. "I think that was because of practicing on his poor sister. It seemed like every time I turned around, poor Jessica was on the receiving end of a Stone Cold Stunner or a Doomsday Device."

Before you think James was as stone-cold-hearted as "Stone Cold" Steve Austin, understand that Jessica was a willing participant in the family wrestling stunts. Nearly every summer day in the backyard pool, James would hoist Jessica upon his shoulders before half-brother Joe Jr. jumped from the diving board to clothesline his sister into the water. That particular move was called the Doomsday Device, the acrobatic decapitating move used by the Road Warriors to finish off their opponents.

"It was fun," James said. "Well, at least Joe and I thought it was fun."

In addition to studying his father's professional wrestling moves, James became a student of football at an early age. "Since James could walk, I just knew there was something special about this kid," his father said. "We would sit and watch football, and he would study every move. I used to say, 'Watch those guys in the middle,' and he would say, 'Who are those guys, Daddy?' I'd say, 'Those are the linebackers,' and he would just nod."

James excelled in a variety of sports at Wayzata High School, a huge 500,000-square-foot facility located on a sprawling campus just west of the Twin Cities where athletics is a passion. The school has an overflowing trophy case boasting nearly sixty state championships in fifteen different sports. James narrowly missed out being able to hoist one of those title trophies when he led the Trojans to the Class 5A championship game during his senior season before Wayzata lost a hard-fought 23–14 decision to Minnetonka. Still, he was named the state's Defensive Mr. Football, an award that eventually led to an explosion in his being recruited.

That explosion was slow in coming, however. Shortly before his senior season began, James verbally committed to his hometown school, the University of Minnesota. Golden Gophers head coach Glen Mason didn't exactly have to make a tough sell—his school was the only major-conference program to offer Laurinaitis a scholarship. But Wayzata head coach Brad Anderson, used to turning out star linebackers, knew he had a prodigy on his hands and cautioned James to wait.

"I was a big fan of Glen's and liked the program and all of that, and I remember James was all excited," Anderson said. "But I told him, 'This is kind of like getting engaged to be married. You don't make a commitment unless you're planning on going through with getting married.' I told him when he committed to the Gophers that if that's what he wanted, that was great, but just make sure it's what you want. He said he was sure."

And then Ohio State stepped into the picture. The Buckeyes hadn't signed a Minnesota high school player since Sid Gillman in 1930, but that didn't stop Tressel, who dispatched his older brother, Dick, to the Twin Cities to pursue Laurinaitis. Dick Tressel, called "Doc" by his younger brother because of his Ph.D., was comfortable in Minnesota, having spent more than twenty years as head football coach at Hamline University, a Division III school in St. Paul.

"As soon as Ohio State came in and started really recruiting him hard, and when he saw their facilities and everything they had going for them at that time, James changed his mind," Anderson said. "Minnesota's loss was going to be Ohio State's gain."

Laurinaitis passed his fiery freshman baptism against Michigan and then saw only token playing time during a 34–20 Fiesta Bowl victory against Notre Dame. But he cracked the starting lineup at middle linebacker as a sophomore in 2006 and won the Bronko Nagurski Trophy as college football's top defensive player.

As his college career continued, James sculpted his 6-foot-3 frame into a chiseled 244 pounds that combined catlike quickness with leverage techniques he had perfected from watching his father on the wrestling mat. He led the Buckeyes in tackles during his sophomore, junior, and senior seasons, helped the team appear in back-to-back national championship games, and became only the eighth Ohio State player in history to earn three consecutive first-team All-America honors.

Following a senior campaign that included winning the Dick Butkus Award as the nation's best linebacker, Laurinaitis was selected by the St. Louis Rams early in the second round of the 2009 National Football League draft. He was an immediate starter for the Rams and led the team in tackles in each of his first four seasons as a pro. Acknowledged as one of the NFL's finest young defensive stars, Laurinaitis continues to drive himself relentlessly to get better.

"I get that from my dad," James said. "He always taught me that today's preparation determines tomorrow's success, and that's something I have lived by my entire life. He kind of messed me up mentally, though, because any time I just want to take a day off, I can't relax because I'm freaking out about someone else outworking me."

Meanwhile, Joe has pretty much turned in his Animal face paint and spiked shoulder pads for the role of a proud father.

"James says to me, 'Dad, our dream is coming true.' Well, I get choked up at that because it ain't *our* dream," Joe said. "I'm here living his dream, and to be able to live his dream and live it alongside him, that just makes it even better. It just makes me say, 'Wow! He really made it.'"

BIBLIOGRAPHY

60 Years of the Outland Trophy, by Gene Duffey, Atriad Press LLC, Dallas, Texas, 2006

1968: The Year That Saved Ohio State Football, by David Hyde, Orange Frazer Press, Wilmington, Ohio, 2008

A Beautiful Mind, by Tim Layden, Sports Illustrated, August 11, 2003

A Fire To Win: The Life and Times of Woody Hayes, by John Lombardo, Thomas Dunne Books, New York City, New York, 2005

A Football Life: Chris Spielman, NFL Network, 2012

An Ohio State Man: Coach Esco Sarkkinen Remembers OSU Football, by William L. Harper, Enthea Press, Marble Hill, Georgia, 2000

Archie: The Archie Griffin Story, by Archie Griffin with Dave Diles, Doubleday & Co. Inc., Garden City, New York, 1977

Big Ten's Man of Troy, by Teddy Greenstein, Chicago Tribune, December 8, 2006

Black Without Malice: The Bill Bell Story, by Dr. William M. Bell Sr., 1983

Blue Plate Special, by Michael Farber, Sports Illustrated, April 25, 1994

Buckeye Bumper Crops, by Bill Conley with J.C. Phillips, 2005

Busted: The Rise & Fall of Art Schlichter, by Art Schlichter with Jeff Snook, Orange Frazer Press, Wilmington, Ohio, 2009

CFL Coaching Survivors Honor Shaw, by Bob Hughes, The Leader Post, Regina, Saskatchewan, January 20, 1977

Cardiologist's Widow Keeps His Memory Alive In Charity Housing, by Gina Potthoff, The Columbus Dispatch, February 4, 2011

Carmen Ohio Centennial Speech, by Robert B. Stevenson, October 25, 2005

Carter's Career Comes Full Circle, by John Breech, CBSSports.com, August 3, 2013

Charles Csuri Is An Old Master In A New Medium, by Paul Trachtman, Smithsonian magazine, Washington, D.C., February 1995

Chic: The Extraordinary Rise of Ohio State Football and the Tragic Schoolboy Athlete Who Made It Happen, by Bob Hunter with Marc Katz, Orange Frazer Press, Wilmington, Ohio, 2008

Chris Spielman, by Austin Murphy, Sports Illustrated, August 31, 1987

Cut 'Em Off At Forward Pass, by William Barry Furlong, Sports Illustrated, October 19, 1964

Dick Schafrath: Carving Out A Life, by Rich Passan, Orange and Brown Report, July 11, 2007

Dr. Wilce Dies: Started OSU As Gridiron Power, by Irven Schiebeck, The Columbus Dispatch, May 18, 1963

Earle: A Coach's Life, by Earle Bruce with George and Darcy Lehner, Orange Frazer Press, Wilmington, Ohio, 2000

Educator's Book Includes Local Family, by M.D. Garmon, The Gadsden Times, Gadsden, Georgia, September 13, 1981

Ex-OSU Coach Wilce Dies At 75, Columbus Citizen-Journal, May 18, 1963

Ex-Green Bay Packer Still Means Business, by Fred Dickey, UTSanDiego.com, November 26, 2012

Ex-Soldier Comes Back To Football, LIFE Magazine, October 22, 1945

Expanding Your Horizons: Collegiate Football's Greatest Team, by Donald Steinberg, M.D., Dauvid Press, Boynton Beach, Florida, 1992

Fanatic Francis: How One Coach's Madness Changed Football, by Brett Perkins, University of Nebraska Press, Lincoln, Nebraska, 2009

Former Buckeye Shaw Made NFL History, by Eric Loughry, Buckeye Sports Bulletin, March 31, 2007

Former Fayetteville State AD Dies, by Brian J. Dulay, Fayetteville Observer, Fayetteville, North Carolina, May 12, 1991

Game of My Life: Ohio State, by Steve Greenberg and Laura Lanese, Sports Publishing LLC, Champaign, Illinois, 2006

George Dreamed Early Of Winning Heisman, by Jeff Rapp, Buckeye Sports Bulletin, December 1995

Given Shot, He Runs With It, by Andrew Bagnato, Chicago Tribune, December 9, 1998

Greene Made Color Irrelevant, by Austin Ward, ESPN.com, March 14, 2013

Grind-It-Out Coach Still Wins, by Harry Grayson, Newspaper Enterprise Association, November 21, 1963

Heart Of A Mule: The Dick Schafrath Story, by Dick Schafrath, Gray & Company Publishers, Cleveland, Ohio, 2006

High On The Scale, by Ken Murray, The Baltimore Sun, April 15, 1997

Hop's Had A Trophy Life, by Dave Schiber, Tampa Bay Times, March 31, 2005

Janowicz Excelled Wherever He Was, by Bob Baptist, The Columbus Dispatch, February 29, 1996

Jim Parker, by Don Smith, Pro Football Hall of Fame, The Coffin Corner, Vol. 2, No. 1, 1980

Kern and Otis Were Home Grown, Newspaper Enterprise Association, October 30, 1969

Legendary Class, by Jason Ohlson, The Columbus Magazine, June 2010

Losing Their Luster, by Peter King, Sports Illustrated, November 10, 1997

Lost Legend: The Chic Harley Story, DAC Productions LLC, Columbus, Ohio, 2009

Meeting Papa, Mount Kilimanjaro & A New Land, by Eric Loughry, Buckeye Sports Bulletin, March 12, 2005

More Than A Coach, by David Lee Morgan Jr., Triumph Books, Chicago, Illinois, 2009

NFL Retirement Very Different For Fred 'Curly' Morrison And The Late Joe 'The Jet' Perry, by Bill Dwyre, Los Angeles Times, April 30, 2011

No Bones About It, by Jill Lieber, Sports Illustrated, August 28, 1989

Ohio State: 100 Years Of Football, by Marv Homan and Paul Hornung, 1990

Ohio State Athletics 1879-1959, by James E. Pollard, Ohio State University Athletic Department, Columbus, Ohio, 1959

Ohio State Renaissance Man William H.H. Tippy Dye Remembered After Death, by Aaron Green, The Lantern, August 24, 2012

Ohio State's 1950 Rose Bowl MVP: 'We Weren't Going To Come Back With Our Tails Between Our Legs,' by Doug Lesmerises, The (Cleveland) Plain Dealer, December 16, 2009

Ohio State's Unforgettables, by Bruce Hooley, Sports Publishing LLC, Champaign, Illinois, 2002

Paul Brown: The Man Who Invented Modern Football, by George Cantor, Triumph Books, Chicago, Illinois, 2008

PB: The Paul Brown Story, by Paul Brown with Jack Clary, Atheneum, New York City, New York, 1979

Requiem For A Viking, by Steven Rushin, Sports Illustrated, August 13, 2001

Runnin' Son Of A Preacher Man, by Jack McCallum, Sports Illustrated, November 5, 1984

Saint Woody: The History and Fanaticism of Ohio State Football, by Bob Hunter, Potomac Books, Washington, D.C., 2012

Shaw's Life Was Stuff Of Hollywood, by Rob Oller, The Columbus Dispatch, April 14, 2011

Show Stopper, by Tim Layden, Sports Illustrated, October 7, 1996

Sid Gillman: Father of the Passing Game, by Josh Katzowitz, Clerisy Press, Covington, Kentucky, 2012

Stringer Leaves Legacy Of Awareness, by Virginia Shank, Warren (Ohio) Tribune Chronicle, July 31, 2011

Teammates Cite Ability, Attitude Of Stringer, by Dave Woolford, The (Toledo) Blade, August 2, 2001

The All-America Foot Ball Team, by Walter Camp, Collier's Weekly, 1920.

The Animal In Him, by Austin Murphy, Sports Illustrated, August 19, 2008

The Ohio Player, by Ray Kennedy, Sports Illustrated, August 19, 2008

The Two Sides of Jim Tressel, by Jeré Longman, The New York Times, January 3, 2007

That's Why I'm Here, by Chris Spielman with Bruce Hooley, Zondervan Publishing, Grand Rapids, Michigan, 2012

The New Thinking Man's Guide to Pro Football, by Paul Zimmerman, HarperCollins, New York City, New York, 1984

The Official Ohio State Football Encyclopedia, by Jack Park, Sports Publishing LLC, Champaign, Illinois 2001

The Ohio State Story: Win Or Else, by Robert Shaplen, Sports Illustrated, Oct. 24, 1955

The One And Only, by Todd C. Wessell, Pepperdine Press, Sarasota, Florida, 2009

Then Tress Said To Troy – The Best Ohio State Football Stories Ever Told, by Jeff Snook, Triumph Books, Chicago, Illinois, 2007

They Call Me Assassin, by Jack Tatum with Bill Kushner, Avon Books, New York City, 1979

Three Yards and a Cloud of Dust, by Bill Levy, World Publishing Co., Cleveland, Ohio, 1966

Tough Love, by Austin Murphy, Sports Illustrated, September 30, 1996

Two Big Decisions, by Alfred Wright, Sports Illustrated, November 13, 1961

Ohio State '68: All The Way To The Top, by Steve Greenberg and Larry Zelina, Sports Publishing Inc., Champaign, Illinois, 1998

Weed Has Faced His Interesting Life Head-On, by Eric Loughry, Buckeye Sports Bulletin, March 5, 2005

What It Means To Be A Buckeye, edited by Jeff Snook, Triumph Books, Chicago, Illinois, 2003

Woody's Boys: 20 Famous Buckeyes Talk Amongst Themselves, by Alan Natali, Orange Frazer Press, Wilmington, Ohio, 1995

Woody Hayes: A Reflection, by Paul Hornung, Sagamore Publishing Inc., Champaign, Illinois, 1991

You Win With People! by Woody Hayes, Typographic Printing, Columbus, Ohio, 1973

ABOUT THE AUTHOR

Mark Rea is managing editor emeritus of Columbus Sports Publications, a Columbus, Ohio-based firm that publishes sports-related fan newspapers including *Buckeye Sports Bulletin* and manages the Internet website Buckeye-Sports.com.

For more than 30 years, Rea has been a writer, journalist, editor and columnist at newspapers and magazines for such companies as Scripps-Howard and McGraw-Hill.

Throughout the course of his career, Rea has won several writing awards, including national first-place honors from McGraw-Hill in 2002 and 2003, and an honorable mention in 2004 from the Football Writers Association of America. In 2009, he authored the book *The Die-Hard Fan's Guide To Buckeye Football*.

Rea and his wife, Lisa, reside in Washington Court House and have a daughter Jessica, who is currently a graduate student working on her Ph.D. in psychology at Ohio State.